IT Project Management

A Geek's Guide to Leadership

Best Practices and Advances in Program Management Series

Series Editor
Ginger Levin

RECENTLY PUBLISHED TITLES

Benefits Realization Management: Strategic Value from Portfolios, Programs, and Projects
Carlos Eduardo Martins Serra

IT Project Management: A Geek's Guide to Leadership
Byron A. Love

Situational Project Management: The Dynamics of Success and Failure
Oliver F. Lehmann

Ethics and Governance in Project Management: Small Sins Allowed and the Line of Impunity
Eduardo Victor Lopez and Alicia Medina

Becoming a Sustainable Organization: A Project and Portfolio Management Approach
Kristina Kohl

Improving Business Performance: A Project Portfolio Management Approach
Ramani S

Leading and Managing Innovation: What Every Executive Team Must Know about Project, Program, and Portfolio Management, Second Edition
Russell D. Archibald and Shane Archibald

Program Management in Defense and High Tech Environments
Charles Christopher McCarthy

The Self-Made Program Leader: Taking Charge in Matrix Organizations
Steve Tkalcevich

Transforming Business with Program Management: Integrating Strategy, People, Process, Technology, Structure, and Measurement
Satish P. Subramanian

Stakeholder Engagement: The Game Changer for Program Management
Amy Baugh

Making Projects Work: Effective Stakeholder and Communication Management
Lynda Bourne

Agile for Project Managers
Denise Canty

IT Project Management

A Geek's Guide to Leadership

Byron A. Love

MBA, PgMP, PMP, CompTIA Project+, CISSP

CRC Press
Taylor & Francis Group
Boca Raton   London   New York

CRC Press is an imprint of the
Taylor & Francis Group, an **informa** business
AN AUERBACH BOOK

CRC Press
Taylor & Francis Group
6000 Broken Sound Parkway NW, Suite 300
Boca Raton, FL 33487-2742

First issued in hardback 2017

ISBN 13: 978-1-138-42317-6 (hbk)
ISBN 13: 978-1-4987-3650-3 (pbk)

Visit the Taylor & Francis Web site at
http://www.taylorandfrancis.com

and the CRC Press Web site at
http://www.crcpress.com

Contents

Foreword

Information technology (IT) is increasingly complex and changes quickly. Successful IT professionals constantly pursue technical training in order to keep up with technological change. They have to be smart, flexible, and committed. They value technology training because without it, they could not deliver the solutions business leaders need. The high pace of technological change, however, leaves little time for leadership development training. As a result, many IT professionals are promoted into leadership positions based on their technical performance, not on their leadership ability. An unintended consequence of this practice may be ineffective performance of IT teams.

Without leadership at the team level, IT and other business executives are at risk of being unable to obtain the information they need to make critical decisions. This risk often occurs because many IT professionals tend to enjoy interfacing with computers rather than interacting with people. However, if people are not involved, often the results are IT projects that are late, are over budget, and do not meet performance requirements. Additionally, many IT team members feel managers may not be interested in their future careers and individual needs, which leads to lack of staff retention and the need to hire others with specialized IT skills. Leadership is required to motivate team members to provide the intense effort required to develop, deliver, and support IT solutions.

I was thrilled when Byron Love approached me about writing this book. Byron has over 31 years of IT experience that ranges from writing code on mainframes in the 1980s to leading large IT programs today. He has had the opportunity to take world-class technical and leadership training from the US Air Force. As one of the few people in the world who have both the PMI®'s PgMP® certification and the (ISC)² CISSP® certification, he is uniquely qualified to address the topic of IT leadership. He is a geek who has learned to be a leader, and his book in turn helps people recognize the importance of geek leadership.

IT Project Management: A Geek's Guide to Leadership fills the leadership void for IT professionals. It provides detailed coverage of leadership, communications, followership, personal credibility, and self-development concepts to address the specific leadership challenges IT professionals face. To me, this book is interesting because it incorporates engaging business fables and stories to demonstrate the IT leadership concepts he describes.

This book further provides IT professionals the tools they need to become more effective leaders, followers, and communicators. But they are not the only people who can benefit from this book:

- Human resources professionals can use this book to create leadership development programs for IT professionals.
- Companies that provide professional development services can use this book to provide IT leadership training for their clients.
- Business leaders, working with IT professionals, can develop more effective technical solutions and services to meet their specific requirements, and they can help IT professionals advance in their fields.

IT Project Management: A Geek's Guide to Leadership is not only a joy to read, it is also an excellent reference for IT practitioners challenged with the complexities of leading teams and engaging stakeholders. Ensure that the IT professionals in your organization read this book and apply its concepts so your organization can benefit from IT leadership at every level!

Ginger Levin, DPA, PgMP®, PMP®

Preface

Most people in the IT industry are familiar with the trite phrase "people, process, and technology." There are manifold technology and process standards that enable the IT industry to impact society in profound ways. From government and defense, to medicine, to finance, and to entertainment, no realm of the human experience is unaffected by information technology.

Technology and processes, when properly designed, are based on logical principles, principles mostly unaffected by human emotions, such as commitment and loyalty, or even envy and greed—emotions that motivate human beings. Although technology is created by people and is supported by people for the benefit of human interests, the innate "people" component of technology development and management is many times neglected.

Consider this short business fable: Tim, a talented software development team leader with a driving and sometimes confrontational leadership style, was under pressure from his program manager, James. "I could write you up for insubordination," James told him. "Your interpretation of the user interface requirements is wrong," Tim retorted. "I've met with the customer and I know what he wants," Tim continued. "He doesn't like the mockup. Why won't you listen?" "I told you to proceed with the approved requirements. You have a very bad attitude," James said as he stormed away.

The conflict between Tim and James may be related to processes, and technology is certainly involved. However, the solution to their squabble is found in neither the process domain nor the technology domain. This is a *people* problem, a *leadership* problem, and the manner in which it is resolved could have profound impact both on their ability to satisfy their customer and on their careers.

IT project managers may manage processes and technologies, but people must be led. The IT industry attracts people who think in logical ways—analytical types who have a propensity to place more emphasis on tasks and technology than on people. This has led to leadership challenges such as poor communication, poor relationship management, and poor stakeholder engagement. Critical IT projects and programs have failed because IT leaders neglect the people component of "people, process, and technology."

When I transitioned from Air Force active duty to the commercial IT industry around the year 2000, I found that the industry was more interested in my Microsoft Certified Systems Engineer certification than in my leadership experience as an Air Force Communications and Information Systems Officer. Employers were more interested in my ability to solve technical problems than in my ability to lead technical people. I found that many people in IT leadership positions had never been taught how to lead. They were promoted based on their technical abilities and their technical training—training that excluded leadership—yet they were expected to lead. Some had natural leadership abilities, others did not. Some imitated the leadership practices of their previous managers, many times mimicking their dysfunctional leadership behaviors. Many times, this led to poor team performance, high turnover, and troubled or failed projects.

As a geek—a moniker I wear proudly—I have written code, designed and developed databases, and administered systems and networks. As a leader, I have led multi-million-dollar projects and programs. The US Air Force equipped me with world-class technical training as an enlisted Airman and with world-class leadership training as an Air Force officer. I have obtained top-tier IT certifications, such as the (ISC)^2 Certified Information Systems Security Professional (CISSP®) certification, and top-tier management certifications, such as the Project Management Institute's Program Management Professional (PgMP®) certification. I am one of the very few people in the world with both of those certifications. During my career of over 31 years, I have made the transition from geek to geek leader, and this book will help other geeks do the same.

I wrote this book to address the leadership issues in the IT industry, to help IT practitioners lead from the lowest level. Unlike other leadership books that provide a one-size-fits-all approach to leadership, this book focuses on the unique challenges that IT practitioners face. It is a book I wish I could have referred to, one that I wish I could have provided as a reference, as I traversed the IT leadership ranks.

Geek leaders are challenged to deliver results in a complex domain that is prone to failed projects, as I discuss in Chapter 1, *Initiation*. Leading IT personnel and projects is different than leading in, say, civil engineering, as I explain in Chapter 2, *Why Geek Leadership Is Different*. In Chapter 3, *Emotionally Intelligent Communications*, I provide an in-depth discussion of the communications cycle and emotional intelligence, providing geek leaders with tools to improve their understanding of others and to help others understand them.

Transforming from a geek to a geek leader requires *Self-Leadership,* which is the subject of Chapter 4. Geek leaders must also be good followers, and they need to be equipped to assist their team members to be good followers. Chapter 5, *Followership,* satisfies this requirement. In Chapter 6, *Personal Credibility and Leadership,* I explain how a geek leader's ability to navigate disparate social styles leads to greater credibility and influence. In order for leadership to be applied consistently across IT projects and programs within organizations, leadership needs to be integrated into technology development processes and project management standards. Chapter 7, *Systems Integration,* provides a methodology for performing this integration. Chapters 2 through 7 conclude with practical instruments, such as leadership assessments and checklists, that can assist geeks to assess and improve their leadership abilities. Finally, in Chapter 8, *Closeout,* I provide a business fable that summarizes the concepts presented in this book.

This is not another vapid and prosaic IT project management book. Business fables such as Tim's story provide life and context. Personal anecdotes from my career provide real-world experiences. This book is replete with graphics that illustrate and emphasize essential concepts. It covers diverse topics, providing a multifaceted view of geek leadership. For example, you will learn about Bill Gates's success as a geek and as a leader; you will learn how to use self-talk to grow new neural pathways; you will learn how to read body language; and you will learn how to differentiate between the Driver social style and the Amiable social style. Yes, this book is about IT geek leadership, but it can benefit anyone, including those of you who can relate to Tim, or to James, or to their team members, their non-IT leaders, or their customers.

I would like to express my gratitude to Dr. Ginger Levin for this opportunity, and to Mr. John Wyzalek, Ms. Susan Culligan, and the superb team at Taylor and Francis and CRC Press for their hard work and assistance. Because of their influence and hard work, I'm sure you'll find *IT Project Management: A Geek's Guide to Leadership* edifying and enjoyable!

Odenton, MD, May 31, 2016
Byron A. Love, MBA, PgMP®, PMP®, CompTIA Project+, CISSP®
Sr. Director, IT Programs, Intrepid Solutions and Services, Inc.
Chairman, Unity Economic Development Corporation

Acknowledgments

Love and truth form a good leader;
sound leadership is founded on loving integrity.
—Proverbs 20:28 (The Message)

My wife Pam, our son Christian, and our twin daughters Aliyah and Alycia have brought me more joy than I ever imagined I would experience. Every day, I thank my Lord and Savior Jesus Christ for my wonderful family. I could not have completed this work without their support.

The late Lou Tice, past chairman and co-founder of The Pacific Institute®, changed my life. Through his *Investment in Excellence*® program, he taught me the power of Smart Talk, which influenced my thinking in significant ways.

John Wyzalek of Taylor & Francis is an outstanding editor. I am extremely grateful to John for working with me to produce this book.

Over the past 18 years, Rev. Dr. Harry L. Seawright of Union Bethel AME Church and Rev. Dr. Jonathan L. Weaver of Greater Mount Nebo AME Church have been my spiritual leaders. These two outstanding pastors are excellent examples of what it means to be a Man of God.

Larry Hebert, Chairman and CEO of Intrepid Solutions and Services, Inc., is the best boss anyone could hope to work for. I appreciate the leadership and opportunities Larry has provided me over the years.

Finally, this book would not be possible without the generosity of Dr. Ginger Levin. She is a role model to many of us in the portfolio, program, and project management profession, and I am deeply grateful to her for taking a chance on me.

—B.L.
ITProjectLeadership.com

About the Author

Byron Love has over 31 years of experience in information technology, working in positions ranging from systems administrator, to applications and database developer, to project and program manager. He retired from the Air Force Reserves as a Communications and Information Systems Officer after 21 years of service on active duty and in the Reserves, rising through the enlisted and officer ranks to become a Major. During his Air Force career, Mr. Love won many awards, including Reserve Officer of the Year for his division, and was an honor graduate of USAF NCO Leadership School and USAF Basic Computer Officer Training School.

As a civilian, Mr. Love has led projects and programs at over a dozen government organizations. Mr. Love led a successful four-year program to convert every Air Force dental clinic worldwide from film-based to digital dental processing, a historic program that impacts every Air Force member and their dependents. Mr. Love successfully performed as Senior Program Manager for the Department of State (DoS) Vanguard 2.1 contract, a 270-person, $26-million-a-year contract for managing the DoS global IT Service Center and for providing desktop support for their 29,000 desktops in the Continental US.

Mr. Love holds an MBA from Averett University, a BA in Computer Science from Thomas Edison State College, and associate degrees from Brevard Community College and the Community College of the Air Force. He holds Program Management Professional (PgMP®), Project Management Professional (PMP®), Certified Information Systems Security Professional (CISSP®), CompTIA Project+, Information Technology Infrastructure Library (ITIL) Foundation, and Toastmasters Competent Communicator certifications. As of January 2016, he is one of fewer than 1,500 PgMP® certified professionals worldwide, and one of very few professionals in the world with both PgMP® and CISSP® certifications.

Mr. Love is the author of *The Golden Rhythm: Righteous and Empowered Living.* He is employed as the Senior Director of IT Programs for Intrepid Solutions and Services, Inc. (www.intrepidsolutions.com) and serves as chairman of the award-winning Unity Economic Development Corporation (www.unityedc.org). You can read Mr. Love's blog at www.ITProjectLeadership.com.

Disclaimer

This book contains references to CompTIA standards. CompTIA has not approved the accuracy of the contents of this book. Specifically, none of the content of this book has been reviewed by or is authorized by CompTIA. This book is not designed to serve as training material in order to prepare for any CompTIA certification exam.

Chapter 1

Initiation

I love promoting qualified and competent Information Technology (IT) professionals into leadership positions. It is one of the most fulfilling privileges of being an IT executive. I have had the pleasure of interviewing, hiring, and promoting many IT professionals during my 30-year career, and many of them have gone on to become executives themselves.

Studies have shown that IT professionals—i.e., geeks—in general are emotionally resilient, tough minded, and open to new ideas, and that they have a customer-service orientation (Lounsbury et al., n.d.). Over the years, as I have worked as a computer operator, a developer, a database administrator, a systems administrator, a project manager, and a program manager, I have found the results of this study to be true. I am proud to be a geek because we have the power to make an impact. The work we do improves lives.

In this chapter, I provide the criteria I look for when selecting a geek leader so that you can understand the characteristics required to succeed as a geek leader. Then, I also describe the geek leadership challenge. Finally, I provide an overview for this book to give you a roadmap for learning to be a better geek leader. My goal is to coach you on the characteristics needed to advance your career. My goal is to provide you with information that empowers you with confidence, enabling you to face and overcome leadership challenges.

1.1 Selecting a Geek Leader

When I hire and promote geeks into leadership positions, I look for answers to several questions concerning criteria that experts have found present in great leaders:

1. ***Does the geek have courage?*** Leaders need the mental and moral strength to take reasonable risks, persist during difficult times, and endure when situations seem difficult or dangerous. Leaders who are able to perform in the face of fear and difficulty inspire and motivate others. The passion to succeed fuels this courage.

2. ***Does the geek communicate well?*** Research has shown that project managers spend 90% of their time communicating (Rajkumar and KP, 2010). Leaders value the people around them and ensure that they receive the right information, in the right format, at the right time. Effective leaders listen closely before they respond, seeking understanding as well as feedback. They synchronize their responses with the stakeholder's needs. A leader's customers, team members, peers, and up-channel leadership are all his or her clients. Leaders restate crucial points for emphasis, requesting feedback as well as clarification to ensure understanding. Leaders establish a regular reporting rhythm utilizing the standard templates. They conduct regular meetings with their customers and their team members to review those reports.

3. ***Is the geek proactive?*** Leaders need to understand their priorities, then organize and execute in accordance with those priorities. Leaders take action to obtain realistic goals in a proactive manner. In order to deliver quality, effective leaders need to understand and implement the Deming Cycle:

   - **Plan:** Plan the work, making use of input from team members and from various other stakeholders. Leaders are responsible for envisioning and communicating the future state and inspiring their team members to achieve this vision.
   - **Do:** Do the job according to the strategy and the timetable.
   - **Check:** Check the work, making an assessment of quality as well as risk.
   - **Act:** Take action on the results of the assessment, ensuring quality and mitigating threats.

4. ***Is the geek capable of establishing and pursuing a unified vision?*** Leaders align their team's tasks with the organization's business objectives. Leaders comply with established policies and procedures for their team and their organization. Leaders must comply with both client requirements and business needs all at once. Leaders relate to people as individuals, no matter their function or position. They make sure everyone understands how their individual objectives align with the organization's objectives.

5. ***Is the geek accountable?*** Leaders must take responsibility and hold their team members accountable. Leaders should know what is expected of them and use performance coaching to ensure their team members

understand what is expected of them. Leaders must be capable of establishing a rhythm that results in meeting client requirements as part of a day-to-day routine:

- Document the criteria for performance expected in a work guideline, SOP, or other document.
- Train team members on the documented criteria. Do not hold individuals accountable for adhering to standards that have not been communicated through training.
- Measure and document results as team members execute the tasks they were trained to perform.
- Praise, incentivize, and reinforce achievement of standards, as well as redirect off-base performance as it happens.

6. ***Does the geek have personal credibility?*** Leaders need to be believable. They need the respect and trust of their customers, their managers, their peers, and their team members. They understand how their honesty, humility, and humor enable them to connect people at all levels within their organization.

7. ***Is the geek trustworthy and reliable?*** Leaders need to take a clear stance on issues and hold their ground. Management of trust is one of the essential factors in a leader's perceived dependability.

8. ***Does the geek manage feelings?*** Charismatic leaders generate meaningful feelings in others. People feel that their job is more significant when they are the masters of their own behavior—that is, they feel competent. They feel a sense of comradery with their team mates. Leaders must be emotionally intelligent; they must be aware of their own feelings and their impact on the people around them.

9. ***Does the geek manage himself or herself well?*** Leaders are expected to have the ability to develop and modify habits to produce behaviors that result in organizational success. Self-management skills enable leaders to live a more efficient and effective daily life, break bad habits and obtain brand-new ones, complete difficult tasks, and obtain individual goals.

10. ***Does the geek lead by example?*** Leaders should model the actions they expect from their team members. Leaders set the example for continuous learning. They treat everyone fairly and with respect. Many people spend about 95% of their time thinking about themselves (Carnegie, 2010); leaders lead by spending time considering what they can do to meet the needs of others. Jackie Robinson said, "A life is not significant except for its impact on other lives."

11. ***Can the geek manage risk?*** Leaders forecast risks and develop contingency as well as mitigation plans early. Leaders ask for assistance to make

certain that risks are not realized—that they do not become problems. Leaders address and report both the good news and the bad news.

12. *Is the geek a problem solver?* Leaders create an environment in which issues are resolved at the lowest level. Effective leaders exercise Servant Leadership, solving their customers', managers', as well as team members' problems before solving their own. Leaders search for creative solutions that enable everyone to succeed, creating synergistic solutions to problems. When leaders present problems to their managers and customers, they also present recommended solutions.

13. *Is the geek capable of continuously improving processes?* Leaders establish processes to gather and record lessons learned, continuously improving efficiency. Leaders identify and implement guides and tools that will improve their team's capabilities. Leaders speak out, providing feedback to their management when processes are not working.

14. *Does the geek understand the organization?* Organizational behavior is the examination of both team and individual performance with respect to the organization. Leaders need to be aware of internal as well as external perceptions of the organization's performance. Leaders who understand organizational behavior are more effective at leading change.

15. *Does the geek balance work and life priorities?* Leaders balance work requirements with personal and family requirements for both themselves and their team members. They make sure their team members are refreshed and prepared to contribute to project delivery.

Not every candidate that I have promoted or hired meets every one of these criteria. As we discuss in Chapter 2, Why Geek Leadership Is Different, many of these attributes do not come naturally to geek leaders. The IT geek leaders who were successful had strong communications skills. Not all of them were strong technically, but they understood enough about the technology to hold their IT team members accountable and to communicate well with stakeholders. They demonstrated the courage to be proactive and to make process improvements. If they came from outside the organization, they made the effort to learn how things worked and how their projects aligned with the organization. The unsuccessful IT geek leaders could not connect with their team members. They could not establish a unified vision for their team and could not build personal credibility. Some were simply not accountable, behaved poorly, and did not set a good example.

Some call the skills needed to become an effective leader "soft skills." They place a higher value on mastering technical skills, such as programming routers with Internetworking Operating System commands or designing databases using Structured Query Language. But "soft skills" are not easy, and "soft" does not equate to "weak." The IT industry's best and most effective leaders know how to inspire their teams, how to connect with their customers, and how to influence people and situations in a manner that gives them control and enables success. When a leader accomplishes those feats, it seems like magic. These people are powerful—there is nothing "soft" or "weak" about them, and their work is not "easy."

The skills needed to be a great engineer, developer, or systems administrator do not help you become a great leader. If you feel you cannot identify with the leadership criteria presented above, and if you aspire to become a leader, then this book is for you. You *can* have the strength, power, and success of other successful IT geek leaders. To become a better leader, you need to develop new skills, a task you are perfectly capable of performing. By becoming an IT professional, you have demonstrated your power, your ability to learn complex concepts. If you apply yourself, you can also use this power to become an effective leader and earn the increased prestige and higher pay that you deserve. And I am here to help you along the way.

A mountain climber may set out to reach the peak of a high mountain range. He may set his sight on a destination—an elevation he has never achieved, perhaps one that no one has ever achieved. He trains, plans his journey, obtains his supplies, sets out along the trail. Along the way, he endures significant challenges and setbacks, perhaps facing extreme conditions, perhaps running into mountain lions, or bears, or even snakes. If he persists and survives, he reaches his goal.

Leadership is not a destination. There is no peak, no summit, because there is always more to learn and because there is no perfect leader. Leadership is about the journey itself. During your climb, you need to pay attention, because there are lessons to be learned along the way. There are things to discover about yourself, your team, your organization, and your world. You need the mindset of a student who is eager to learn about leadership, understanding that you will never know it all. Each leadership experience, each assent up the mountain, is an opportunity to learn something new, an insight about yourself that will make you a better climber, an observation that will help you mentor an aspiring leader on his or her first climb. Effective leaders are lifelong learners.

1.2 The Geek Leadership Challenge

Ladies and gentlemen, the stakes in IT have never been higher, and the higher the stakes, the more critical solid leadership becomes. Please forgive me for being dramatic, but I feel as though the IT profession is under a curse. I am reminded of a man in the Bible's Old Testament named Amos, who was not professionally trained to be a prophet but became one, just as many geeks are not professionally trained to be leaders but are put in leadership positions. Amos predicted dark days for ancient Israel, saying, "In that day you will be like a man who runs from a lion—only to meet a bear. Escaping from the bear, he leans his hand against a wall in his house—and he's bitten by a snake" (Amos 5:19).

1.2.1 The Lion

In the United States, President Obama's healthcare.gov rollout is infamous for its technical glitches and delays. New York City's payroll modernization project was cancelled after costs grew from $63 million to $700 million. The state of Texas's seven-year, $863-million outsourcing contract with IBM was plagued by problems (Newcombe, 2014). In Britain, the BBC's leadership was severely criticized for the failure of a 100-million-pound ($170-million) digital media initiative (Goldsmith, 2014). In Australia, a 2011 Victorian Ombudsman's report into 10 projects found that each failed to meet expectations and added an additional $1.44 billion in costs (Clarke, 2014). Experts estimate the global cost of IT failure to be $3 trillion annually (Krigsman, 2012).

This is one angry lion that has us on the run, a tremendous problem that will not be solved without leadership. It takes leadership to inject leadership. "Attention to the time and skills required for expert collaboration and coordination is often overlooked," says Theresa Pardo, director of the Center for Technology in Government at the University of Albany. "You need 'super' project managers, who have the skill-sets to ensure all actions are coordinated across multiple boundaries and are sensitive to shifting realities" (Newcombe, 2014).

1.2.2 The Bear

As we attempt to escape the lion, we run into a bear of a problem. Few geeks have these "super" project management and leadership skill sets. A study of over 100 project managers revealed that the most critical characteristics for effective project managers are leadership by example, vision, technical competence, decisiveness, good communication skills, and good motivation skills (Zimmerer and Yasin, 1998). Yet the majority of IT professionals are not visionary (Lounsbury et al., n.d.).

As two-thirds of IT professionals are introverts, and many introverts prefer working alone and avoiding social contact, effective communication and motivation is challenging if not impossible for these IT professionals (Institute for Management Excellence, 2003).

1.2.3 The Snake

In the IT industry, one can be promoted into a leadership position without ever attending college or obtaining leadership training and experience. These promotions are based on skills gained on the job and credentials obtained through technical certification. With the high costs of developing and deploying technology and the ever-increasing rate of technological change, the world needs capable IT leaders to drive solution development and delivery. The industry needs to be able to lean on our technologists without fear of being bitten by a snake. We must instill confidence in our geek leaders.

Coaching front-line leaders, many of whom have never obtained leadership training, enables organizations to build leaders from the bottom up. These field commanders are in a position to aid the organization's top leadership to develop and articulate the vision for success. They work at ground level to motivate technologists to take the actions required for technology projects to succeed. This book provides tools to address this leadership void in the IT industry.

1.3 Overview of This Book

In Chapter 2, Why Geek Leadership is Different, we examine the definition of a leader and the challenges geeks face in leadership roles. We explore the Information Technology industry, taking a look at failed IT projects. We expound on the leadership potential that is intrinsic to geek leaders. In order to increase the success rate of IT projects, geeks need to understand their intrinsic power and utilize it to lead projects and organizations. This chapter concludes with a Leadership Assessment Questionnaire that can help you analyze and understand your leadership strengths and weaknesses.

This leads to Emotionally Intelligent Communications, which is discussed in Chapter 3. Good communication skills are essential to effective leadership. Helping geek leaders to communicate with emotional intelligence enables them to connect with their team members, their management, and their customers. In this chapter, I introduce the "Missed Signals" use case, which is based on a couple of actual events. Then, we describe three building blocks: (1) emotional intelligence, (2) the Communications Cycle, and (3) the basics of reading body language. These three building blocks are then combined to describe the process of communicating with emotional intelligence. The chapter concludes with an Implementation Checklist designed to assist the geek leader to become a more effective communicator.

Emotionally intelligent communications require the geek leader to know himself or herself. Chapter 4, Self-Leadership, begins with a use case that describes a challenging self-leadership situation. I then provide tools to help the geek leader discover himself or herself and to define the type of leader he or she would like to be. Then I explain how geek leaders can "rewrite their code" and take incremental steps to become the leaders they need and desire to be over time. At the end of this chapter, you will find a checklist that can help you take a proactive approach to improving your self-leadership.

Followers must accept being led. In Chapter 5, Followership, I present a use case describing a situation in which a geek leader has trouble obtaining support from her followers. I describe what it means to be an effective follower and the relationship between effective leadership and effective followership. We will discuss the leader's responsibility for resolving conflicts among followers and for creating synergistic solutions. I introduce a technique I call "Reverse Micromanagement," which I have effectively employed on several occasions to ensure that my leadership has the information they need to make decisions and up-channel status. The chapter concludes with a Followership Assessment to help you analyze how well your team members engage in followership.

A geek leader without personal credibility will be frustrated and ineffective. In Chapter 6, Personal Credibility, we discuss the importance of being an organized leader. We discuss the meaning of acting in a proactive manner. I will introduce techniques for prioritizing initiatives. We discuss keeping commitments, as an essential element of leadership is accountability—accountable geek leaders prevent IT project failures. Putting these principles into action produces a geek leader with a good reputation and substantial influence, which we will explore. We will conclude with an Implementation Checklist the geek leader can use to increase his or her personal credibility.

In Chapter 7, Project Leadership Systems Integration, we bring it all together with an overview of the CompTIA Project+ project management life cycle and product life cycles. Systems integration in this context means integrating IT leadership into the project management life cycle. I will introduce the Leadership Integration Plan, which provides guidance for defining, implementing, and assessing leadership within the context of the CompTIA Project+ project management life cycle. This chapter concludes with a Leadership Integration Plan template.

In Chapter 8, Closeout, we finish our examination of geek project leadership with a business fable about a CEO facing the challenge of injecting leadership into the project management practices within his company. We will explore three established and pertinent leadership models: the Exemplary Leadership Model, the Team Leadership Model, and the Situational Leadership Model. Each provides leadership concepts that can aid the geek leader in overcoming leadership challenges.

This book provides geek leaders with resources to assist them to continually improve their leadership abilities. My goal is to provide information to help geeks in leadership roles better understand leadership and become better leaders. This information can help geeks aspiring to advance their careers into management and earn more money and prestige. As presented in the overview, this book is designed to coach IT professionals in leadership positions on how to lead their teams within the context of being a leader in their organization. After you complete this book, you will be able to overcome leadership challenges with emotionally intelligent communication.

I am confident that this book will help geeks become better, more effective leaders, embodying the leadership characteristics described earlier that have made others successful leaders. This book can also help non-geeks better understand geeks, IT projects, and the impact of leadership on the success of IT projects. The management instruments at the end of Chapters 2 through 7 can help you put what you have learned into practice.

The information I provide in this book will help geeks progress in their careers by being aware of leadership expectations and adapting their styles accordingly. I hope you enjoy reading this book as much as I enjoyed writing it for you. Now, let's continue with Chapter 2, Why Geek Leadership Is Different.

Chapter 2

Why Geek Leadership
Is Different

It has been said that in any group of people, a small fraction will be leaders, a larger fraction will be followers, and a substantial portion just will not want to get involved. A leader is part artist, and in IT, this art requires blending technology skills, process skills, and, most importantly, people skills to produce products and services that deliver value to customers. You can administer networks, servers, and databases; you can program computers; you can design and implement processes; and you can manage projects—but people must be led. This means motivating them to achieve their highest performance by creating a vision, building teams, providing direction, and resolving conflict. This means building relationships—having frequent dialogues and making connections with team members and other project stakeholders. You can judge the success of leaders by the success of their followers and by their ability to perform in a manner that achieves their vision.

But people are the wildcards in the game of IT projects. They are unpredictable and sometimes chaotic. They are influenced by their instincts and emotions. They see and hear things differently based on their individual perceptions, filters, and experiences. They have different backgrounds and preferences. They don't always understand each other or even like each other. But mostly, in my experience and in accordance with McGregor's Theory Y (McGregor, 1960), IT people want to do a good job—they want to learn, achieve, and do well at work, and they look for their leaders to provide the support and coaching they need to perform well. Management tools and techniques such as quality control and risk management are important, but projects will not succeed unless people receive the leadership they need.

In 2015, for the first time, the US Government Accountability Office added "Improving the Management of IT Acquisitions and Operations" to its annual High Risk Report, stating, "Although the executive branch has undertaken numerous initiatives to better manage the more than $80 billion that is annually invested in information technology (IT), federal IT investments too frequently fail or incur cost overruns and schedule slippages while contributing little to mission-related outcomes" (GAO, 2015). The Standish Group International reports that in 2012, 61% of IT projects worldwide were challenged or failed altogether.

As a program manager, I once supervised a team leader, let's call him John, who was responsible for Information Technology Infrastructure Library (ITIL) Configuration Management processes for a large IT support operation. We needed to mature our processes, so it was important that John establish relationships with the other leaders within the enterprise in order to integrate processes across the organization. We needed him to lead the integration effort, and we provided him with clear objectives for his positon. After several months, we did not see the progress we expected. Instead, John focused his efforts on a network engineering project that was only tangentially related to his position. This effort did not require him to talk to anyone. "I just want a job where I can put my head under a hood all day, do my work, and then go home," he told me. Realizing that he was not a good fit for the role, and also that he was not willing to make the effort to adapt his style to fit the position, he soon left. Fortunately, we were able to fill the position with someone with strong leadership skills soon after his departure.

As mentioned in Chapter 1, many front-line leaders in IT have never obtained leadership training, and John was one of them. To increase the rate of success of IT programs and projects, we need leadership from the bottom of organizations up. IT personnel such as programmers, database administrators, and network engineers are accustomed to being evaluated on the quality of their individual contributions. Leadership is different—it requires different skills because the leader is responsible for the performance of his or her group and for managing relationships with stakeholders. IT geek leadership is different because IT geek leaders are not natural leaders. As we will explore in this chapter, most IT geek leaders are introverts and are more comfortable being "under the hood all day" and not talking to people. Yet, research indicates that 90% of project management is communications. The IT leader who does not know how to communicate with people will fail. This book can help IT geek leaders understand the art of leadership, enabling them to adapt to the requirements of IT leadership and increase the rate of IT project success.

2.1 What Is a Leader?

Leadership is an abstract term that invokes philosophical perceptions concerning the impact of one person's influence on others. Many have described and defined leadership in various ways.

Businessdictionary.com defines leadership as:

1. The individuals who are the leaders in an organization, regarded collectively.
2. The activity of leading a group of people or an organization or the ability to do this.

Leadership involves establishing a clear vision; sharing that vision with others so that they will follow willingly; providing the information, knowledge and methods to realize that vision; and coordinating and balancing the conflicting interests of all members and stakeholders (Leadership, n.d.).

Table 2-1 lists a variety of leadership attributes from different reputable sources.

"Are leaders born or made?" This question has served as a source of intellectual nourishment for ages. There are two major perspectives on leadership: the *trait perspective* and the *process perspective*.

Table 2-1 Leadership Attributes

Leaders are:		
Team builders	Bold	Intelligent
Motivators	Risk takers	Articulate
Communicators	Planners	Perceptive
Influencers	Inspiring	Self-confident
Decision makers	Courageous	Self-assured
Politically aware	Listeners	Persistent
Culturally aware	Decisive	Determined
Negotiators	Visionaries	Trustworthy
Trust builders	Passionate	Dependable
Conflict managers	Motivators	Friendly
Coaches[a]	Organizers	Outgoing[c]
	Critical thinkers[b]	

[a] Data derived from Project Management Institute (2013). *Guide to the Project Management Body of Knowledge, (PMBOK® Guide),* 5th ed. Newton Square, PA: Project Management Institute.

[b] Data derived from Toastmasters International (2005). *A Practical Guide to Becoming a Better Leader—Competent Leadership Guide.* Mission Viejo, CA: Toastmasters International.

[c] Data derived from Northouse (2007). *Leadership: Theory and Practice,* 4th ed. London, UK: Sage.

According to the trait perspective, leaders have special inborn, innate characteristics that set them apart from others. These factors include physical traits such as height, personality features such as extraversion, and abilities such as fluency of speech (Northouse, 2007).

The process viewpoint sees leadership as a set of behaviors. From this perspective, leadership can be learned (Northouse, 2007). Those seeking to become leaders can improve how they interact with followers, enhancing their leadership effectiveness.

There were several studies of the trait approach to leadership in the 20th century. These studies have resulted in a list of traits that are desirable to those of us who seek to be perceived as leaders: intelligence, self-confidence, determination, integrity, and sociability.

- *Intelligence.* Researchers have found that leaders tend to be more intelligent than non-leaders. However, if a leader's intellectual ability far exceeds his or her followers, there could be a counterproductive impact on leadership.
- *Self-confidence.* Self-confidence, including self-esteem, self-assurance, and the belief that one can make a difference, invokes positive feelings within leaders concerning the actions they take to influence their followers.
- *Determination.* Effective leaders are perceived to be determined, to exercise initiative, to be persistent, and to drive toward results. They assert themselves proactively to overcome obstacles.
- *Integrity.* Lastly, leaders exhibit integrity, demonstrating honesty and trustworthiness. They take responsibility and hold themselves accountable, inspiring confidence in others because they are trusted to keep their word (Northouse, 2007).

There are core leadership skills that researchers have found to be advantageous to those seeking promotion into leadership positions. These skills can be learned, enabling the prospective leader to become more effective.

- *Strategy,* including vision, acumen, planning, and the courage to lead:
  - **Vision.** Leaders have the ability to envision a new reality and inspire followers to take action to realize it.
  - **Acumen.** Leaders see the big picture and understand how it impacts their present situation.
  - **Planning.** Leaders perceive and anticipate future events and design goals and activities to prepare for those events.
  - **Courage to Lead.** Leaders take calculated risks—they stand firm in the face of adversity.
- *Action,* including decision making, communication, and mobilizing others:

- o **Decision Making.** Leaders consider and weigh alternatives and then determine the course of action.
- o **Communication.** Leaders facilitate free-flowing thoughts and information sharing.
- o **Mobilizing Others.** Leaders convince others to take actions toward the envisioned future state.
- **Results,** including risk taking, result-focused actions, and agility:
  - o **Risk Taking.** Leaders venture into uncharted territories in order to achieve their objectives.
  - o **Results Focus.** Leaders avoid distractions and help their subordinates avoid them as well, staying on course to achieve the desired goals.
  - o **Agility.** Leaders adapt to changing situations and address uncertainty creatively (Bradberry and Greaves, 2012).

Erika Andersen, author of *Leading So People Will Follow* (Andersen, 2012a), provides a rational and balanced viewpoint that attempts to reconcile the contradiction between born and made leadership perspectives. At Forbes.com, she posted, "What I've learned by observing thousands of people in business over the past 30 years, though, is that—like most things—leadership capability falls along a bell curve. Some people are, indeed, born leaders. These folks at the top of the leadership bell curve start out very good, and tend to get even better as they go along. Then there are the folks at the bottom of the curve: that bottom 10–15% of people who, no matter how hard they try, simply aren't ever going to be very good leaders. They just don't have the innate wiring.

"Then there's the big middle of the curve, where the vast majority of us live. And that's where the real potential for 'made' leaders lies. It's what most of my interviewers assume isn't true—when, in fact, it is: most folks who start out with a modicum of innate leadership capability can actually become very good, even great leaders" (Andersen, 2012b).

Many IT solutions are delivered in programs and projects. Program managers provide high-level leadership for programs. According to the Project Management Institute (PMI®), a program is "a group of related projects, subprograms, and program activities that are managed in a coordinated way to deliver benefits not available from managing them individually" (Program Management Institute, 2013a). An IT program to develop a point of sale system for a restaurant chain, for example, may comprise software development, hardware configuration, and network configuration projects.

Also according to the PMI®, program managers are responsible for defining the program vision, mission, goals, and objectives. They define the program components (projects and subprograms) to develop deliverables that, when integrated, achieve the vision. Program managers apply leadership throughout the program life cycle, setting goals for the project team and expectations for stakeholders (PMI®, 2013b).

Not only must program managers apply leadership skills to align the program with organizational objectives, they must also develop the leadership skills of the project managers on their team.

PMI® advises that project managers require leadership skills to be personally effective (PMI®, 2013a). The project leader leads project activities such as initiating, planning, executing, monitoring, controlling, and closing out projects. The program manager relies on the project leader to influence the team's behavior in a manner that leads to successful development of deliverables, which enable the program to deliver the desired benefits. The program manager needs the project leader to communicate effectively, manage conflict, motivate team members, and facilitate problem resolution.

Because IT projects are complex and subject to frequent changes, IT project leaders need a flexible leadership style and excellent communication skills to influence the reduction of complexity and to effectively control change.

IT project leaders are responsible for organizing and leading team-building activities for their project teams. The complexities of IT projects require team members to be comfortable working with each other. They need to trust each other to perform their assigned tasks well. This trust goes beyond appreciation of technical skill sets and application of sound processes. Relationships are required to develop trust. People more easily communicate and work well with people they like. If people like each other, they are more likely to have synergy, to produce far more together than they would on their own. The project leader is responsible for creating environments that enable relationships and synergy to grow. If people do not know each other, perhaps fear each other, and do not trust each other, synergy be will difficult to develop, and complexity will be difficult to defeat.

At the team level, it is the project leader's responsibility to encourage positive behaviors—those that lead to successful outcomes; and discourage negative behaviors—those that lead to project failures. These behaviors include not only technical performance, but also behaviors that lead to the establishment and enhancement of relationships that lead to synergies—synergies that will enable team members to overcome complexity and drive project initiatives toward meeting the mission requirements and achieving the projected vision.

I once managed a large IT operations program for a US government agency. The program had over a dozen team leaders, each leading teams of between five and fifteen administrators and analysts. Within a month of starting the position, I conducted a leadership questionnaire to get an understanding of the leadership and management training these team leaders had received. The results were all over the map—some were trained and experienced leaders, others had never attended any leadership training. Some of the team leaders who had no leadership training had complaints from the customer because of their poor communications. Some of them had team members that were not happy. Most of them had accountability issues—they were not accountable and they did not hold their people accountable. As a result, morale was low and our customer was not satisfied.

I responded by developing and communicating a strategic vision of the program, establishing initiatives for the calendar year. I documented leadership and management standards for each team leader in the program. I met with them individually in order to build relationships and to gain an understanding of the issues they faced. I made myself available to speak with them whenever they needed assistance. I established quarterly awards for Valor, Customer Service, and Leadership, recognizing personnel that exemplified the behavior we needed in order to improve. I met with them as a group on a weekly basis, facilitating resolution of issues and providing leadership training. I established a system consisting of team assessments, analysis of those assessments to identify strengths and weaknesses, and team planning to bolster strengths and reduce weaknesses. Instead of providing them leadership briefings every week, the system required the team leaders to brief their groups on the status of implementing their plan. During these briefings, the team leaders received feedback from their peers on how to deal with operations, customer, and personnel issues and how to improve morale. They learned to be better communicators. Through this process, the team leaders obtained on-the-job training in leadership, IT operations continuously improved, and morale issues were identified and addressed.

Now that you have an introduction to leadership, let's explore the career of a great geek leader to understand how you can become one yourself.

2.2 Great Geek Leadership

William Henry Gates III is the epitome of a great geek leader. He is a geek's geek, a highly intelligent and voracious learner, nurtured on technology, driven to solve the most complex problems. Bill demonstrated core leadership skills early in his career. He then practiced exemplary leadership skills as he built Microsoft into the world's largest software company.

Bill Gates was first exposed to computers in 1968 when he was only 13 years old. He attended Lakeside School, an all-male institution with grades seven through twelve in Seattle, Washington, USA. The Mothers' Club at Lakeside used the proceeds from a rummage sale to buy an ASR-33 Teletype terminal and computer time on a General Electric mainframe (Andrews and Manes, 2013). "The Lakeside's Mothers' Club had a rummage sale every year to raise money for the school," Gates said in a 2010 interview. "And instead of just funding the budget, they always would fund something kind of new and interesting in addition. And without too much understanding, they decided having a computer terminal at the school would be a novel thing. It was a teletype—upper case only, ten characters a second—and you had to share a phone line to call into a big time-sharing computer that was very expensive. When you were connected up it would charge, and then when you actually had a program running it would charge a lot more." It was here that Gates learned to program in BASIC. "The programming language was BASIC, which was quite novel at the time. It had been invented by some Dartmouth professors. So that was the first computer language I learned, and I wrote increasingly complex programs. So that eighth grade exposure was a pretty neat thing, even though the machine we were working on was quite limited" (Academy of Achievement, 2010).

Gates and his classmates in the Lakeside Computer Club, including Paul Allen, who co-founded Microsoft with Gates, eventually wrote a complex class scheduling system for the Lakeside School. (Lakeside had asked some adults to write the program, but they could not figure it out.) After completing this project, the students wrote a payroll application for the Computer Center Corporation (C Cubed) in exchange for computer time. "So we agreed to write this payroll program," Gates explained. "And a payroll program is surprisingly complicated. There's all these taxes and reports and things at the state level and federal level (Academy of Achievement, 2010)." This experience exposed Gates to the inner workings of a business at a very young age.

C Cubed asked Gates and his friends if they could find problems with the Digital Equipment Corporation computer that the company rented. "These C Cubed people have this computer, which is a time-sharing computer, and they're letting us come in at night," Gate explained. "And they had this deal with the company who made the computer, Digital Equipment Corporation (DEC), that they had this acceptance period. If they could find problems with it, they could delay their rental payments. So they thought of us as kind of monkeys that might find some problems and help them delay their rental payments. Well, that was a fair analysis, because at first we were just completely goofing around. Like, we'd try to run hundreds of jobs at the same time, or have all the jobs try and grab the same resources, to see if we could get the system to fail. And we did, in kind of this brute force approach. So they would report that as a problem and delay their rental payment. Well, a few months went by, actually about four months by the end of it. We had gotten very sophisticated. In fact, we'd gotten the source code of the operating system out of the garbage can, and were reading it, and the kind of problems we were finding were far more subtle. In fact, we would not only find the problem, we'd look and we'd suggest how they might fix it" (Academy of Achievement, 2010).

The team's exploits gained them a reputation at DEC, and when TRW needed top programming talent for a large DEC PDP-10 and PDP-11 programming project at the Bonneville Power Administration in Vancouver, Washington, USA, DEC recommended Gates and Allen (Andrews and Manes, 2013). "I was 16 when they interviewed me," Gates explains. "So they were like, 'We can't hire you.' But then they talked to us about software and we clearly know a lot. And when you're young and you know a lot, people don't have any kind of intermediate thing. You're either what you're supposed to be, which is a kid that doesn't know that much, or they think, 'Whoa, this guy is the limit!' We were pretty good programmers. But anyway, so we got jobs at this TRW and that exposed me to some programmers, who were way better than I was, who critiqued my work. I could look at their work."

It is widely known that Gates attended Harvard and left the university to start Microsoft. But Gates was a geek's geek, a proven problem solver prior to even being accepted at Harvard.

While at Harvard, Micro Instrumentation and Telemetry Systems (MITS) created the Altair 8800 based on Intel's 8800 chip. However, the machine did not ship with software, and no one at MITS had time to develop it. Gates and Allen called MITS and said they had an installation of BASIC that would run on the new Altair 8800. When they made the call, the software did not exist. They had six weeks to develop it. Allen built an Altair 8800 simulator based on previous work they had done with an Altair 8080 (Andrews and Manes, 2013). "So I'm a student at Harvard," Gates explained. "Paul's working at Honeywell, but we spend—what was it?—six weeks, and really write this thing, which— you know, my whole career has sort of been building after this thing. It's one of the most—probably the *most* fun piece of software I ever wrote. I mean, it's unbelievable, because it has to be very small—there's only 4K bytes of memory—and we don't have the real machine, so you have to be very careful you get everything right. Anyway, so Paul takes it out, and these guys mostly sell kit computers, they'd only assembled a few of them, and so they got it connected up and Paul puts it in and it runs the first time!" (Academy of Achievement, 2010). Gates left Harvard, Gates and Allen signed a contract with MITS, and Microsoft was born!

In the early years at Microsoft, Bill Gates developed and refined his core leadership skills as demonstrated through his strategy, action, and results.

Strategically, Gates defined the Microsoft *vision* as "a computer on every desktop and in every home, running Microsoft software" (Andrews and Manes,

2013). Gates always had the big picture in mind, yet he kept an eye on every detail of the business. He *planned* a strategy in the early years that Microsoft still uses very effectively today. "Microsoft was only a few people and we'd written this BASIC, and the idea was to license it to lots of companies and then to write other software. So the head of MITS said he could help us market it to other people and take a sales commission for that, and I wrote the contract so that if they weren't serious about promoting it and putting a lot of investment into that, they would lose that right" (Academy of Achievement, 2010).

Recognizing that software piracy was eroding Microsoft profits, Gates demonstrated the *courage to lead,* writing an open letter to the Altair computer users group that discouraged the pirating of the Altair BASIC software Microsoft developed. "Most directly, the thing you do is theft," Gates wrote (Andrews and Manes, 2013).

Bill Gates *took action* in the early days of Microsoft. He made the decision to purchase 86-DOS from Seattle Computer Products and then license it to IBM just in time for the release of the IBM Personal Computer (PC), capitalizing on an opportunity to position tiny Microsoft predominately with giant IBM (Andrews and Manes, 2013).

Gates, an effective *communicator,* became the chief spokesman for Microsoft, constructing business deals with partners such as Apple and Texas Instruments and making sales to customers. His efforts *mobilized others* to follow his lead, all in pursuit of a single vision—a computer on every desk in every home running Microsoft software. Gates achieved results through risk taking, staying focused, and being agile. The software that Microsoft released was not always free of bugs, but Gates took the risk and released it regardless. He did not give up when he received poor reviews; instead, he stayed focused on results. Word 3.0 was a great example. Word 1.0 and Word 2.0 were riddled with bugs, but Microsoft listened to the customer, remained focused, and developed Word 3.0—which unseated Corel WordPerfect, the leading word processor since 1979—as the dominant word processor in the industry in 1992 (Andrews and Manes, 2013).

Windows development took a similar path. When Windows 1.0 was released in 1985, it was not successful, but Gates was not deterred. Microsoft released Windows 2.0 in 1987, which did better, but was not widely successful. In 1990, Microsoft released Windows 3.0, and the company finally achieved a breakthrough, selling 10 million units in two years and raking in millions in profits. This is an example of resiliency, the determination to continue to pursue a vision in the face of obstacles (Chandomba, 2014).

Microsoft demonstrated *agility* by developing the capacity to excel not only in the areas of programing languages, but also in operating systems and productivity applications. Their actions, led by Gates, enabled attainment of their vision (Andrews and Manes, 2013).

2.3 Transformational Leadership

Businessdictionary.com defines transformational leadership as a "style of leadership in which the leader identifies the needed change, creates a vision to guide the change through inspiration, and executes the change with the commitment of members of the group" (Transformational Leadership, n.d.). In 1983, Jim Kouzes and Barry Posner of Santa Clara University started researching thousands of personal best leadership experiences. Their research included 75,000 people from all over the world. They used this research to develop their Five Practices of Exemplary Leadership Model. This transformational leadership model consists of these five elements: Model the Way, Inspire a Shared Vision, Challenge the Process, Enable Others to Act, and Encourage the Heart. Bill Gates's leadership at Microsoft not only transformed the computer industry, it also transformed the business world. Table 2-2 demonstrates Gates's exemplary transformational leadership impact based on Kouzes and Posner's model (Kouzes and Posner, 2010).

Table 2-2 Five Practices of Exemplary Leadership Model

Element	Description	Gates's Behavior
Model the Way	The leader is clear about his/her values and philosophy, setting a positive example.	Bill Gates was an expert programmer. He worked long hours and rarely took vacations. He expected his employees to show the same commitment.
Inspire a Shared Vision	The leader creates a compelling vision that drives people's behavior to achieve the goals.	Microsoft employees were inspired by Gates's vision of ruling the microcomputer software world.
Challenge the Process	The leader is willing to change the status quo and take risks, stepping out into the unknown as pioneer.	No other company shared Gates's vision for writing software for inexpensive microcomputers. Ken Olsen, the president of Digital Equipment Corporation, a company Gates admired, thought the notion that people would want to have a computer was "silly" (Academy of Achievement 2002).

(Continued on next page)

Table 2-2 Five Practices of Exemplary Leadership Model *(Continued)*

Element	Description	Gates's Behavior
Enable Others to Act	The leader is effective at working with people. The leader values teamwork and collaboration.	Although Gates has a tough and challenging management style, his employees respected him and were compelled to follow his leadership.
Encourage the Heart	The leader recognizes and rewards team members for their contributions and accomplishments toward achieving the vision.	Bill Gates rewarded his employees with excellent pay and recognition. Many Microsoft employees became millionaires during their tenure with the company.

Data derived from Northouse (2007). *Leadership: Theory and Practice.* London, UK: Sage.

Bill Gates was an effective communicator who kept his employees motivated. He invested in their future and made many of them wealthy. He delivered the right information to the right people for the right purpose. "The vision is really about empowering workers," Gates said, "giving them all of the information about what's going on so they can do a lot more than they've done in the past" (Chandomba, 2014).

2.4 IT Geeks Are Different

When it comes to IT geeks in leadership positions, Bill Gates is the exception, not the rule. Considering the traits and behaviors of effective leaders, most geeks face more challenges that hinder their ability to lead than they have intrinsic capabilities for leadership. Studies have shown that IT geeks (1) are generally not visionary, an attribute that is key to effective, transformational leadership (Lounsbury et al., n.d.); (2) are generally introverted, preferring to work alone, which makes motiving others and being an effective communicator difficult if not impossible (Institute for Management Excellence, 2003); (3) are generally not conscientious, meaning they have an inclination to disregard rules, norms, and values (Lounsbury et al., n.d.); (4) are not concerned about image management, which makes modeling the way a challenge (Lounsbury et al., n.d.); and (5) generally prefer thinking to feeling, which makes leading from the heart challenging (Institute for Management Excellence, 2003).

There are three personality preferences that give IT geeks hope to become effective leaders: (1) IT professionals are predominantly thinkers, a trait they share with people in management and executive positions; (2) two thirds of IT geeks prefer judging over perceiving, meaning they are generally decisive and organized; and (3) some IT geeks have intuition, and therefore have the ability to think strategically and systematically (Institute for Management Excellence, 2003). IT geeks are also emotionally resilient, open to change and new ideas, intrinsically motivated, and tough minded (Lounsbury et al., n.d.).

Let's explore a few studies that produce these findings.

2.4.1 The Big Five Personality Traits

In the 1970s, two independent research teams studied personality traits of thousands of people and found the same results. The first team was Paul Costa and Robert McCrae at the National Institutes of Health, and the second team was Warren Norman of the University of Michigan and Lewis Goldberg of the University of Oregon. Analysis of each team's data revealed that most human personality traits, regardless of language or culture, fall within five dimensions, known as the Big Five: Agreeableness/Teamwork, Conscientiousness, Emotional Resilience/Neuroticism, Extraversion, and Openness (The Big Five Personality Test, n.d.).

John Lounsbury of the University of Tennessee, R. Scott Studham of Oak Ridge National Laboratory, Robert Steel of the University of Michigan, and Lucy Gibson and Adam Drost of eCareerFit.com conducted a study of 9,011 IT professionals, extracting data from eCareerfit.com's archival database, a database that included 2,000 unique IT job titles (Lounsbury et al., n.d.). Their study analyzed IT professionals according to the Big Five personality traits. In addition, because the Big Five traits were deemed to be too broad, they included seven narrow-scope personality constructs in their analysis: Assertiveness, Customer Service Orientation, Intrinsic Motivation, Image Management, Optimism, Tough-Mindedness, and Visionary Style. For these 12 factors, they compared the results for IT professionals against 200,000 individuals from all occupations in their database to determine how those traits related to career satisfaction. The study examined two research questions:

1. On which personality traits do IT professionals differ from other occupations?
2. Which personality traits are related to career satisfaction for IT professionals?

Their findings are summarized in Table 2-3.

In 2002, another group of researchers (Timothy A. Judge, University of Florida; Joyce E. Bono, University of Minnesota; Remus Ilies, University of Florida; and Megan W. Gerhardt, University of Iowa) analyzed 78 leadership and personality studies published between 1967 and 1998 against the Big Five traits. They found that extraversion was the factor most strongly related to leadership, followed by conscientiousness, emotional resilience, and openness. Agreeableness was only weakly associated with leadership (Northouse, 2007).

Table 2-3 Big Five Personality Traits Study Results

Personality Trait	Description	Finding
Big Five:		
Agreeableness/ Teamwork	Propensity to work as part of a team and cooperatively function on group efforts.	IT professionals' mean scores not significantly different from norm group.
Conscientiousness	Dependability, reliability, trustworthiness, and inclination to adhere to company rules, norms, and values.	**IT professionals' mean scores were BELOW other occupations.**
Emotional Resilience	Overall level of emotional resilience in the face of job stress and pressure.	*IT professionals had significantly HIGHER mean scores compared to other occupations.*
Extraversion[a]	Tendency to be sociable, outgoing, gregarious, expressive, warmhearted, and talkative.	IT professionals' mean s Mission Viejo, CA: Toastmasters International. cores not significantly different from norm group.
Openness	Receptivity/openness to change, innovation, novel experience, and new learning.	*IT professionals had significantly HIGHER mean scores compared to other occupations.*
Narrow-Scope:		
Assertiveness	Disposition to speak up on matters of importance, express ideas and opinions confidently, defend personal beliefs, seize the initiative, and exert influence in a forthright but not aggressive manner.	IT professionals' mean scores not significantly different from norm group.
Customer Service Orientation	Striving to provide highly responsive, personalized, quality service to customers, putting them first, and trying to make them feel satisfied.	*IT professionals had significantly HIGHER mean scores compared to other occupations.*

(Continued on next page)

[a] This is a career satisfaction study. Extraverted IT professionals are as satisfied with their careers as extraverts in other occupations. However, two-thirds of IT professionals are considered introverts (Institute for Management Excellence, 2003).

Table 2-3 Big Five Personality Traits Study Results *(Continued)*

Personality Trait	Description	Finding
Intrinsic Motivation	Disposition to be motivated by intrinsic work factors such as challenge, meaning, autonomy, variety, and significance.	*IT professionals had significantly HIGHER mean scores compared to other occupations.*
Image Management	Disposition to monitor, observe, regulate, and control the self-presentation and image projected during interactions with others.	**IT professionals' mean scores were BELOW other occupations.**
Optimism	Have an upbeat, hopeful outlook concerning people, situations, prospects, and the future, even in the face of difficulty and adversity; a tendency to minimize problems and persist in the face of setbacks.	IT professionals' mean scores not significantly different from norm group.
Tough-Mindedness	Appraise information, draw conclusions, and make decisions based on logic, facts, and data rather than on feelings, values, and intuition; disposition to be analytical, realistic, objective, and unsentimental.	*IT professionals had significantly HIGHER mean scores compared to other occupations.*
Visionary Style	Focusing on long-term planning, strategy, envisioning future possibilities and contingencies.	**IT professionals' mean scores were BELOW other occupations.**

Data derived from Lounsbury et al. (2009). "Personality Traits and Career Satisfaction of Information Technology Professionals." eCareerFit.Com.

2.4.2 Myers-Briggs Type Indicator Study

Katherine Briggs and her daughter, Isabel Briggs Myers, developed the Myers-Briggs Type Indicator (MBTI) instrument in the 1940s. MBTI is based on the work of Carl Jung, a Swiss-born psychiatrist who researched and published studies on psychological types in the 1920s. The instrument was designed to determine individual preferences and to promote more constructive use of differences among people. MBTI test results enable organizations to assign personnel to tasks that fit their abilities. It is one of the most widely known psychological instruments today and is used all over the world (Kroeger, Thuesen, and Rutledge, 2002).

The MBTI instrument analyzes our preferences using four dichotomies: Energy, Information, Decision, and Action. Each dichotomy consists of two personality areas. Energy and Action are attitudes observed by the outside world. Information and Decision are internal processes that we use to make sense of the outside world. The preferences are not right or wrong, good or bad. They are our inclinations, our first choice in our approach to dealing with the world.

- *Energy*. Extraverts (E) receive their energy from their experiences with people. They refuel through personal interaction. Introverts (I) focus internally and are energized through their own internal experiences.
- *Information*. People with a Sensing (S) preference make sense of the world using their five senses. People who prefer iNtuition (N) understand the world through insight.
- *Decision*. Those who prefer Thinking (T) make decisions based on logic and principles, whereas those who prefer Feeling (F) make decisions based on personal and social values.
- *Action*. If one's preference is Judging (J), this person likes a structured approach, living life in a controlled way. Those who prefer Perceiving (P), on the other hand, are spontaneous and open ended in their approach to life (Hewertson, 2015).

The MBTI instrument assigns a four-letter type indicator that summarizes an individual's preference. For example, ESFP indicates an individual with a preference for Extraversion, Sensing, Feeling, and Perceiving (Kroeger et al., 2002).

Individuals develop preferences early in life, and these preferences usually do not change. We become comfortable with our preferences, which allows us to cope with confidence in this complex world. We are capable of using our non-preferences when necessary, and as we mature, our non-preferences enhance our ability to perform in new ways. But our non-preferences do not become our preferences, just has left-handed people do not become right-handed people (Kroeger et al., 2002).

Right-handed people can learn to write with their left hand, but it takes hard work and a lot of practice. I have known programmers that prefer Visual Basic over C#, and programmers that prefer C# over Visual Basic. Give them the same requirements, and each of them was capable of writing excellent code to solve a problem in a reasonable amount of time. They did it in their own way using their preferred development language. Could the C# programmer write code in Visual Basic, or the Visual Basic programmer develop solutions in

C#? Absolutely! But it would take more time and more effort for them to write code in their non-preferred languages. You can think of the Myers Briggs Type Indicators in the same way.

Tables 2-4 through 2-6 contain a summary of MBTI and a comparison of the MBTI scores of the general population verses IT professionals. If you have never taken an MBTI test, write down the temperament preference that agrees with you as you read the descriptions.

In contrast to the findings of Judge et al. (Northouse 2007) concerning leadership and extraversion, MBTI studies of IT professionals have found that two-thirds of IT geeks are introverted. This comes as no surprise to anyone that has spent time with IT geeks. IT geeks are generally less extraverted and more introverted than the general population. According to Carl Jung, the preference between introversion and extraversion is the biggest discriminator among people (Kroeger et al., 2002).

As discussed earlier, researchers have found that extraversion is the most important trait of the Big Five concerning leadership. This finding puts most IT geeks at a disadvantage when it comes to being an effective leader.

Generally, introverted people are more comfortable working alone than in groups and find themselves drained after prolonged social interactions (Kroeger et al., 2002). Such a predilection does not lend itself well to being a strong communicator or motivator. These introverted geeks must work hard at communication and motivation tasks; they generally don't like those tasks, and those tasks don't come naturally to them.

Introverts are energized by their own thoughts, ideas, and concepts and are generally not motivated to influence others. As discussed earlier, leaders are required to motivate and influence their team members. IT geeks in leadership positions generally are challenged when it comes to motivating others.

Introverts generally require time to think about situations before making decisions (Kroeger et al., 2002). This predilection may put IT geek leaders at a disadvantage when the situation requires a quick decision.

Leaders are expected to model the way, to set a positive example. Considering the Big Five study results, IT geeks scored below the norm on image management, indicating a lack of concern for projecting a smooth, polished self-presentation in interpersonal settings. IT geeks that do not care about their appearance will have a difficult time attracting followers. Their predilection for poor image management is likely related to their introverted inner focus and lack of conscientiousness. Non-geek leadership will frown upon a geek leader who does not monitor the image he or she portrays.

As Erika Andersen stated (Andersen, 2012b), most of us can learn to be more effective leaders. IT geeks can learn to use their less-preferred extraverted style just as a Visual Basic programmer can learn to code in C#. It may take some effort, but you *can* learn to lead out loud!

Table 2-4 MBTI Extraversion and Introversion Study Results

Temperament Preferences	General Population (CAPT Study)	General Population (Keirsey/Myers)	Computer Professionals (Management)
Extraversion (E):	54%	75%	33%
Need for sociability; energized by people and contact with lots of people			
Prefers to work with other people (teams, parties, gatherings, work groups)			
Speaks first, thinks later			
Finds listening more difficult than talking			
Needs affirmation from others to feel confident in own performance			
Introversion (I):	46%	25%	67%
Territorial—needs own private space; drained by a lot of people contact			
Prefers working alone (reading, writing, studying) or working with a limited number of people			
Prefers depth over breadth			
Rehearses things before saying them			
Perceived as a "great listener"			
Believes "talk is cheap," respects people who use words efficiently			

Data derived from Institute for Management Excellence. (2003). "Differences between 'Computer' Folks and the General Population." itstime.com; and Kroeger, et al. (2002). *Type Talk at Work.* New York, NY: Dell.

Table 2-5 MBTI Sensing and Intuition Study Results

Temperament Preferences	General Population (CAPT Study)	General Population (Keirsey/Myers)	Computer Professionals (Management)
Sensing (S):	54%	75%	46%
Practical and realistic; wants facts, trusts facts, and remembers facts			
Focuses on details and may miss the big picture			
Focuses on the external (what is observed); does not use or trust intuition			
Likes to focus on the moment; would rather take action than think about taking action			
"Fantasy" is a dirty word; "seeing is believing"			
Intuition (N):	46%	25%	54%
Innovative; seeks a better way			
Wants ideas; likes metaphors and vivid imagery			
Focuses on the internal (own inner voice); may find ideas coming to them with no idea of where they come from			
Thinks about several things at once			
Believes time is relative			
Gives general answers to questions instead of specifics			

Data derived from Institute for Management Excellence. (2003). "Differences between 'Computer' Folks and the General Population." itstime.com; and Kroeger, et al. (2002). *Type Talk at Work.* New York, NY: Dell.

Table 2-6 MBTI Thinking and Feeling Study Results

Temperament Preferences	General Population (CAPT Study)	General Population (Keirsey/Myers)	Computer Professionals (Management)
Thinking (T):	41%	50%	81%
More comfortable with impersonal, objective judgments; makes decisions based on logic and objectivity			
Prefers and follows rules, principles, laws, criteria			
Good at logical arguments			
Stays calm in situations in which others are upset			
Will argue both sides of a discussion			
Believes it is more important to be right than to be liked			
Feeling (F):	59%	50%	19%
More comfortable with value judgments, may be put off by rule-governed choices			
Makes decisions based on personal preferences and others' feelings			
Good at persuasion			
Will over-extend personally to accommodate others			
Easily takes back comments that may offend others			
Empathetic toward others			

Data derived from Institute for Management Excellence. (2003). "Differences between 'Computer' Folks and the General Population." itstime.com; and Kroeger, et al. (2002). *Type Talk at Work*. New York, NY: Dell.

IT geeks are generally less sensing and more intuitive than the general population. There are slightly more IT geeks who prefer intuition over sensing.

IT geeks in leadership positions with a preference for sensing have a natural sense of the movement of time (Kroeger et al., 2002). While not an identified leadership trait, this is an advantageous preference for estimating how long tasks and projects will take.

IT geeks with a preference for sensing tend to focus on individual pieces of the puzzle instead of the picture the completed puzzle produces. For geek leaders, this can be a disadvantage. There could be a tendency to fix what is seen as individual performance issues rather than take actions that motivate and energize the entire team to work together to reach a goal.

Leaders who prefer intuition have no problem seeing the picture, but may not see how all of the puzzle pieces fit together. They easily see patterns and future possibilities. For IT geek leaders with this preference, intuition is a strength that enables them to think strategically and systematically, to create a vision for the future of their team and project. It enables them to use their vision to drive creative change. Unfortunately, almost half of IT geeks tested did not have this preference.

Bill Gates's ability to simultaneously conceive and pursue a big-picture vision, a computer on every desk in every home running Microsoft software, and to be as detailed oriented as necessary to write great software, is extraordinary.

IT geeks prefer thinking much more than the general population does. There are far more thinkers than feelers in the IT profession.

Cross-cultural research has shown that thinkers make up about 86% of middle managers, 93% of senior managers, and 95% of executives. Leaders of all temperaments tend to clone themselves, hiring and nurturing other leaders who think as they do (Kroeger et al., 2002).

Because IT professionals are predominantly thinkers, this trait is an indicator that IT professionals have the ability to advance within their organizations if they can develop other complimentary leadership skills and if they can overcome their natural leadership challenges.

From a thinker's perspective, the world is a series of problems to be solved (Kroeger et al., 2002). IT geeks solve technical problems for a living, and IT geek leaders with a thinking preference are driven to solve problems with little regard to the human element. They may come across as critical and harsh concerning their subordinates' performance. As discussed earlier, this preference makes encouraging the heart a challenge for IT geek leaders.

Whereas MBTI studies may show that IT geeks prefer thinking over feeling, this does not make geeks more intelligent than people who prefer feeling over thinking, and it does not mean that IT geeks do not have emotions. It does mean that IT geeks prefer thinking over feelings when they make decisions. Instead of preferring to make a decision based on what people care about and their different points of view, IT geeks generally prefer to look at the principles that are applied and to analyze the pros and cons. Instead of being primarily concerned about values and what is best for the people involved, IT geeks generally prefer to be logical and impersonal.

Dale Carnegie first published *How to Win Friends and Influence People* in 1937, and the lessons taught in that book are still relevant today. Part Two of the book is called "Six Ways to Make People Like You" (Carnegie, 2010). The six principles Carnegie presented are summarized in Table 2-7.

Table 2-7 Dale Carnegie's Six Ways to Make People Like You

#	Principle	Quote
1	Be genuinely interested in others.	"It is the individual who is not interested in his fellow men who has the greatest difficulties in life and provides the greatest injury to others. It is from among such individuals that all human failures spring."
2	Smile.	"Action seems to follow feeling, but really action and feeling go together; and by regulating the action, which is under the more direct control of the will, we can indirectly regulate the feelings, which are not."
3	Remember that a person's name to that person is the sweetest and most important sound in any language.	"Franklin D. Roosevelt knew that one of the simplest ways of gaining good will was by remembering names and making people feel important—yet how many of us do it?"
4	Be a good listener. Encourage others to talk about themselves.	"Isaac F. Marcosson, a journalist who interviewed hundreds of celebrities, declared that many people fail to make a favorable impression because they don't listen attentively. 'They have been so much concerned with what they are going to say next that they do not keep their ears open. . . . Very important people have told me they prefer good listeners to good talkers, but the ability to listen seems rarer than almost any other good trait."
5	Talk in terms of the other person's interests.	"For Roosevelt knew, as all leaders know, that the royal road to a person's heart is to talk about the things he or she treasures the most."
6	Make the other person feel important—and do it sincerely.	"The unvarnished truth is that almost all the people you meet feel themselves superior to you in some way, and a sure way to their hearts is to let them realize in some subtle way that you recognize their importance, and recognize it sincerely. Remember that Emerson said: 'Every man I meet is my superior in some way. In that, I learn from him.'"

Data derived from Carnegie, D. (2010). *How to Win Friends and Influence People*. New York, NY: Simon & Schuster.

IT geeks generally do not try to appear caring, warm, or tactful—this disposition is not their first preference. Instead they generally prefer to be impersonal, to avoid allowing their personal wishes or other people's wishes to influence their decisions. This general preference makes leading by encouraging the heart very challenging for IT geeks.

As Bill Gates has shown, IT geeks are capable of encouraging the heart, but they need to be cognizant of the disparity between their personal preference and the behavior required and expected of effective leaders.

IT geeks generally prefer judging over perceiving more than the general population does. As described in Table 2-8, two-thirds of IT geeks tested prefer judging over perceiving.

This general preference toward judging gives IT geeks a leadership advantage. Leaders are expected to establish plans for their teams and manage the implementation of those plans. They need to be decisive and to work hard to set a positive example. IT geeks with a preference toward judging are capable of leading in this way.

Keirsey.com lists Bill Gates as an INTJ (Rational™ Portrait of the Mastermind, n.d.), meaning that he is an Introvert (I) verses an extrovert and he prefers Thinking (T) over feeling. Yet Gates is a visionary, an effective communicator and motivator, and he has demonstrated that he encourages the heart. He is proof that IT geeks can come to be great leaders, and he sets the example for other IT geeks, demonstrating how they can adapt their preferred style and

Table 2-8 MBTI Judging and Perceiving Study Results

Temperament Preferences	General Population (CAPT Study)	General Pop. (Keirsey/ Myers)	Computer Professionals (Management)
Judging (J):	54%	50%	66%
Likes closure and solid plans, goals, and timetables			
Work comes before play			
Likes to make decisions and move on and to complete things and get them out of the way			
Organized: keeps things in order			
Does not like surprises			

(Continued on next page)

Table 2-8 MBTI Judging and Perceiving Study Results *(Continued)*

Temperament Preferences	General Population (CAPT Study)	General Pop. (Keirsey/ Myers)	Computer Professionals (Management)
Perceiving (P):	44%	50%	34%
Likes open and fluid options			
More playful and less serious; work does not always come first; work must be enjoyable			
Likes to keep options open and explore; resists making final decisions			
Easily distracted			
Prefers creativity and spontaneity to neatness and order			
Changes the subject often during conversations			

Data derived from Institute for Management Excellence. (2003). "Differences between 'Computer' Folks and the General Population." itstime.com; and Kroeger, et al. (2002). *Type Talk at Work.* New York, NY: Dell.

make a difference for their team, their project, their organization, and maybe even the IT industry and the business world.

The differences in personality preferences are the source of miscommunications, politics, interpersonal conflicts, and the like. But if everyone were an introvert, our projects would not benefit from ideas generated in lively brainstorming sessions fueled with the energy of extraverts. And, if everyone were an extravert, our projects would not benefit from the introvert's deep thinking and listening skills required to develop solutions. Each temperament preference brings its own strengths, and as leaders, we must manage the inevitable conflict among people with different styles and leverage their ability to contribute to the success of our projects.

2.5 Information Technology Projects are Different

IT projects are sickly creatures, prone to ailments that threaten their survival. If you are an IT project leader, your project may be at risk of failing.

Since 1985, The Standish Group has documented success and failure rates of real-life IT environments and software development projects. The group produces

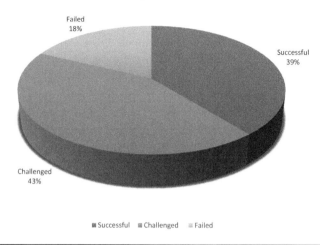

2012 IT Project Outcomes

Figure 2-1 2012 IT project outcomes. (Data derived from The Standish Group International. "The CHAOS Manifesto 2013: Think Big, Act Small." Versionone.com.)

the CHAOS Manifesto, which is based on research that encompasses 90,000 completed IT projects over 18 years. Sixty percent (60%) of the projects analyzed for the CHAOS Manifesto are US based, 25% are European, and the remaining 15% represent the rest of the world.

According to the CHAOS Manifesto 2013 (see Figure 2-1), 39% of all projects were successful, meaning they were delivered on time, on budget, with required features and functions; 43% were challenged, meaning they were late, over budget, and/or provided less than the required features and functions; and 18% failed, meaning they were cancelled prior to completion or delivered and never used (The Standish Group International, 2013). Experts estimate the global cost of IT failure to be $3 trillion annually (Krigsman, 2012).

If the civil engineering community experienced the same statistics, 43% of housing would be substandard and 18% of houses would be unfinished, littering our cities and towns with ramshackle buildings. If the IT projects were patients, they would have a survival rate of 39%, a chance of becoming sick of 43%, and an 18% chance of dying.

2.6 Why Are IT Projects So Sickly?

Although not as complex as the human body, IT projects are born and raised in an environment with its own inherent complexities.

According to Robert Goatham of Calleam Consulting Ltd, IT projects are complex because of the number of interrelated decisions that are required in order for the project to be successful. Goatham reports that IT projects require practitioners to expend over five times as much effort making decisions as civil engineering practitioners expend on making decisions for construction projects (Goatham, 2009).

The environments in which IT projects are developed and deployed exacerbate the complexity. "While it would be comforting to think that all decisions are made in a fully rational and informed way, in practice many other dynamics influence the way decisions are made," Goatham writes. "Diverse factors such as cognitive biases, training, prior experiences, interpersonal relationships and personality type can shape the decisions made on an individual basis and in the broader context factors such as politics, organizational goals (both spoken and unspoken) and the structure of incentives within the organization can also influence the choices that get made. When other environmental factors that affect decision making (such as the amount of schedule or budget pressure the team is working under) are considered, it becomes clear that the domain within which decisions are made is an extremely complex one and that complexity brings with it the ever present danger of project failure" (Goatham, 2009).

According to the 2013 CHAOS Manifesto, "The real key to being a good PM is to take a complex process and make it simple and executable. Projects follow a natural progression. The PM's job is to administer this progression to a successful resolution. The Standish Group research clearly shows that projects that have the leadership and judgment of a talented PM and an organization that supports its PM will fare much better than those that do not have such capability and posture in place" (The Standish Group International, 2013).

In the United States, the 2013 Healthcare.gov rollout is an excellent example of IT project failure due to extreme complexity. Healthcare.gov was one of the most complex IT projects ever undertaken by the US federal government. It communicates in real time with about 112 different computer systems across the United States (Cha and Sun, 2013).

Heathcare.gov did not get exhaustive testing and had undergone late changes before its October 2013 release. The public found the site difficult to use, and it caused significant embarrassment for the Obama administration. CGI Group Inc, the contractor responsible for developing the site, said the government made late requirements changes, not providing the final requirements until May 2013. This lead to a requirement to rework about one-third of the development effort (Olsen, 2014).

Commenting on the complexity of Healthcare.gov and other government IT projects, Theresa Pardo, Director of the Center for Technology in Government at the University of Albany, State University of New York, said, "Greater complexity leads to greater risk. Most traditional system development efforts do not account for the level of coordination necessary in the development of such complex systems. . . . Our work shows, the more boundaries crossed, the more critical coordination becomes" (Newcombe, 2014).

As discussed in Chapter 1, managing this level of complexity requires excellent leadership. "Attention to the time and skills required for expert collaboration and coordination is often overlooked," Pardo says. "You need 'super' project managers, who have the skill-sets to ensure all actions are coordinated across multiple boundaries and are sensitive to shifting realities" (Newcombe, 2014).

IT project leadership requirements are like the complex requirements human bodies have for antioxidants. In the human body, free radicals are atoms or groups of atoms that are formed when oxygen interacts with certain molecules. Free radicals can cause a chain reaction within the human body, damaging cellular components such as DNA or the cell membrane, causing cells to function poorly or to die.

The body's defense system for free radicals is antioxidants. Antioxidants are molecules that interact with free radicals and terminate the chain reactions, preventing cellular damage and diseases such as cancer. The principle antioxidant micronutrients are vitamin E, beta-carotene, and vitamin C. The body cannot create the micronutrients—they must be supplied in the diet.

Complexity rampages through IT projects like free radicals. Complexity both damages projects at the lowest level, causing miscommunication and low morale, and hastens technological failure.

Antioxidants are composed of vitamin E, beta-carotene, and vitamin C. Similarly, the 2013 CHAOS Manifesto provides 10 success points that together make up a prescription for the leadership qualities needed in IT leaders. Table 2-9 details these success points and potential scotomas (blind spots) for IT project leaders—these blind spots impair the IT geek's ability to successfully lead in the prescribed area. A subjective, nonscientific scoring of each CHAOS Manifesto Success Point against the Big Five Personality Trait Study and MBTI preference for IT professionals produces an IT geeks' score of 0 out of 10 possible points. IT geeks are not natural leaders. They have to work hard to overcome their natural preferences—to gain sight in their blind spots—in order to become effective leaders. Just as antioxidants are required to combat free radicals at the atomic and molecular level, leadership is required to combat complexity at the project team level (see Figure 2-2).

Just as antioxidants are not found naturally in the human body, leadership is not found naturally in IT project teams. IT project leaders need the right diet. They need to feed their minds with the right information and change their behavior in such a manner that they strengthen their teams and protect their projects from failure.

Table 2-9 Project Leaders Success Points and IT Geek Temperaments

Success Point	Description	IT Geek Temperament	Score
Point 1: Basic	Execute basic PM and process skills.	Strength: Per MBTI, Intuitive, Sensing, Judging, Thinking IT professionals have basic PM and process skills.	1
Point 2: Executive bonds	Maintain a relationship with the Executive Sponsor.	Neutral: Per Big Five Study, IT professionals scored low on image management, which makes executive bonds challenging. IT professionals are not Feelers and are not adept at persuasion. IT Professionals are generally Thinkers, a trait shared with executives.	0
Point 3: Details	Organize and manage details through planning, tracking, and controlling.	Strength: Per MBTI, strength for Sensing IT professionals.	1
Point 4: Team leadership	Keep focus on main goal, think analytically, recognize and leverage team member potential.	Weakness: Per MBTI, weakness for introverted IT professionals which makes effective communications and motivation challenging.	−1
Point 5: Connections	Lead stakeholder communications that lead to successful resolution.	Weakness: Per MBTI, weakness for introverted IT professionals which makes effective communications challenging.	−1
Point 6: Ownership	Own the process for doing things well.	Strength: Per MBTI, strength for Intuitive IT professionals.	1
Point 7: Bad news bearers	Deliver bad news early.	Weakness: Per MBTI, weakness for introverted IT professionals which makes effective communications challenging.	−1

(Continued on next page)

Table 2-9 Project Leaders Success Points and IT Geek Temperaments *(Continued)*

Success Point	Description	IT Geek Temperament	Score
Point 8: Business understanding	Envision project components and how the parts incorporate the business as a whole.	Weakness: Per Big Five Study, IT professionals scored low on visionary style and may have trouble thinking strategically.	−1
Point 9: Good judgment	Exercise the discipline, hard work, experience, and maturity required for sound judgment.	Neutral: Per MBTI, strength for IT professionals, however Big Five Study conscientiousness score threatens judgment.	0
Point 10: Seasoned	Learn from mistakes and control resources to make timely corrections.	Strength: Per Big Five Study, strength for IT professionals as they have high emotional resilience, enabling them to bounce back from mistakes.	1
Total			0

Scoring model: 1, Strength; 0, Neither Strength nor Weakness; −1, Weakness

Data derived from: The Standish Group International. "The CHAOS Manifesto 2013: Think Big, Act Small." Versionone.com.

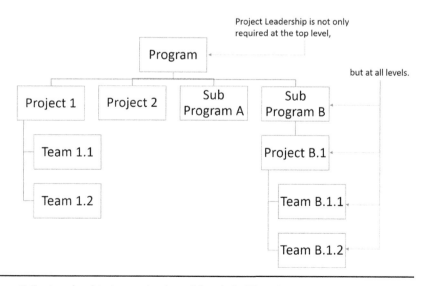

Figure 2-2   Leadership is required at all levels in IT projects.

While it is important that organizations provide training, just as individuals are responsible for eating a healthy diet, IT project leaders are responsible for their own leadership self-improvement.

This book is designed for you, the frontline IT geek leader faced with the challenge of healing and maintaining the health of a sickly IT project. You do not have to treat this patient alone. I am here to help you understand your patient's ailments and to provide you the leadership prescription needed for preventive and responsive care.

2.7 We Need IT Geeks to Lead IT Geeks

Great leadership is required in order for information technology and computer engineering to gain the same type of standing in the world as civil or electrical engineering. Civil, electrical, and mechanical engineers have developed methods that enable consistent delivery of projects on time, within budget, and at the expected levels of quality and customer satisfaction. When is the last time you heard about a new building that collapsed or a new refrigerator that exploded? We take for granted that these solutions work.

As discussed, IT projects are complex, risky, and more prone to failure. The developers and technologists—the IT geeks who attempt to develop, deliver, and maintain these solutions—must be brave and emotionally resilient. They must be able to visualize a successful outcome and motivate their teams to fight through the setbacks and obstacles in order to achieve this success. IT geeks must care enough to understand the stakeholders' feelings and desires, not just what makes sense to the geek's logical mind. This requires IT geeks to behave in ways outside of their comfort zone. To some, it may not seem fair to require a geek to perform in a way that is contrary to his or her instincts in order for IT projects to be successful. Others, those of a determined ilk, those whose self-esteem and character will not allow them fail, will put on a hero's cape and demonstrate the courage required for IT geek leaders.

I had an opportunity to lead with a very determined and agile group of IT technologists when I was the program manager for the US Air Force Digital Dental Radiography Solution (DDRS) Implementation Program. The goal of this program was to replace film-based X-rays with digital radiography at 77 US Air Force Active Duty Bases around the world and 24 US Air Force Reserves units in the United States. The program consisted of various component projects that were expected to deliver coordinated program benefits resulting from the deployment of servers, workstations, storage, software, digital sensors, digital panoramic radiographs, and other digital imaging devices at dental clinics and dental training facilities.

As a contract program manager, I led engagement efforts with the Air Force program sponsor, clinical lead, and other program management stakeholders prior to Request for Proposal (RFP) release to collaborate on the high-level program requirements and the intrinsic and extrinsic benefits that the program expected to deliver.

I established a Program Management Office (PMO), developing the vision, mission, goals, and objectives for managing the global deployment of the component projects and establishing the program management infrastructure to govern all the components. I developed the DDRS implementation program plan, documenting all the high-level planning elements, including roles and responsibilities, work breakdown structure, schedule management plan, communications plan, and risk management procedures.

In order to set expectations, I communicated the scope of the program to the clinic leaders and dental professionals, establishing boundaries for the products and services that were available in the program and those that were not. I performed this task by making use of a combination of various techniques: workshops, brainstorming sessions, presentations, etc. I took this opportunity to understand the voice of the stakeholders' viewpoint and translate their expectations into reality within the grounds of the agreed contractual obligations. As the program manager, I understood how each piece fit into the DDRS puzzle. It was my job to communicate how each stakeholder, whether a supplier, engineer, sales person, logistics coordinator, web developer, trainer, or training video production staff—no matter which puzzle piece—fit into the overall DDRS picture.

This was a very complex program with many moving parts. Many of the disciplines involved were not accustomed to working together. For example, dentists and dental technicians don't usually work with IT engineers. My leadership skills were challenged on many occasions. I led more conference calls and meetings during that four-year program than I can remember. As an introvert, this did not come naturally to me; facilitation was a skill I had to learn earlier in my career. It was a lot of hard work, but when the program was completed, we had successfully implemented a historic solution that touches every member of the US Air Force and their dependents around the world! Fortunately, I had several IT heroes on my team that refused to fail.

Dictionary.com defines a hero as someone who is of "distinguished courage or ability, admired for his [or her] brave deeds and noble qualities." IT leaders must be heroes to their followers. They must be willing to sacrifice for the good of the customer, the organization, and their team members without expecting anything in return. They work hard to set an example by consistently sharpening their intellect, enabling themselves to handle complexity and to navigate through chaos and uncertainty. They willingly risk their hearts, demonstrating that they care for their people. They have the courage to consistently step outside of their comfort zone, being conscientious when their preference is to rebel, speaking out when their instincts are to internalize.

Chaos creates uncertainty. IT geek leaders must identify the uncertainty, uncover it, and take initiatives to resolve it. Geek leaders need to assemble teams of the right resources to address uncertainty and bring order to chaos. As a hero performs a heroic effort, a leader builds a system, working to bring order to chaotic situations, resolving uncertainties in the environment to deliver successful projects that satisfy customers.

IT leaders are motivated by these nobler causes. They have learned how to visualize a future status of success, how to build a strategy to achieve it, and how to articulate it to their followers in an inspirational way. In this group of followers, they recognize future leaders, detecting traces of a hero's soul, and they purposefully empower, encourage, and mentor those future leaders. Their geek followers may have access to other leaders in the organization, those with oversight of their projects and performance, but they want to look up to their project leader—the leader who knows them best and who shares their backgrounds, perspectives, and experiences.

As an IT geek leader, you may be tempted to dive into the technical aspects of your project, but you have to focus on tasks that only you as a leader can do. Morale, coordination with senior leaders, strategic planning, rewards, discipline, accountability—these and many other leadership tasks take time and are your responsibility. Confine your work on technical problems to those that only you can solve. After you resolve the problem, obtain the resources and put a system in place that will allow you to delegate so that you will not have to resolve the next similar technical problem yourself.

There was LinkedIn post in a CIO group that invited comments concerning failed IT projects and the reasons for their failure. Some participants cited communications failures, others cited leadership failures. Their opinions are correct—leadership and communications failures, not only at the top of the organization, but also at the lowest leadership level, contribute to IT project failure. At this lowest level, we expect team leaders and project managers to be effective leaders, to overcome tremendous complexity; but as an industry, we do not provide the training required for them to be successful. If the cells of the body are compromised, the patient will be sick. This book equips the heroic IT geek to apply leadership at the cellular level. We can heal the cells by combating the free radicals of IT complexity, by learning to connect with people as well as we connect with technology. We can heal our patients, our IT projects, and be more successful more often.

IT geeks are some of the most brilliant people on the planet, having developed and delivered solutions that affect all of humanity. "Be nice to nerds," Bill Gates said, "chances are you'll end up working for one" (Walters, 2014).

If you are an IT geek who is willing to put forth a hero's effort, if you learn to overcome tendencies that impair your ability to lead, both geeks and non-geeks alike will gladly serve on your staff. In the next chapter, Emotionally Intelligent Communications, we will explore emotional intelligence, providing a framework for understanding yourself and your communication partners. Because communication is fundamental to effective leadership, I want to equip you to effectively send, receive, and understand information in a way that empowers you to influence people and situations.

Leadership Assessment Questionnaire

The statements in the questionnaire on the following page are designed to help you analyze your leadership style with respect to the 2013 CHAOS Manifesto 10 Success Points and the Five Practices of Exemplary Leadership. By thinking about your leadership performance with respect to these two models, you can get a sense of your own IT geek leadership strengths and weakness.

Leadership Assessment Questionnaire

Use the following key for this assessment:

Not at all	Once in a while	Sometimes	Fairly often	Frequently, if not always
0	1	2	3	4

#		0	1	2	3	4
1	I execute basic project management and process skills.					
2	I maintain a relationship with my project's Executive Sponsor.					
3	I organize and manage details through planning, tracking, and controlling.					
4	I keep focus on the main goal, think analytically, recognizing and leveraging each team member's potential.					
5	I lead stakeholder communications that lead to successful outcomes.					
6	I have ownership of the processes for doing things well.					
7	I deliver bad news early.					
8	I envision project components and how the parts incorporate the business as a whole.					
9	I exercise the discipline, hard work, experience, and maturity required for sound judgment.					
10	I learn from mistakes and control resources to make timely corrections.					
11	I am clear about my values and philosophy, setting a positive example.					
12	I create a compelling vision that drives people's behavior to achieve the desired goals.					
13	I am willing to change the status quo and take risks, stepping out into the unknown as a pioneer.					
14	I am effective at working with people. I value teamwork and collaboration.					
15	I recognize and reward team members for their contributions and accomplishments toward achieving the vision.					

Chapter 3

Emotionally Intelligent Communications

Because most IT professionals are introverts, IT geek communication requires energy and concentration to convert thoughts into words. Communication is also an emotional process. People not only hear what is said and interpret body language, they also associate feelings to the conversation, feelings that impact their understanding. Communicating with emotional intelligence means connecting with people at a level that enables transition of meaning and understanding from one person to another person or group of people. Dr. Sanford Berman wrote in *Words, Meanings, and People* (Berman, 2001) that meanings are in people, not in words. The goal is to ensure that the meaning the sender intends for the message is the meaning the receiver interprets from the message. Because words have different connotations to different people, because people interpret nonverbal signals differently, and because the political din in organizations is deafening, the communications process is plagued by complexity and errors.

3.1 The Importance of Effective Communication

Research has shown that project managers spend 90% of their time communicating (Rajkumar and KP, 2010). IT project managers trying to find success in complex environments that are prone to failure have their work cut out for them. It is like trying to climb Mount Everest during a blizzard while being pursued by a snow leopard. For IT professionals that are introverts, the communication process needs to proceed as efficiently and effectively as possible, without wasting precious energy. Efficient communication enables IT professionals to channel their energy toward delivering solutions that meet business objectives and that satisfy customers.

One morning I was working in my office when I heard my best project manager and my new project manager arguing. They were screaming at each other as they walked toward my office to escalate their situation to me. I was very concerned because I needed the two of them to work closely together on several critical projects and because they were distracting others in the office. We were under pressure to perform and stress levels were high.

The body language of the two PMs was contentious. I was afraid that one PM would strike the other. I knew that my body language would influence their behavior. I needed them to focus on our critical project because their bickering was not contributing to our success. If they did not work together, the project schedule would slip, we would overrun the budget, and the quality of delivery would suffer.

My initial impulse was to raise my voice and berate them for creating a scene in the office. However, I understood that I had to remain calm in order to influence them, to calm them down so that we could sort out the matter. I ushered them into my office, closed the door, and told them to sit down. No matter how loud they were, I kept my voice calm and low. When they were talking over each other, I'd raise my hand, palms out, facing them, signifying "stop," to give the one that was explaining his or her frustration the opportunity to finish their thought. After a few minutes of this, the PMs were able to calmly explain their positions.

The new PM felt frustrated and disrespected. She felt the seasoned PM was not sharing information with her because of her gender. The experienced PM denied the allegation.

At the end of the conversation, they were both calm. It was a misunderstanding that could be cleared up if they engaged in dialogue. The experienced PM agreed to work harder at sharing information in order to get the new PM up to speed on the project. There was an obvious need for the two PMs to learn to trust and communicate with each other more effectively. I knew I needed to keep a close eye on them and to work with them to facilitate establishing an effective working relationship.

The walls of my office were paper-thin. A coworker in the next office said to me later, "I have no idea how you stayed calm during that situation."

In order to understand how to lead people through complexity, you need to understand how they think. If you have a basic understanding of how the human mind works and why people behave the way they do, you can more effectively communicate with them and influence their behavior. IT projects are generally very complex and include a significant amount of uncertainty. Communication at a person-to-person level facilitates understanding and combats complexity. This type of communication enables team leaders, team members, and stakeholders to understand each other. If a team understands the problems they face and can work together with cohesion, they can find solutions, even in complex environments. A leader is responsible for bridging gaps when the individuals involved in a project do not understand each other and do not understand the problems they are tasked to solve. This is especially true when team members do not understand each other, a team does not understand its customer, or the customer does not understand the team. By understanding the basics of how people think, an IT project leader is better equipped to facilitate communication and understanding, reducing complexity and uncertainty and increasing the probability of project success.

Because the human mind is considered the most complicated structure in the universe, emotionally intelligent communication is complex. You, the intelligent IT geek, are more than capable of handling this complexity.

My goal for this chapter is to introduce you to the workings of the mind, as reported in recent psychology and neuroscience publications, and to relate this information to the communication process. At the end of this chapter, you will have a basic understanding of how the mind functions during the communication process. This understanding can enable you to tailor your communications in a manner that provides the greatest efficacy, enhancing your ability to influence people and situations—a core leadership purpose.

Let's start our journey by reviewing a use case called "Missed Signals." This use case is based on actual events that I have experienced. The characters in the story are based on real people. I am playing the role of Tony, the program manager. I will refer to this use case at various points throughout this book.

3.2 Missed Signals

"You people are just lazy!" Karen screamed. "I don't understand why it is so hard for you to correctly complete the inventory sheets! This data is useless! You need to go back and get the correct data! Our customer is furious about the inaccuracies in our daily reports!" Karen had just taken over a troubled team working on a high-visibility workstation migration project. Her face was flushed red when she spoke. Everyone could sense that her heart was racing.

Mark, a team member, sat quietly in his chair, wringing his hands beneath the table. Then he decided that he had heard enough. He was offended. His defense mechanism was activated, and he tuned Karen out.

Karen didn't know that Mark had been passively looking for a new job. After Karen's rant, a lashing similar to one he had endured from the previous project lead just a week before, he called a recruiter during his lunch break and set up an interview.

Three weeks later, Mark was attending an exit interview with Sandra in Human Resources (HR). "That Karen is a piece of work," he said. "I hate how she talks to us. I know it's an important project, and I know there are issues, but she makes me hate coming to work."

Sandra and Tony, the program manager, had a monthly meeting to discuss HR issues on the program. "We received a complaint during an exit interview about Karen's communication style," Sandra explained, leaning forward, steepling her hands on the table, her fingertips touching. "She comes across as overbearing," she continued.

"I've spoken to her about this," Tony replied, leaning back in his chair, hand on his chin. "I've explained to her and to the other leads on the project that this type of behavior can be perceived by the people on the team as hostile, perhaps giving them grounds for a 'hostile work environment' claim. They all committed to toning it down. But please understand: our customer is getting yelled at by his superiors, and when he faces pressure, he applies pressure to the team. There's not much we can do about that," he said while raising his hands. "We do what we can to provide encouragement, but at the end of the day, it's a high-pressure project in a high-pressure environment. On top of that, I asked one of the technical leads why we had so much trouble gathering the required inventory information, and the response was 'they just don't want to do it.' These are the same people that are dogging Karen during their exit interviews. I find it hard to give them any credibility. Lastly, after Karen counseled the team, their performance did improve."

"I understand," Sandra said, "but no matter what the leads are feeling, they do not have an excuse to berate the employees so harshly." "That's why I asked for help with leadership and supervisory training earlier this year," Tony replied. "Our techs are trained and experienced in information technology; they're experts in Microsoft Windows 7, MS Active Directory, TCP/IP, and the like. They are leads because of how well they deploy and maintain technology. Karen has over 20 years of experience in this area, as do I. But Karen never received training on how to deal with difficult people, both difficult customers and difficult employees. She's never had any type of leadership training."

"You're right," Sandra said. "This is an issue we face across the company—across the industry, really. But we're concerned that the company will not be in a position to defend itself if this situation ends up in court," Sandra continued, crossing her legs so that her knees formed a barrier between her and Tony. "I have a couple of online communications courses I'd like for Karen to attend. I will send them to you so that you can instruct her to take them. This will show that the company has recognized the problem and that we're taking action to prevent this situation from occurring in the future."

"I'm all for training," Tony replied, "but I think it would be better if some-one from HR spoke with Karen first." "Speak to her about what?" Sandra asked in a higher tone of voice. "About the complaint," Tony replied. "Doesn't she have a right to know who made the accusations, and doesn't she have a right to respond?" "That's not necessary," Sandra explained. "Our only requirement is for Karen to take the courses."

The next day Tony spoke to Karen about his conversation with HR. "I for-warded you an email from Sandra in HR," Tony told Karen. "Apparently, one of the technicians who left the project recently said something about your com-munication style during an exit interview. I'm not privy to the details of the exit interview, but HR needs you to take a couple of online communications courses, the courses I sent you in the email. The courses only take about an hour apiece to complete, and you have 30 days to complete the courses. How do you feel about this?"

"I don't understand. What did I do wrong?" replied Karen, holding up her hands below shoulder level, palms facing up. "Apparently, one of the techs was offended by how you spoke to him about the inventory data issue. HR was not forthcoming with the details," Tony replied.

"But why didn't they reach out to me to discuss this?" asked Karen. "I don't know," said Tony, shaking his head. "Look," Tony continued, lowering his voice to almost a whisper, "if you just take the courses, which are good training for you anyway, all of this will blow over, it will just go away." "Ok, Tony," Karen said, as she turned on her high heels and walked away. "Whatever you need."

A couple of weeks later, Karen knocked on Tony's door. "Come in," he said. "Do you have a minute?" replied Karen. "Absolutely. What can I do for you?" Karen entered the office, closed the door behind her, and sat down in a chair in front of Tony's desk. She then placed a piece of paper on the desk and slid it to him. "I'm resigning," she said. "This is my two-week notice." Tony leaned back in his chair, threw back his head, and put his hands over his eyes. "Oh no!" he said. "Why? What happened? We just gave you a raise!" "I know, I know," Karen said, leaning toward Tony, "and you transferred me from my position in service operations to be the special project lead. And I do appreciate that. But the com-munications course was the last straw. There were several incidents that occurred before you got here. I don't like the way some people have been treated around here. I know that you've tried to fix some things since you've been here, but the fact that HR made me take that training without talking to me about what hap-pened pisses me off. I never got the chance tell my side of the story, and now that incident is in my file. That was the last straw." "Is there anything I can do?" asked

Tony, sounding desperate. "I don't have a problem working for you or this project," replied Karen, "I just don't want to work for this company."

There were many different emotions expressed in this use case. We are going to analyze this use case later in this chapter to help you understand it within the context of emotionally intelligent communications. Let's begin with a basic understanding of how the brain operates.

3.3 Basic Brain Operations

Many scientists feel that the human brain is the most complex creation in the universe. I cannot explain all of these complexities. However, in order to understand emotional intelligence, you need to understand the basics of the human brain, the source of emotions and intelligence. Our discussion of brain functions begins with the reptilian brain, then progresses to the limbic system, and ends with the cortex. Figure 3-1 illustrates the basic anatomy of the human brain.

The oldest part of the brain is known as the *reptilian brain,* consisting of the brain stem and the cerebellum. The reptilian brain controls heart beat, breathing,

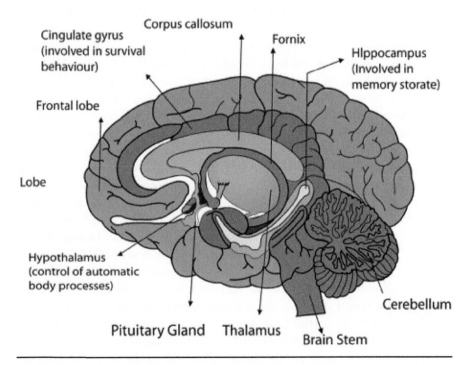

Figure 3-1   Anatomy of the brain. © Gnanamdesigns | Dreamstime.com—Brain Photo. Used with permission from Dreamstime.com.

swallowing, body temperature, digestion, and other functions necessary for survival. Although reliable, the reptilian brain is considered to be rigid and compulsive. It controls our flight-or-fight response and urges such as hunger and sex (Chopra and Tanzi, 2012; The Evolutionary Layers of the Human Brain, n.d.).

After the reptilian brain was developed, the *limbic brain* evolved. This type of brain emerged first in animals. The limbic system consists of three components. The first is the *amygdala,* which is associated with events and emotions such as fear, anger, indignation, rage, and pity. Another key component of the limbic system is the *hippocampus,* which processes information from the present into long-term memory and assists in recalling those memories. The last component of the limbic system is the *hypothalamus,* which controls automatic body processes. The limbic system is the source of our value judgments, which impact our behavior, judgments that are made unconsciously (Fogel, 2014; The Evolutionary Layers of the Human Brain, n.d.).

The region of the brain that was developed most recently is the *neocortex,* which represents the majority of the cerebral cortex. This region of the brain has between 10 and 14 billion tightly packed neurons. The neocortex is divided into four lobes that process sensor information: *frontal, parietal, temporal,* and *occipital.* Because it is the outermost layer that surrounds the brain, it gives the brain its wrinkly appearance. It is in the neocortex that higher thought takes place, including decision making, learning, logic, language, and planning. It receives and processes sensory information and controls voluntary movement. These higher thought functions allow us to be self-aware; to observe and reflect on our own thinking; to have free will, choice, and self-control; and to develop human cultures (Chopra and Tanzi, 2012; Fogel, 2014; The Evolutionary Layers of the Human Brain, n.d.; Swenson, 2006).

IT project leadership takes place in the neocortex, which allows us to logically plan, make decisions, and communicate with others. This conscious activity is influenced by unconscious activity processed in the limbic system, resulting in emotions and body language that impact communication. Our reptilian brain causes automatic reactions to events we sense in the outside world and the emotions we feel. For example, fear and anger may result in a faster heartbeat.

Now that we understand the basic brain operations, let's explore four phases of the brain: Instinctive, Emotional, Intellectual, and Intuitive. A brief description of each phase is provided in Table 3-1.

3.3.1 Instinct

With respect to evolution, instincts developed in our reptilian brain, the part of the brain that existed before emotions. The anxiety we feel partly stems from the instinctive brain. It sends signals of fear, and it cannot tell the difference

Table 3-1 Four Phases of the Brain

Instinctive Phase	Intellectual Phase
Brain Area: *Reptilian*	Brain Area: *Neocortex*
Instincts are a necessary part of who we are.	Intellectual thought is blended with emotion and instinct.
Mindfully manage fear and anger.	Intellect develops rational responses to fears and desires.
Be aware of fear and desire to keep them in balance; acknowledge feelings of guilt.	Intellectual responses should be ethical.
Mindfully live in the gap between impulse and response.	
Emotional Phase	**Intuitive Phase**
Brain Area: *Limbic*	Brain Area: *Neocortex*
Letting feelings come and go helps us understand ourselves and the world.	You can trust your intuition and "feel" your way through life.
Understanding our own emotions enables us to respond mindfully rather than to react mindlessly.	Snap judgments are accurate and are faster than reasoning.
	Reasoning is used to justify intuition.

Data derived from Chopra, D. and Tanzi, R. (2012). *Super Brain.* New York: Random House Publishing.

between fear of public speaking and fear of an approaching snow leopard. We struggle to manage our impulses—to distinguish between true dangers and those that are exacerbated by our instinctive brain. We control the impulses we can and respond to those we can't. This is the source of courage—to feel the impulse of fear, assess it, and take rational action despite it. Our instincts are part of who we are—part of the human condition. We need to approach our fear and anger patiently, controlling them and not allowing them to control us. There may be times when it is appropriate to express our fear and anger freely, but that should be a conscious decision, not a mindless reaction.

When faced with situations that challenge our sense of self, our understanding of the world and our place in it, we feel psychologically threatened. At an unconscious level, our cognitive unconscious (subconscious) lets us know in subtle ways that danger is present, regardless of whether it is physical danger or psychological danger. The instinctual signals, in the form of "gut feelings" and stress indicators, impact our decisions in the cognitive unconscious mind, before our conscious mind contemplates the decision. It is constantly analyzing patterns and comparing what it perceives with patterns stored in memory (Kehoe, 2011).

As long as situations are positive, the processes work well. But if the situation quickly changes from positive to negative, the cognitive unconscious can give off signals that are not in line with the actual situation. We put our words (which are minor representations of ourselves) out there, and if someone disagrees with us and it comes as a surprise, or if it comes in a way that seems to diminish our sense of who we are, the cognitive unconscious reads this as a threat. A threat is a threat to your cognitive unconscious, whether it is a psychological threat to self-esteem or a physical threat to your body. This takes place very, very quickly, before your conscious mind even knows what is going on. Changes in the facial expressions and mannerisms of our critics signal our cognitive unconscious and cause reactions in our bodies before their words reach our ears. Our heart beats faster, increasing the sweat on our palms, raising the hair on our forearms, tightening our neck and throat muscles, forcing blood from our gut to our limbs, all in an effort to signal us that the threat is about to manifest. It is an "amygdala hijack" that invokes a fight-or-flight response—a sudden emotion that comes very quickly and that leads to irrational or inappropriate actions or talk. This system, which is intended to protect us from threats, actually makes the situation worse by matching patterns erroneously and causing us to respond from the place where we learned our judgments instead of from the present moment. At the same time, the person we are talking to is reading our automatic reactions and is invoking a cognitive unconscious response to them. This cycle feeds itself, and communications spiral out of control (Kehoe, 2011).

As leaders we must train our conscious minds to recognize when this process is playing out and allow our conscious selves to slow down the process and be mindful of the current situation, to react to the here and now and not to the situation that provoked the emotional response when the "threat" was detected. We have to live in the gap between the stimulus and the response. Not only must we control our own reactions, but we must help those with whom we are communicating—our communication partners—do the same.

3.3.2 Emotions

Instincts and emotions are tightly aligned. Emotions allow us to name the feelings we experience as a result of our stimulated instincts. Whether we are sexually aroused or frightened to the point where we want to fight or flee, the alignment between instinct and emotions provokes a mindless reaction.

Somatic markers are the biochemical changes deep within the mind-body. These changes, known as "somatic" or "body" states, impact posture, blood flow, heart rate, muscle contractions, hormones, and other bodily conditions. For example, when someone is happy, the associated bodily change may be a smile as well as a change in breathing pattern.

These changes in somatic markers may be pleasant or unpleasant, and they may impact a person's attitude concerning the event or object that influenced the change. For example, if someone experiences their "stomach being tied up in knots" before speaking in public, the mere thought of public speaking may elicit a similar experience, albeit to a lesser extent (Moss, 2011).

When we become aware of somatic markers, we name them, and they become our feelings. Becoming aware of our feelings, naming them, and describing them in a way that is accurate and useful to ourselves and to others is a fundamental component of effective communications (Kehoe, 2011).

The cognitive unconscious mind, the automatic function that operates out of our limbic system, supports rational decision making in our conscious, intellectual mind. It assesses the biochemical patterns in our minds to sense our environment before our conscious mind can do so. The cognitive unconscious enables us to quickly recall the meaning of words and to detect subtle nonverbal signals. However, the more automatic our thinking, the less effort is required, and the more prone we are to mistakes. It is easier, requires less energy, to react than to think; to say what comes to mind first instead of to carefully choose our words (Kehoe, 2011).

Basic Emotions

Hurtful speech damages relationships because it causes emotional pain. The listener's brain recalls similar hurtful experiences stored in the limbic system and again experiences the psychic pain associated with that memory. The speaker may apologize, and may try to take back what was said, but the impression from the offensive speech lingers and impacts how the listener interacts with the speaker for the rest of their lives. As the great poet Maya Angelou said, "I've learned that people will forget what you said, people will forget what you did, but people will never forget how you made them feel" (Shriver, 2014).

Table 3-2 describes views on a few basic emotions from Dr. Robert C. Solomon, a philosophy professor from the University of Texas at Austin.

Resentment is a particularly important emotion for IT leaders to understand. I have found that after resentment builds up within employees over time, they seek their vengeance by resigning. A colleague of mine was resentful because he felt that his supervisor did not respect his skills and experience. He became very irritated by his supervisor's habit of second-guessing all of the consultation he provided. His team was at a critical juncture in their project. He shared with me that he found another position and that he could not wait to leave his team so that they would be short of resources and facing failure.

LeRoy Ward writes at ProjectConnections.com, "While there's a long list of risks any organization faces when starting an IT project, certainly one of the biggest risks has to be the potential that the team members you start with might

Table 3-2 Description of Basic Emotions

Emotion	Description
Anger	Most explosive and dangerous emotion. Violent anger is called rage. Anger can be used strategically.
Fear	Perhaps the most important emotion—keeps us from being vulnerable to danger. Fears can be mistaken, exaggerated, and irrational. Panic, anxiety, and horror are related to fear.
Love	Most complex emotion. *Eros, philia,* and *agape* are forms of love.
Empathy	Sharing an emotion with another person, whether sorrow or joy.
Sympathy	A "moral sentiment" at the very heart of human nature. Compassion.
Pride	A positive evaluation of something one has done. A social emotion.
Shame	Opposite of pride. One takes responsibility for the event or act. Guilt, embarrassment, regret, and remorse are similar.
Envy	A desire to have what someone else has. Envy separates us, love is inclusive. Personal in nature. Spite is an escalation of envy.
Jealousy	A social emotion that binds one with a rival who has the same desire.
Resentment	The feeling that there is nothing one can do about one's frustrations.
Vengeance	The most violent and dangerous of emotions. The natural extension of resentment. It is an attempt to right a wrong.
Grief	Grossly misunderstood emotion. Triggers thoughts of a lost loved one, but also provoke thoughts of one's own mortality.

Data derived from Solomon, R. (2006). *Passions: Philosophy and the Intelligence of Emotions.* Chantilly, VA: The Great Courses.

not be the same ones you end with; and changing team members in the middle of a critical project can be very disruptive. If you lose a key technical person, or one who's doing a great job at client relationship management, this could pose serious obstacles to project success" (Ward 2014). According to *Baseline Magazine,* 81% of IT professionals surveyed in 2014 said they were open to new job opportunities. This was true even for happily employed IT geeks that were in the job market. Taking actions to prevent resentment, such as maintaining a dialogue with your team members, treating everyone fairly and respectfully, standing up on your team members' behalf, and involving team members in decisions, can prevent turnover and save your project.

Like instincts, emotions are essential to our humanity. As we have evolved beyond solely identifying with the instincts transmitted by our reptilian brain, our emotions do not define us. We can separate ourselves from our emotions if we choose to. By separating ourselves from our emotions, by being mindful, our emotions do not control our behavior. We can choose to behave in a rational way no matter what emotion we are feeling. Being mindful—engaging our intellect to live in the gap between the stimuli and the response—causes fears to subside and anger to cool, preventing us from saying or doing things that are inappropriate and that we may later regret.

Once an emotion manifests itself, it intends to run its course, to be acknowledged and satisfied (Chopra and Tanzi, 2012). Emotions are not concerned with your efforts to be mindful and not to express them. In our mindful state, we can use our emotions to gain perspective on the situation without anyone else ever knowing what we are feeling. We may subconsciously display cues through body language, but most people will only be able to guess at what we are feeling. In this way, we experience life and enable ourselves to understand how others feel—their perspectives and the reasons for their behavior.

Two particular feelings—fear and desire—are closely linked. They both are rooted in our instinctive brains. They manifest themselves in our emotions, provoking us to act to resolve them, to alleviate the fear or to satisfy the desire. Unbridled fear and desire are dangerous. Unbridled fear can cause us to cower from trivial threats, such as the irrational fear of harmless bugs. Unbridled desire entices us to lust after things and people that are forbidden, even dangerous. We use our intellectual brains to keep our emotions in check, to control or prevent our response to these stimuli (Kehoe, 2011).

The limbic system is the control center for our emotions, but it also stores our long-term memories. It unites our senses—smell, sight, sound, touch—with memories and the emotions associated with those memories (Kehoe, 2011). Through these experiences and this link between memory, senses, and emotion, we learn and grow. These experiences are captured in long-term memory, anchored in emotions. They are triggered by senses and shape who are. They leave indelible impressions concerning our likes and dislikes, shaping our preferences.

Emotions and Subtle Forms of Communication

Let's examine how emotions impact three forms of subtle forms communications, communications that do not rely on words: *body language, tone of voice,* and *mirror neurons.*

- *Body Language.* The activities in our limbic system influence our nonverbal behavior, our body language. Our body language provides indicators concerning how we feel, whether we are feeling comfortable and relaxed or whether we are feeling uncomfortable and stressed in response to events within our environment. Table 3-3 provides signals our bodies transmit unconsciously, signals that we can learn to observe in order to understand how those around us are feeling so that we can respond appropriately.

It is important to make a concerted effort to observe the body language of your team and coworkers. If you are an introvert, it may be natural for you to be absorbed in your own thoughts, but in order to have effective situational awareness so that you can be an effective leader, you must pay attention to others. This can help you establish a baseline of behavior for those around you. Then, when you notice that they perform an action that is different from the baseline, you will know that whatever is being said or is taking place in the environment has caused them some form of comfort or discomfort. If something stressful occurs, people engage in pacifying behaviors to make themselves more comfortable, and the greater the stress, the greater the likelihood of the behavior. Their body communicates messages to you that that they did not verbalize, messages that are important to you as a leader. If you observe and mimic their behavior, you will get a sense of how they are feeling.

Table 3-3 Body Language Activities and Interpretations

Body Part	Signs of Comfort or Pacification	Signs of Discomfort
Face	People puff out their cheeks to release stress and to pacify themselves. People touch their cheeks to pacify feelings of nervousness, irritation, and concern.	People rub their foreheads when they are very uncomfortable or if they are struggling with something. People under stress may yawn excessively. People block the eye with their fingers and hands as a display of consternation, disbelief, or disagreement.
Neck	People cover their neck dimple to pacify insecurities, concerns, even fears. People "ventilate" their neck areas to reduce stress and pacify themselves.	People touch their neck when they feel uncomfortable, doubtful, or insecure. Men adjust their ties when feeling insecure or uncomfortable.

(Continued on next page)

Table 3-3 Body Language Activities and Interpretations *(Continued)*

Body Part	Signs of Comfort or Pacification	Signs of Discomfort
Shoulders	People shrug both shoulders when they don't know something—there is nothing wrong with this.	People raise their shoulders toward the ears like a turtle hiding in its shell if the person is feeling humbled or suddenly loses confidence. People who shrug only one shoulder are sending an unconvincing message concerning their doubt or lack of knowledge.
Torso	People bring themselves closer to each other when they are comfortable with each other. People splay out on chairs when feeling territorial and comfortable. People puff up their chests to establish territorial dominance.	People lean away from each other when they disagree. People suddenly cross their arms across their torsos and grip their arms when feeling discomfort. People breathe deeply, indicated by an expanding and contracting chest, when under stress.
Arms	People raise their arms and perform other gravity-defying motions when they are happy and energized. People spread their arms over chairs to indicate they are confident and comfortable.	People withdraw their arms when they are fearful or upset. People put their arms behind their back when they do not want to make contact.
Hands	People under stress will "cleanse" their palms on their laps to pacify themselves. This may occur under the table. People wring their hands when feeling stressed or concerned. People bite their nails when they are nervous or insecure.	People stand with their hands on their hips to establish dominance and to communicate their dissatisfaction. Around the world, finger pointing is considered offensive. People steeple their hands fingertip-to-fingertip when feeling confident.

(Continued on next page)

Table 3-3 Body Language Activities and Interpretations *(Continued)*

Body Part	Signs of Comfort or Pacification	Signs of Discomfort
Legs	People cross their legs when they are comfortable. When people cross their legs and place their knee farther away from the person they are talking to, they are removing the barrier between themselves and the person they are talking to.	While sitting, people clasp their knees and shift their weight to their feet when they are ready to stand up and leave. When people cross their legs and place their knee between themselves and the person they are talking to, they are using their knee as a barrier.
Feet	People point their toes upward when they are in a good mood, thinking or hearing something positive. People step toward other people when they feel comfortable with each other.	When standing, people turn their feet away from the person they are talking to when they are ready to leave, to end the conversation. People shift their feet from being flat-footed to "starter position" when they are ready to leave. People maintain a distance from or step away from other people who they do not feel comfortable with. When sitting, people kick their feet when they feel discomfort. Someone who normally wiggles or bounces their feet while sitting and then suddenly stops when something is said or occurs is feeling stressed or threatened by the event. People will suddenly interlock their legs or lock their legs around a chair when feeling discomfort, anxiety, or insecurity.

Data derived from Navarro, J. and Karins, M. (2008). *What Every BODY is Saying: An Ex-FBI Agent's Guide to Speed-Reading People.* [Kindle]. William Morrow Paperbacks.

- **_Tone of Voice._** Researchers performed a study to analyze the tone of the human voice and the information communicated in tone. The research group was presented with recordings of doctors speaking to their patients. Some of the doctors had been sued for malpractice. The words in the recordings were muffled so that the audience could not tell what the doctors were saying and could only make out their tone. The audience accurately identified the doctors who had been sued for malpractice based on their tone alone. The doctors could not hide their frustration and resentment—their cognitive unconscious revealed their feelings in the tone of their voices (Kehoe, 2011).

- **_Mirror Neurons._** Has someone ever smiled at you and you found yourself automatically smiling back? Have you ever looked at someone who was upset or sad and found yourself feeling the same way, even when you did not know why the other person was down? Many times when I yawn, my wife also yawns, and I find myself mimicking her when she yawns. Dr. Shad Helmstetter attributes these reactions to _mirror_ or _simulating_ neurons. This is an activity that simulates or infers the actions, feelings, or intentions of others. These neurons fire in our brains as though we are taking the action, even though all we are doing is observing the action. Dr. Helmstetter writes that mirror neurons also cause us to mimic the feelings and attitudes of others. These feelings and attitudes imprint on our brains, causing us to unconsciously respond to what they are experiencing. Neither you nor your communication partner realizes the communication is occurring (Helmstetter, 2013).

  The phenomenon of mirror neurons is essential to communications. Critical communications, in which important information needs to be exchanged between IT project leaders and their key stakeholders, need to occur face to face as much as possible. Such a dialogue facilitates the processes of mirror neurons transmitting information, feelings, and attitudes between the IT project leader and the stakeholder. This transmission does not take place in email or video teleconference communications. Introverted IT project leaders can't be shy about engaging in these face-to-face dialogues. The conversation enables them to communicate ground truth to the stakeholder and the stakeholder to communicate requirements to the IT project leader. Then, when the IT project leader communicates with team members, the stakeholder's feelings and attitudes can be transmitted from the stakeholder, via the IT project leader, to the team.

3.3.3 Intellect

In our mindful state, we are capable of using our intellect to develop more creative solutions than running away or fighting back. Our instincts sense a situation; our emotions process and categorize it, relating it to similar situations;

and our intellectual brain creates a strategy—a plan of action—to satisfy the feeling. Instead of fighting the bully when attacked, we can devise a way to conduct a surprise attack; instead of forcing ourselves on a potential mate like a Neanderthal, we develop a strategy to woo her.

Humans have an internal voice—self-talk—consisting of continuous communion between the emotions and the intellect. This speech may be an internal monologue for some or an internal dialogue for others (Chopra and Tanzi, 2012). Should we listen to our brain's internal monologue, drawn from irrelevant habits, old memories, and obsolete programming? Or should we engage in internal dialogue and explore new ideas and approaches? As leaders, we must learn from and then influence our environment to achieve project success.

Intellect is driven by our internal dialogue, enabling us to ask questions and seek knowledge. We not only experience life, we also analyze it and learn from it. Not only do we learn about experiences, we learn how to think about our experiences (Kehoe, 2011). When events occur in life, our instincts, emotions, and intellect help us react to those events in sophisticated ways, as Figure 3-2 indicates.

Thinking about our experiences requires self-awareness. Self-awareness dwells in our consciousness and requires intellect. Our instincts and emotions reside in our subconscious. We blend our conscious and our subconscious instincts, emotions, and the knowledge gained from experience in our intellectual brain. When our subconscious thoughts and impulses drive us into situations in which we find ourselves unhappy, our intellect seeks better experiences (Chopra and Tanzi, 2012).

The intellect enables understanding. Instead of mindlessly reacting to situations, intellect enables us to analyze a situation and create a response (Chopra and Tanzi, 2012). The intellect is capable of analyzing instinctual impulses and preventing mindless reactions. It is capable of corralling emotions, holding them back or expressing them consciously. It is capable of anticipating and understanding the instincts and emotions of others and preparing a mindful response to their words and behavior.

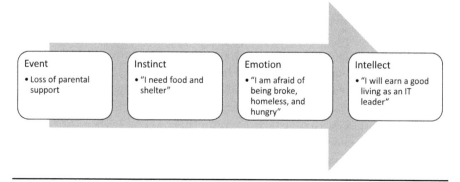

Figure 3-2   Instinct, emotions, and intellect.

Our intellect enables us to make connections with others, to have empathy for them so that we can relate to their instincts and what they are feeling. This connection leads to understanding. We craft verbal communication to engage their intellect, asking questions to understand what they are sensing, how they are feeling, and the rational for their reasoning—what and how they are thinking. We share what we are sensing, our feelings, our memories of relevant experiences, and our judgment. Through dialogue, we learn about each other, and we are able to teach one another. Our verbal and nonverbal communications, subconsciously transmitting our inner anxieties, desires, and preferences, enable us to connect at a deeper, more human level, a level of understanding that connects us emotionally and spiritually. We can find common ground through a a shared vision and mission, understand each other's objectives and approach, and understand each other's needs and how we can help each other fulfill those needs.

Using our intellect in this manner—being mindful of our own impulses, emotions, and thoughts and their relation to our situation and that of others, being mindful of how our words and actions as leaders impact others' behavior—gives us the ability to influence situations. We have a responsibility to influence others in positive ways and to avoid being manipulative and abusive. The International Information Systems Security Certification Consortium (ISC)[2] provides an excellent example of an ethical standard that individuals and organizations should adopt and strive to implement consistently. This code demands adherence to individual integrity, including honesty, respect for the law, avoidance of conflict of interest, and treating others with respect ([ISC][2], 2010). Employing power as leaders must be done with care and understanding, as we are depositing memories and invoking emotions in other human beings. We are responsible for making this a rewarding experience and for avoiding creation of painful memories.

3.3.4 Intuition

The conscious mind thinks in words and pictures. Intellect and intuition use words and pictures to help us understand and respond to the world around us. The conscious mind does not access the cognitive unconscious mind directly because its memories are composed of biochemical patterns, not words and pictures. The cognitive unconscious mind lives in the limbic system, the source of our feelings and long-term memories. It continuously receives input from all of our senses while we are awake, looking for and remembering patterns, annotating those patterns with emotions, with somatic markers for later retrieval (Kehoe, 2011).

Dictionary.com defines *gestalt* as "a configuration, pattern, or organized field having specific properties that cannot be derived from the summation of its component parts, a united whole." As leaders, we are bombarded with information from a multitude of sources, such as users, team members, peers, our senior managers, other teams, and competitors. The complexity of implementing and supporting high-tech solutions, the difficulties of communicating abstract ideas concerning technical requirements to developers and engineers and of explaining abstract technical solutions to customers and users, the myriad unpredictable personnel issues—all of these chaotic elements come together to create a dynamic challenge for IT leaders. The summation of these complex elements can create on overwhelming morass, a morass that is larger than the sum of the individual organizational elements.

This situation may seem difficult to manage effectively. The stimuli from the various sources is received too quickly to process in a timely manner using rational, logic-based thought. A typical decision-making process includes defining the problem, collecting data, developing and testing alternative solutions, and choosing the best solution. There is not enough time or enough management manpower within organizations to execute this process for all decision requirements within IT environments.

Intuition enables IT leaders to navigate through the morass of complexity in their environments. Gestalt psychology enables us to build dynamic correlations between our perceptions and experiences. It combines our instincts, emotions, and intellect to produce an overall image of reality, enabling us to make snap decisions. Recent studies have shown that intuition is a faster process than rational decision making. These intuitive decisions are influenced by what we sense, our memories, and our experiences.

Intuitive leaders can prevent problems. Like the Jethro Gibbs character in the American television series "NCIS," their "gut" warns them of issues and directs them toward solutions. They sense when issues are likely so they can then take proactive measures to prevent them. This requires leaders to be in tune with their environment through the management and monitoring of communications, having dialogue with stakeholders on a regular basis, performing informal and formal relationship management.

First impressions and snap judgments—those based on the combination of our instincts, emotions, intellect, and intuition—are often the most accurate (Chopra and Tanzi, 2012). Our intuition enables us to make creative leaps, to understand facial expressions and body language, to know when someone is lying, and to otherwise feel our way through complex situations. As IT leaders in complex and dynamic environments, we must trust our intuition, using our minds in a holistic way, in order to navigate our way to project success.

3.3.5 Schemas and Communications

Our intuitive mind automatically refers to *schemas*. A schema is a concept or framework used to organize and interpret information. Schemas are mental molds into which we pour our experiences, like data stored in database tuples. We then, in our cognitive unconscious, use these schemas to organize and interpret unfamiliar information. We draw on these schemas to understand our world and to communicate with each other. During communication, we endeavor to connect the schema in our own minds to the schemas in the minds of others such that it correctly describes our message. When our schemas are different, when we do not have the same experiences, when we do not use the same language or use unfamiliar jargon, communication becomes difficult. When there are no references between the data in our databases and the data in our communication partner's databases, we can't understand each other.

When the ideas we formed about reality are wrong, and we are not seeing the same truth, communication becomes even more challenging, as the schemas we draw from would not make sense to our communication partners.

It takes very little effort to create a first impression. When we take things at face value in conscious thought, and when we are wrong, we create an erroneous schema within the mind of our communication partner, a schema that becomes the basis of decision making. When we use abstract words and judgmental language to explain ourselves, but the listener does not understand and does not ask for clarification, the listener applies his or her own schemas to fill in the blanks, whether correctly or incorrectly (most likely incorrectly when little effort is expended). It is easier for the listener to make assumptions—assumptions easily regarded as facts—than to make the effort to obtain clarification and understanding. These assumptions will most likely be made based on their past experiences—different schemas that are not relevant to the situation at hand. The easier it is to recall those experiences, the more likely our communication partners believe their recollections and associations are true (Kehoe, 2011).

The more abstract our talk, the more we leave out information, and the more we rely on others to fill in information using their own schemas, which may be different from ours and not what we intend. As mentioned earlier, meanings are in people, not in words. Our communication partner fills in this information at the cognitive unconscious level; it is filled in automatically and faster than the conscious mind can process the data. The conscious mind then draws conclusions based on the stimuli from the cognitive unconscious, stimuli that is packaged with emotions and memories, stimuli that our conscious minds integrate with our beliefs. Once our beliefs are added to the package that includes our emotions and assumptions, we are ready to respond through words and actions—a conscious response that can be far removed from the current reality, a response that could be based on a distorted and garbled message.

No wonder Osmo Wiio, a Finnish professor of communications, was so sarcastic when he developed his communications "laws." He said, "Communication usually fails, except by accident." He also said, "If a message can be interpreted in several ways, it will be interpreted in a manner that maximizes the damage." Finally, he said "There is always someone who knows better than you what you meant with your message" (A Commentary on Wiio's Laws, 2015).

Organizations have their own norms for communications, influenced by society. Similar to the manner in which organizations have different dress codes, organizational norms dictate the methods and forms of acceptable communication: who is allowed to deliver messages to whom; acceptable ways to express emotions. There is knowledge, processes (habits), history, and tradition in organizations that create common schemas in their members' minds. When new people join those organizations, they are indoctrinated into those schemas. To effectively communicate, leaders must understand the organization's norms and know when to utilize them to deliver and receive information, or when to exercise the courage to defy them when important messages are not being heard.

I once led a Microsoft Active Directory and Exchange migration project for a critical government customer. Our team was not getting the information we needed from the infrastructure group to move the project forward. I had numerous meetings with the project sponsor to stress that we needed their cooperation in order to stay on schedule. The senior members of my project team and I became frustrated, and together we crafted an email message that expressed our concerns and frustration. We were less than diplomatic, calling out senior members of the infrastructure group in our message. As we were contractors, we violated a norm or two by sending this message without clearing it with our government sponsor. Our message caused political problems for our sponsor and his superiors. They had to perform political damage control. If I were not the PM for the contract, and if the project were not as critical as it was, I could have been relieved of my position. Partly because of our courageous act, we did eventually get the cooperation we needed. However, it came at a political cost.

The schemas in our minds help us organize and interpret information about the world we live in. Let's take a look at how our interpretations of these data influence our behavior.

3.4 The Rational-Emotive Behavior Model

The Rational-Emotive Behavior (REB) Model (Ellis, 1962) explores how individuals process external events and how the results of this processing impacts their behavior. It describes the relationships among values, assumptions, beliefs, and expectations (VABEs). People are emotionally impacted, feel psychological discomfort, when their VABEs are threatened, and they use defense mechanisms to protect their psychological well-being. People draw conclusions about themselves and about their external environment based on what they perceive in comparison to their VABEs. These conclusions impact their behavior, what they do and what they say. If their perceptions are in line with their VABEs, they may behave in a positive way. If their perspectives are out of sync with their VABEs, they experience psychological discomfort and may become defensive if they feel threatened.

Figure 3-3 builds on Albert Ellis's REB Model. I expanded the model to account for the human instincts, emotions, intellect, and intuition discussed earlier. I described the model within the framework of the basic input, processing, and output computing model familiar to IT professionals:

- Input: REB activating experiences or adversities
- Processing: Inside the human mind—REB beliefs, ideas, and philosophies about adversities
- Output: REB consequences and results

Table 3-4 provides definitions for the terms used in Figure 3-3.

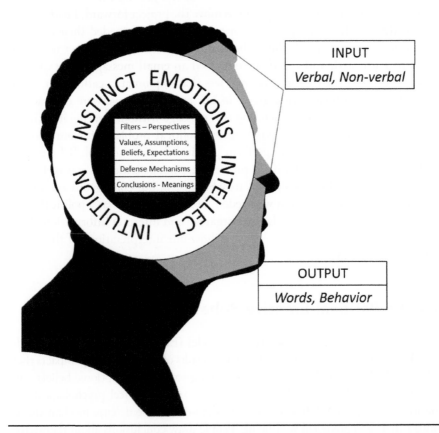

Figure 3-3   REB Model with intuition, emotions, intellect, and intuition. [Data derived from Ellis, A. (1962). *Reason and Emotion in Psychotherapy*. NY: Lyle Stuart.]

Many therapists and researchers consider defense mechanisms when analyzing human behavior. Defense mechanisms have significant influence on our response to the world, as we use them to protect our wellbeing. Several widely used defense mechanisms are provided in Table 3-5.

This modified REB model addresses the instincts, emotions, intellect, and intuition along with the VABEs, perceptions and filters, defense mechanisms, and conclusions within the mind of one person. This framework becomes more interesting when we add a communication partner. Instead of a stand-alone system with its own input, processing, and output, we now have a communication process, a network that integrates those systems.

Table 3-4 REB Model Terms

Term	Definition
Filters— Perceptions	Perceptions result from the process of organizing and interpreting sensory information, enabling us to recognize meaningful objects and events (Meyers, 2007). These activities enable living beings to order and interpret the stimulants received into meaningful insight. We all have different interpretations to stimulants, and therefore, we filter events differently and sometimes inaccurately (Perception, n.d.).
Values	Values are judgments about how important something is to us (Values, n.d.).
Assumptions	Assumptions are the premise or supposition that something is a fact; therefore, this is the act of taking something for granted. Assumptions represent how we think things should be (Assumptions, n.d.).
Beliefs	A belief system is a set of beliefs which guide and govern a person's attitude. Usually, it is directed toward a system such as a religion, philosophy, or ideology. Attitudes and beliefs in these systems are closely associated with one another and are retained in memory (Belief, n.d.).
Expectations	Expectations are the state of tense and emotional anticipation. We experience psychological discomfort when our expectations are not met (Expectation, n.d.).
Defense Mechanisms	Defense mechanisms are the unconscious reaction the ego uses to protect itself from anxiety arising from psychic conflict (Defense Mechanisms, n.d.).
Conclusions	Conclusions are the offer to which a stream of analysis or opposing matter leads. Conclusions lead to feelings (Conclusions, n.d.).

Table 3-5 Defense Mechanisms

Term	Definition
Denial	Refusal to admit a threat is relevant or that it will occur
Avoidance	Refusal to face the threat
Rationalization	Making excuses to explain away threats
Intellectualization	Complex rationalization of threats
Displacement	Redirecting reactions from a more threatening activity to a less threatening activity or action
Projection	Attributing negative emotions to others rather than accepting them
Regression	Reverting back to an earlier, less mature state

Data derived from Kehoe, D. (2011) *Effective Communications Skills.* Chantilly, VA: The Great Courses.

3.5 The Communications Cycle and the REB Model

To communicate with emotional intelligence, you need to consider what we have learned about how the mind works within the context of the classic communications cycle. Figure 3-4 depicts the integration of the modified REB model presented in Figure 3-3 with the classic communications cycle.

The sender, on the left side of the graphic, formulates the message. This message is the result of a conclusion drawn from what the sender senses, how he feels, what he believes, and what he thinks—all of the elements present in the mind of the sender. The sender has a mental picture in his mind that he needs the receiver to understand. He needs to describe his intent with consideration of the meaning that he feels resides within the receiver.

The sender encodes into words that he feels describes his intent and sends it over a communication channel to the receiver. This communication channel may be the sender's voice, an email, an instant message, or some other medium. If the sender and receiver can see each other, the sender may use gestures to emphasize and strengthen his message.

The message, once encoded and transmitted, is subject to noise. The noise may be in the form of distractions, poor encoding, language barriers, and dialects. The sender's emotions will impact the message he delivers, perhaps through voice inflections or body language, and will do so subconsciously.

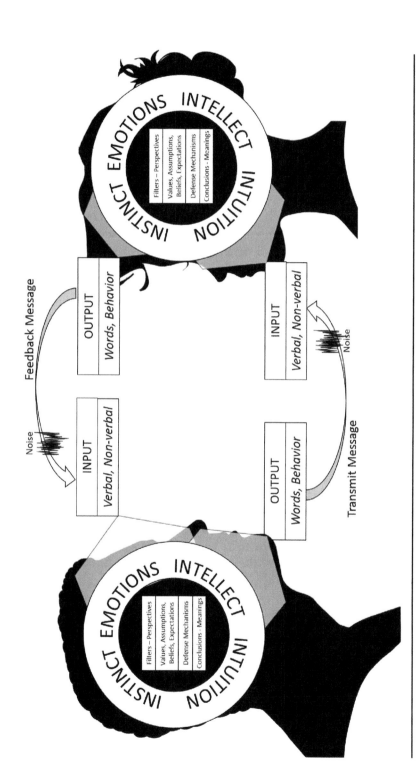

Figure 3-4 The Modified REB Model integrated with the Classic Communications Cycle. [Data derived from Ellis, A. (1962). *Reason and Emotion in Psychotherapy.* NY: Lyle Stuart.]

The receiver receives the message, and immediately her cognitive unconscious mind, influenced by the somatic markers in her limbic system, matches patterns it perceives in the message with previous patterns. This happens very quickly, before the receiver's intellect and intuition can process the signals received and draw meaning from them. She senses and filters both verbal and nonverbal inputs, deciphering the sender's feelings about the message through observation of his voice inflection and body language. She may mimic his actions through her mirror neurons, feeling what he feels. She subconsciously analyzes not only what he says, but how he says it. Once a pattern is found—a schema that helps her perceive the message—she may experience biological changes such as an increased heart rate, sweaty palms, changes in breathing patterns—changes that cause comfort or discomfort depending on her interpretation of the message, on the schema that she relates to the message. She then applies her own values, assumptions, beliefs, and expectations to the message. If she perceives that information is missing or if there is information she does not understand, her cognitive unconscious adds her own assumptions and conclusions to the package. The more abstract the message, the more information that the sender has left out, the more information she fills in on her own.

Research has shown that the receiver will take what she hears at face value, placing a high value on information that is easy for her to recall. She will classify what she hears and perceives based on cases in her past, treating the assumptions she makes as facts (Kehoe, 2011). Her conscious mind applies its intellect and intuition to the message. She will consider her interpretation of the content and the emotions associated with the content to reach her conclusion.

If she feels threatened by the message, she may unconsciously invoke defense mechanisms to protect her own psychological discomfort.

The stream of information from filters and perceptions, VABEs, and defense mechanisms lead to conclusions about the message. These conclusions result in feelings. Now, her intuition will give her a sense of the real meaning of the message, holistically considering all of the stimuli she has received. Does she trust the sender? Does what he is saying seem right?

Her intellect rationalizes the message and seeks to understand it. She may form a question concerning the message or decide on the value of the message. Does it make sense? Is it within context—is it relevant to the discussion? Does she need more information? Perhaps she quickly understands exactly what is being said, or perhaps she forms her own opinion about the message. She may challenge it or support it. She forms a mental picture in her mind and then encodes that picture into words and behaviors. This output needs to address the meaning of the message that she perceives within the sender.

She transmits her message over a communications channel. Her feedback is subject to the same noise that affected the message she received.

The sender of the original message processes her feedback in the same manner as the receiver processed the message she received from him. He applies filters and perceptions, VABEs, defense mechanisms, and conclusions using his cognitive unconscious mind. His intellect enables him to learn from her feedback, and his intuition enables him to draw meaning from all of the stimuli and thoughts he experiences. He makes a determination as to whether the meaning he attempted to convey to her was successfully transmitted, received, and understood, and then he responds accordingly. The cycle begins again and the dialogue continues.

All of this happens very, very quickly, with the instincts, emotions, intellect, intuition, VABEs, filters, perceptions, defense mechanisms, and conclusions firing within the minds of both the sender and receiver simultaneously. Messages are encoded, transmitted, and decoded faster than data packets over a wireless network.

Not only do the sender and receiver focus on the message they are transmitting, but also how they feel about themselves and about each other impacts the success or failure of communications.

3.6 The Communications Cycle and Self-Images

Our self-images give us a sense of our personality. Self-images reflect our success in relationships and our wellbeing (Self-Image, n.d.). During the communications process, we maintain three images in our minds: our own self-image, our image of the receiver, and the image we want to project to the receiver as depicted in Figure 3-5 (Kehoe, 2011).

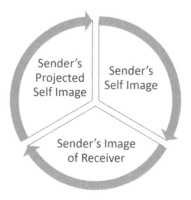

Figure 3-5   Sender's images.

The sender's image of the receiver is based on what the sender believes about the receiver's values, assumptions, beliefs, and expectations. The sender will make judgments about the receiver's ability to understand the message and will try to anticipate her response to the message. He may make assumptions about her background—the schemas she has stored in her mind—and then craft his message accordingly. For example, if the sender is providing the status of a software development effort, and he believes the receiver does not understand software development, he may educate her on the basics of Agile Software Development Methodology before providing the status.

The sender will project the self-image that he wants the receiver to see. For example, if he wants to appear to be educated and competent, he may use Agile jargon in his message such as "scrums" and "sprints" in order to shape the image he projects to the receiver. Think of the projected self-image as your profile on Facebook, LinkedIn, Google+, or some other social network. You post information to present the image of yourself that you want people to see, not the deep, dark secrets that compose who you are.

If the sender is an introvert, as most IT geeks are, his self-image reflects someone who prefers internal communications to external communications. However, the IT geek can present a projected self-image of someone who is an effective communicator. Projecting this image for long periods is draining for most introverts, as it requires a lot of energy. It requires the IT geek to use his or her less preferred Myers Briggs Type Indicator (MBTI) style, as discussed in Chapter 2. However, through positive self-talk, mentorship, and practice, the introverted IT geek can learn to communicate effectively, much as a right-handed person can learn to write with his or her left hand.

The receiver will have her own impression of the sender and will attempt to project the image of herself that she wants him to see. Figure 3-6 represents the receiver's images.

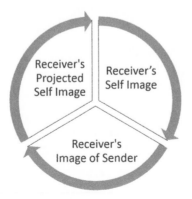

Figure 3-6   Receiver's images.

If the sender and the receiver have negative impressions of one another, there could be negative impacts on the communications process. What if the receiver is a business executive who believes that IT geeks are not sophisticated enough to understand the company's business requirements? This bias creates mental noise that inhibits the sender's message from getting through. What if the sender is an IT leader who is intimidated by his perception of the business executive's image? This fear could lead to a distorted message that leaves out the ground truth concerning a delayed project schedule, for example—information the business executive needs to create accurate forecasts.

Overlaying these images on the communications cycle, with respect to human instinct, emotions, intellect, and intuition, produces a dynamic image of the communications process as shown in Figure 3-7. All of the elements of Figure 3-7 are active simultaneously during the communications cycle, even for the simplest interactions.

Both the higher-order senses and the lower-order, primitive senses are involved in projecting and observing images of the senders and receivers. The senders and receivers may feel sexual attraction, or repulsion, for one another. These primitive stimuli occur automatically, before the intellectual mind can process the signals. The intellectual mind decides how to respond to the feelings, but it does not operate quickly enough to prevent the feeling. I once heard a story about a customer who was on the selection panel for awarding a large US government contract. While she was listening to the oral presentations from the bidders, she found a particular presenter to be quite attractive and had a hard time concentrating on his company's presentation!

Again, the thought processes that take place during communications occur very, very quickly and are extremely complex. Human communications are prone to error. In the complex environment of IT projects, communications cannot be taken for granted but must be approached with diligence in order to promote understanding. IT leaders and team members need to understand each other, and the IT team needs to understand the customer and his or her requirements. This understanding can lead to reduced complexity in the environment, improved communications, and an increased probability of project success.

3.7 The Talk Continuum

Dialogue is the mindful way to make connections with people and to enable people to understand each other. Problems are solved through dialogue. Professor Dalton Kehoe of York University describes what I have labeled the Talk Continuum, provided in Table 3-6. The Talk Continuum provides a framework for understanding the types of communications we engage in. It progresses from internal and automatic evaluations to external and deliberate dialogue. This connection between

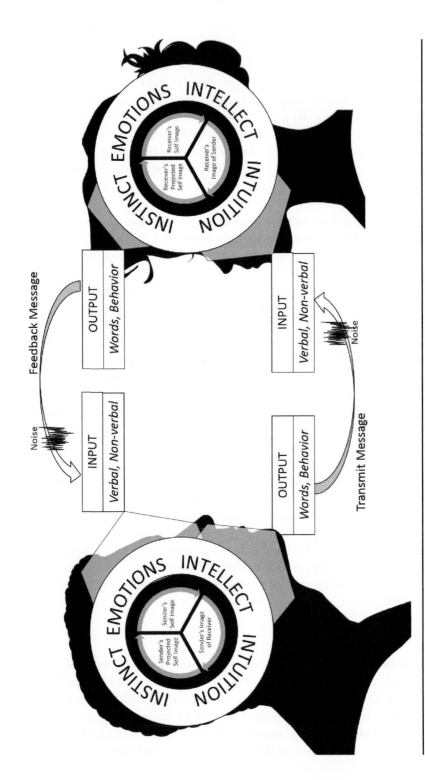

Figure 3-7 Communications cycle with sender and receiver images. [Data derived from Ellis, A. (1962). *Reason and Emotion in Psychotherapy*. NY: Lyle Stuart.]

Table 3-6 Talk Continuum

Talk Type	Description
Self-Talk	Automatic and constant internal self-evaluation and evaluation of those around us. Negative self-talk can emotionally hijack a person and render them ineffective. Positive self-talk builds confidence and self-esteem.
Connect Talk: Procedural	Used to get through every-day situations. This is the conversation we have when making a purchase or ordering food. Procedural control talk is the expected behavior of "normal" people.
Connect Talk: Ritual	Ritual recognition or greetings such as when one asks, "How are you?" and the other responds "fine." Demonstrates ability to participate in social roles in the community.
Connect Talk: Small Talk	Provides a safe way for people to get to know each other. Provides the opportunity for participants to move from first impressions to more significant relationships.
Control Talk: Light	An automatic response to differences and disagreements. A form of problem solving where one person tries to persuade another. One tries to dictate to the other how he or she should think, act, or feel.
Control Talk: Heavy	The escalation of light control talk. A natural, yet ineffective, human response to conflict. Uses more negative tactics to overcome resistance. Undermines the integrative, connective nature of the relationship.
Dialogue	A conscious choice to be mindful and appreciative in order to solve a problem, not to "save face." Requires management of emotions and the pursuit of understanding.

Data derived from Kehoe, D. (2011) *Effective Communication Skills*. Chantilly VA: The Great Courses.

internal thoughts and external communications demonstrates the link between our internal selves and our relationship with others.

The point of emotionally intelligent communication is to maximize dialogue and minimize control talk. It requires active listening, engaging both you and your communication partner. It requires you to focus not on yourself but on your communication partner and what he or she is saying. Most IT professionals are introverts, and if you are one of them, you are probably perceived as a good listener. Active listening is an opportunity for you to exercise this strength.

Your cognitive unconscious will automatically try to relate what you are hearing to your own schemas. You need to be mindful of what your communication partner is saying and what he or she means, not focusing on how you will reply. Dialogue is not a competition of who can talk more or who can make the most points. It's about actively listening and understanding, asking the "who, what, when, and how" questions that will lead to the why. This leads to the efficient attainment of ground truth.

As Steven Covey advises, we should seek first to understand, then to be understood (Covey, 1989). I once worked with a senior leader who had just recently taken on responsibility for a large services firm. This leader had a tremendous amount of experience and was anxious to make his mark on the organization. However, during the first few months of his leadership, all of his meetings were very tense. He struggled to make what he believed to be improvements without understanding how the organization worked and why his predecessors made the decisions they made. His interactions with his staff escalated to a dysfunctional level. He would frequently disparage staff members in formal meetings and curse at them in informal meetings. This heavy control talk did not contribute to resolution of the firm's problems. Instead, it damaged the relationship between the leader and his staff, making problem solving more difficult.

Over time, the leader learned more and more about the organization and felt comfortable enough to engage in dialogue with key staff members. He learned to ask questions about the environment, and he learned from experience what was required for the firm to be successful. The firm moved forward. However, it would have been successful sooner if the leader had heeded Covey's advice and sought to understand before being understood, engaging in dialogue that led to relationships based on mutual respect and so to the resolution of problems.

Emotionally charged control talk distracts from problem solving. With control talk, our energy is spent in emotional and intellectual competition instead of on reducing complexity and increasing understanding.

The enemy of efficiency is complexity, and dialogue defeats complexity. It is the weapon of choice to facilitate understanding, leading to better IT solutions.

3.8 Analysis of the Missed Signals Use Case

In the Missed Signals use case introduced earlier in this chapter, Mark, the disgruntled team member, did not have a favorable perception of Karen, the new supervisor, because of how she addressed the issues of data accuracy. Karen used heavy control talk and did not engage in dialogue concerning the issue. She could have been experiencing an "amygdala hijacking," making it difficult for her to think rationally about her behavior and its impact.

Mark was very uncomfortable while Karen was talking, and he hid his angst by wringing his hands underneath the table. He did not believe he was lazy, and he was hurt by Karen's accusation. Her appearance while she spoke made him nervous and fearful. Karen's behavior did not meet his expectations for a supervisor, did not fit his schema for how a supervisor should treat an employee. Mark had suppressed his desire to search for another job. However, his fears were revived after Karen's rant. He felt powerless to fight, so he decided to flee.

Tony, the project manager, knew about Karen's behavior, and he did speak to her about it, but he did not have a relationship with Mark. He had spoken to Mark in meetings and had offered to speak with any of the team members one-on-one. The conversation between Mark and Tony never happened. Tony had no intuition concerning what Mark was feeling. They did not understand each other. There was no VABE connection between the schemas in Mark's mind and those in Tony's. As a leader, Tony had no impact on Mark's behavior.

Mark did not provide feedback to Karen or to Tony. Karen did not know how she needed to adjust her message to ensure that Mark understood the urgency of the matter and how the team members needed to adjust their behavior. She had no idea of how her message made Mark feel. Mark's feedback was provided to Human Resources, then to Tony, and then back to Karen. By the time Karen received the message, it was too late to have an impact on Karen's relationship with Mark.

Mark's expectation was that the PM would not allow a supervisor to treat team members in the way Karen had treated them. Yes, Mark was assigned to a high-visibility and high-pressure project, but this was not an issue for him because he was as emotionally resilient as any other IT professional. However, Mark's values included self-respect, and he would not allow himself to be disrespected. He concluded that if Tony was not going to handle the problem with Karen, Human Resources would.

Human Resources never made a connection with Karen. Operating in accordance with their policy, Sandra from HR spoke to the PM, Tony, about the personnel situation, and then Tony relayed the message to Karen. It worked like a bad game of "telephone." By the time the message traveled from Sandra, through Tony, to Karen, it had been distorted. Karen never understood HR's intent. She did not know their interpretation of the events, their feedback from Mark, or their rationale for assigning the communications courses.

The corporate picture within the mind of HR was not successfully transmitted from Sandra to Tony to Karen in a way that connected to Karen's values, assumptions, beliefs, and expectations. Karen did not have an opportunity to ask questions, to provide feedback and obtain clarification. This disconnection caused uncertainty within Karen's mind, uncertainty that led to fear concerning her job.

Tony and Karen never made a connection. Karen was close to the previous PM, and her management style was closer to his than to Tony's. But Tony never would have treated the team members the way that Karen had. He had taken steps to coach her and to set expectations concerning how team leaders were to behave. He provided her with the training recommended by Human Resources. However, Karen harbored resentment concerning corporate issues outside of Tony's control. Her expectation and belief was that Human Resources would allow her to rebut complaints against her, would allow her to tell her side of the story.

Karen told Tony she would provide "whatever he needed," but she said this with her back turned to him as she walked away. Her body language was not consistent with what she said. It was, however, an indication of what she meant. Karen made the same choice as Mark did: relieve the psychological discomfort by fleeing rather than fighting.

I have lost good people from my team because I was not in tune with them and the issues they faced. Many times, when key team members left, it took us several months to find replacements. Our productivity for the tasks assigned to those positions suffered. As an introvert, I had to learn to pay more attention to body language and demeanor. I had to pay more attention to the project's most valuable asset, its people. As a leader, it is my job to make them feel important and appreciated.

People issues are complex and can derail your project, whether those people are your team members or your stakeholders. To get and stay ahead, find the ground truth as quickly and efficiently as possible.

3.9 Ground Truth

Bonnie Smith, Senior Vice President of IT and Industrial Sector CIO at Eaton, cites cultivating casual conversations as a secret to project success (Smith, 2014). "As IT leaders who are most often schooled in engineering disciplines, we sometimes forget that the best governance practices are, in the end, executed by a wildcard—namely, people," she told *CIO Magazine* in September 2014. "Often, the people who report to us will, through a surplus of good intentions, suppress any rumblings on the ground in the updates they give us, concealing the fact that milestones are quietly being missed. What is needed is an honest dialogue, which is often stymied by a fear of disappointing the boss.

"As CIO, it is absolutely critical to ensure that you, personally, build relationships with the speakers of truth," she continues. "You must identify the people who will tell you that what you're being told isn't what is really happening. The most common way to gain these insights is through an offhand comment someone makes in casual conversation, since lower-level staffers may worry about stepping on someone's toes during formal meetings."

Bonnie concludes, "Once that communication channel is established, cultivate it carefully, listen very intently and word your responses judiciously. The signals you get from these conversations are what let you hone in on trouble spots or pressure-test more than just a few deliverables. This is absolutely critical to knowing what to adjust, whether it's rearranging resources, changing processes or adding more checks and balances" (Smith, 2014).

As an IT project leader, your job is to provide senior leaders such as Bonnie the ground truth about your project and your ability to successfully achieve objectives. Establishing effective dialogue with senior stakeholders is not only good for your project, it is also good for your career. You will be seen as more than a great technologist who produces outstanding technical products and services. You will be seen as an effective leader on whom senior stakeholders can depend to provide and deliver critical information about your project, building a reputation that can help you get promoted.

3.10 Keys to Emotionally Intelligent Communications for IT Geeks

The following checklist can help the IT geek use dialogue to effectively connect with important project stakeholders, such as business executives and members of the steering committee. Using Dr. W. Edward Deming's Plan-Do-Check-Act cycle as a framework (The Plan, Do, Study, Act [PDSA] Cycle, 2016), this checklist helps you prepare for dialogue, provides do's and don'ts for the conversation, helps you ensure that both your needs and those of the stakeholder are met during the dialogue, and provides guidance on post-dialogue activities.

3.10.1 Plan

- Write down the goals of the conversation you are about to have.
  - What information do you want your communication partner to understand?
  - What do you think your communication partner will need to know from you?
  - What should you be prepared to teach?
- Gather information relevant to the conversation.
  - If possible, use a graphic to help make your case. Use your graphic to explain your point, to transmit the same picture you see into your communication partner's mind.

     o Learn what you can about the stakeholder's area of the business (requirements, previous projects, budget, issues and risks, best practices, etc.) so that you can relate to his or her schemas.

- Like a good introvert, rehearse the conversation in your mind. Anticipate what your communication partner might say and how you will respond.
- Schedule enough time to have the conversation.
- Consider the setting. Should the conversation be on your turf or theirs? Should it be in a neutral environment? Is the conversation formal or informal? Should the conversation take place over a meal? Weigh the pros and cons and make a decision.

3.10.2 Do's and Don'ts

Do:

- If you feel anxiety about the conversation, privately calm yourself using breathing exercises.
- Start the conversation in a friendly way in order to set a positive mood, helping your communication partner to view the conversation in a positive light.
  - o Make eye contact to show that you are paying attention.
  - o Reference the talk continuum—begin with small talk, working your way up to dialogue and avoiding control talk.
- Express appreciation for your communication partner's time and contribution to the project.
- Make your communication partner feel important.
- Ask questions to gain an understanding of your communication partner's background. Find areas where you can connect at a personal level, if possible. Find out how your communication partner feels about the situation or subject matter and why he or she feels that way.
- Find areas of common benefits. Identify common noble motives, such as customer satisfaction.
- Find out where your communication partner will benefit personally from the project. For example, perhaps the business executive is concerned about building his or her legacy.
- Use examples and analogies that resonate with your communication partner, that mean something to him or her.
- Be encouraging, empathizing with your communication partner, getting him or her to continue speaking.

- o Try to see things from his or her perspective—use your imagination to try and feel what he or she is feeling.
- o Reflect your interpretation of how you think your communication partner is feeling back to him or her and ask for clarification.
- Give important stakeholders the opportunity to save face and avoid embarrassment.
- Pay attention to body language and tone of voice so that you can understand how your communication partner normally behaves.
- This will enable you to detect changes in nonverbal communications and understand when your communication partner is uncomfortable or pleased with the conversation.
- Without becoming a distraction, subtly mimic your communication partner's body language to get a sense of what he or she is feeling.
- Capture notes and action items. Agree on timelines to complete action items.
- If necessary, schedule a time to follow up on the conversation.
- Thank your communication partner for his or her time and attention.

Don't:

- Don't start or end the conversation late. Be respectful of the stakeholder's time.
- Don't enter into control talk.
  - o Don't tell your conversation partner how he or she should think, act, or feel, and don't criticize harshly.
  - o Speak in a way that keeps his or her defense mechanisms down. Once defense mechanisms go up, communication stops.
  - o Don't offer your advice unless you are asked.
  - o Don't interrupt your communication partner in order to debate.
- Don't try to hide how you feel. Expect your body language and tone of voice to give you away.
- Don't draw the wrong conclusions from your observation of the stakeholder's body language, especially if you do not know the person very well.
- Don't be afraid to:
  - o Admit when you and your team have made a mistake.
  - o Tell the ground truth, providing the information needed to move the project and organization forward, stating what you agree with and disagree with up front.
  - o Express how you feel about the subject matter or situation.

      o Excuse yourself when you need to get your thoughts together, espe-
cially if the conversation gets heated. Return after you have calmed
down and you are ready to have an adult conversation.

- Unless you are a mental health professional, don't engage in mental health
issues such as rage and depression.

3.10.3 Check

- Review your notes and action items with the stakeholder.
- Ask questions to clarify anything you do not understand.
- Encourage your communication partner to ask clarifying questions.
- Verify what information is confidential and what can be shared.

3.10.4 Act

- Follow up on action items. Delegate tasks to your team as applicable.
Follow-through builds trust and credibility.
- Negotiate enough time for your introverted team members to analyze
and understand the information you are providing from key stakeholders
before preparing a response.
- Continue the momentum—check in on your communication partner
from time to time on a human level, outside of the issue you are discussing.
- File your notes so that you can refer to them. Update your Stakeholder
Engagement Register.
- Conduct dialogue sessions with your team members to share relevant,
non-confidential information.

3.11 Conclusion: Communicating in a Complex Environment

The more complex an environment, the more important a decision, the more
face-to-face dialogue becomes important. Because most communications are
nonverbal, those involved in the communications process need the opportunity
for their cognitive unconscious minds to pick up cues from the speaker and
understand his or her meaning. When these cues and the words spoken are out
of sync, the listener has the opportunity to ask deeper questions to understand
why the speaker feels the way he or she does. The words the speaker uses may have
different connotations, different meanings, so the listener needs opportunities

to ask for clarification. When the speaker receives cognitive unconscious clues that the listener does not understand, he or she has the opportunity to reiterate a point in a different way, giving the listener alternative ways to draw meaning from the words spoken, enabling the listener's cognitive unconscious to use multiple schemas to obtain meaning. If only written words are used, such as email, critical meanings are lost and the communication process is inefficient.

People need to feel safe when they are engaged in the communication process. Fear and inhibitions are psychological noise, distorting the messages both unconsciously—through the impact of automatic reactions—and consciously—where the team member purposefully leaves out information, intentionally spins conclusions, or lies outright in an effort either to protect his or her own self-image and self-esteem or to protect someone else. If team members understand that they can be frank without being judged or punished, leaders get better information, perhaps even ground truth. As leaders, we need to create environments in which team members find it easy to be courageous and are rewarded for doing so.

Because the enemy of efficiency is complexity, and complexity is a major contributor to project failure, our goal is to communicate in a manner that reduces complexity in the most efficient manner possible. We want to minimize time and resources spent communicating and achieving ground truth, enabling us to make more and better decisions in the shortest possible time. Dialogue is the most efficient manner of communication, as time and resources are not wasted with heavy control talk. Instead, precious energy is applied efficiently toward building understanding, leading to solutions that prevent project failure.

Now that you understand emotionally intelligent communications, you are ready to progress to Self-Leadership, the focus of Chapter 4, in which we will further explore self-talk and self-images, important components of the mental make-up of a leader.

Chapter 4

Self-Leadership

Today, most leaders want to empower you. They want to give you the authority and responsibility to deliver successful IT projects. They need you to tell them the ground truth. They need you to help them understand the status of your project. They need to know what you need from them as well in order to meet schedule, cost, and quality requirements. They need you to lead your team members—to motivate them to provide IT solutions that meet the users' requirements.

You need to be ready to perform when they give you the opportunity. The Project Management Institute (PMI®) conducted a Role Delineation Study for the Project Management Professional (PMP®) certification. In this study, they advised project managers to "enhance individual competence by increasing and applying professional knowledge to improve services." Doing this "requires knowledge of personal strengths and weaknesses, appropriate professional competencies. Requires skills in self-assessment, developmental planning, and obtaining and applying new information and practices" (Project Management Institute, 2000).

In this chapter, I describe how to use self-talk to improve your self-leadership, and I provide you with a process called the Self-Leadership Cycle, which will help you enhance your individual competence as a leader. Through this process, you can learn to take initiative and to exercise a growth mindset. You can become a self-directed leader.

In any circumstance, leaders have to adapt to new situations and changes first, before they can lead their team members. Adapting in this manner requires you to change how you think about leading and working with others.

Let's take a look at how Tony, a fictional character based on some of my real-life experiences, faces a challenging situation that requires him to adapt his thinking in order to become a project manager.

4.1 Things Are Changing

"Tony, I need to tell you something," James said. "Not now, man," Tony replied. "I need to finish this systems architecture document for the server farm. I just got the network load balancing configuration working in the lab and I want to make a final update to the document and send it out for review today."

"That's cool—I'll call you after work," James replied.

"I am proactive. I keep my commitments and obtain my goals," Tony thought.

On the drive home, Tony's phone rang, and James' picture appeared on the screen. Tony answered in hands-free mode. "James! What's going on?" he said.

"Hey, I quickly reviewed the architecture doc—man, it looks good. It should get through the review board very quickly," James said. "Thanks," replied Tony. "So what did you want to tell me?" "I just got a promotion and I'm going to another program," said James. "Wow! Congrats!" exclaimed Tony. "What's the new position?"

"I'm going to be a senior architect on the Dillinger program. You know, the word on the street is that the Baker program that we're on is going to be cancelled. The great work we're doing may never go into production, so I decided to apply with Dillinger," replied James.

"Yes, I heard about that. Smart move on your part. Congrats again, man!" Tony said.

As Tony and James hung up, Tony thought, "Wow, James made the right move. The last time a program was cancelled, the whole team got laid off. I'm a good architect, but I'm no James. I need to figure this out."

Then Tony said to himself, "I begin with the end in mind. I create success first in my mind and then in my life."

The next day, Terry, Tony's boss, asked to see him in Terry's office. "Uh oh," Tony thought. Tony sat in a chair across from Terry's desk. He was wringing his hands, but Terry didn't notice because he couldn't see Tony's hands over the desk.

"You did a great job on the architecture document, Tony," Terry said. "Thanks," Tony replied, exhaling. Terry continued, "I've noticed that you're a good architect Tony, but I think you're a better project manager. I've noticed how organized you are, and you're a good writer. Have you ever thought about becoming an IT project manager?" "I do enjoy project management," Tony replied, "but I haven't given it much thought."

"You should," said Terry. "I see you with a Six Sigma certification or a PMP®. You should think about that. Once the Baker program ends, there will be new project management opportunities in the company as we stand up the PMO. I recommend that you prepare yourself."

"Interesting," Tony replied. "Thanks for the feedback and the advice. I'll give this some thought."

That evening, Tony attended the systems engineering class he was taking for his master's degree. Aaron, Tony's professor, made it a habit to mentor the promising students in his classes. Tony admired Aaron because he was smart and successful, and just an overall great person.

Referring to Tony's self-talk statements during their one-on-one session after class, Aaron said to Tony, "OK, let me hear it."

"I am proactive. I keep my commitments and obtain my goals," Tony begins.

"I begin with the end in mind. I create success first in my mind and then in my life.

"I put first things first. I organize and execute around my priorities.

"I seek first to understand and then to be understood. When I listen, I rephrase content and reflect feeling. When I respond, I present my ideas clearly, specifically, visually, and contextually.

"I think win/win. I constantly seek mutually beneficial solutions.

"I seek positive synergy. I utilize conflicting opinions to create third alternative solutions.

"I'm balanced and sharp. I 'sharpen the saw.' I constantly learn, do, and commit to activities that promote physical, mental, social/emotional, and spiritual improvement."

"Great," Aaron said. "You flowed right through those. Everyone morning and every night, right?"

"That's right," Tony replied. "I recorded them on my phone as you suggested. I listened to them every day and every night until I memorized them. Now I recite them at least once a day in the mirror, and throughout the day."

Aaron had attended a seminar with Lou Tice from The Pacific Institute. He combined Tice's ideas on self-talk with Stephen Covey's *The 7 Habits of Highly Effective People* (Covey, 1989) to create specific affirmations—constructive self-talk—which he used to mentor his students.

"You weren't yourself tonight in class," Aaron said. "Something wrong?"

"Things are changing at work," Tony replied. "The program I'm working on may get cancelled before we're complete. My boss says I should think about becoming a project manager to prepare for life after this program. I'm trying to visualize myself as an IT project manager."

"Begin with the end in mind," Aaron said. "Your boss is right, you know. I have noticed your leadership abilities during class, on group projects. IT projects have a high failure rate, and we need good project managers in the industry. Since you're thinking so hard about this, it's obviously something you want to do. Tell you what, why don't you sign up for the Project Management course next quarter, and then take the PMP® once you finish. You should also use the 10-Page Plan to get through the *PMBOK® Guide* (Project Management Institute, 2013a) while you're taking the class. This will help you pass both the PM course and the PMP® exam. The quarter starts next week, so you can begin right away. What do you think?"

"Let me think about it. I'll email you tomorrow and let you know," Tony replied.

"Introverts need time to think," Aaron remembered.

The next day, Tony sent Aaron this message: "I appreciate your advice, as usual. I am ready to make the commitment to become a great IT project manager, and I know with your help, I can achieve this goal."

Tony followed Aaron's advice to the letter. Over the next three months, he joined the Project Management Institute (PMI®) and earned an A in his project management course. He followed the 10-Page Plan that Aaron had taught him, studying 10 pages per day, every day, enabling him to read the *PMBOK® Guide* twice while taking his project management course. This prepared him to pass the PMP® certification exam. Tony then notified the HR department at his employer to add the PMP® certification to his records.

Tony called James at his desk and asked as he picked up, "James, do you have a minute?"

"Absolutely," James replied. "I heard Baker was cancelled. What's going on with you?"

"How do you feel about Dillinger?" Tony asked.

James answered, "Great, man, we're fully funded, and we're leveraging the work we did on the Baker program."

"Yes," Tony said. "Terry told me today that I need to transition my documentation from Baker to you. You'll be hearing about this from your boss soon. The reason I'm calling is to let you know I got promoted to project manager, and I will be in the new PMO. I'll be managing projects on Dillinger, among other projects."

"That's awesome," James said. "I'm looking forward to working with you again!!"

Tony sent Aaron another email: "I got the promotion! I'd like to thank you by taking you to dinner—we can celebrate and talk about the next challenge!"

"Outstanding!" Aaron replied. "You've embarked on your leadership journey!"

"I am a leader who demonstrates excellent project management skills," Tony said to himself.

4.2 Self-Talk

Self-talk is very powerful. What you say to yourself influences who you are in both positive and negative ways. Positive self-talk provides life-giving nutrients to your brain, building neural pathways that enable you to grow and become what you want to become. Negative self-talk is poison. It cripples your mind, debilitates your self-image, and restricts your growth.

We begin our exploration of self-talk with an examination of the self. Then, we will cover inner motivation. Next, you will learn how to rewrite your own code in order to take on the IT geek leadership mindset. Finally, we will talk about improving your self-talk in order to improve your self-leadership.

4.2.1 The Self

The self is created in the conscious mind. We mentally integrate our unique collection of perceptions, beliefs, and feelings to form the self. The self consists of three aspects: personality, self-concept, and self-esteem (Kehoe, 2011).

As self-leaders, our challenge is to know ourselves. We are challenged to observe our own personality—our needs, perceptions, and emotional reactions—and the personality we perceive to be required for leaders, and then we make the effort to adapt. We are challenged to observe our own self-concept and then to understand our strengths and weaknesses in how we define ourselves in relation to leadership.

Our self-concept is based on how we see the world, not necessarily how the world is. Our ability to make these changes, considering the complexity of knowing oneself, is quite challenging. Our success rate for adapting to situations that require leadership impacts how we feel about ourselves—our self-esteem.

Our self-concept is in motion, constantly changing through interactions with others. We enhance certain parts of who we are and hide others. We are constantly changing through interactions with others, growing and adapting to meet their needs while they do the same to meet our needs (Kehoe, 2011).

Researchers have found that most people and organizations are able to perform effectively if they strive to understand themselves and each other, then adjust their behavior and change the way they communicate (Institute for Management Excellence, 2003). They have to work to progress toward better teamwork and productivity. But they must first be committed to positive change. Our personality's enduring characteristics include our needs, perceptions, and emotional reactions. These characteristics influence our reactions to the world across a variety of situations (Kehoe, 2011). Psychologists have found that personality is a consequential system, in which personality characteristics follow as a result or effect of the situations we face. Just as individuals develop Myers-Briggs Type Indicator (MBTI) preferences early in life that usually do not change, our personalities exhibit persistent patterns over time that influence our lives (Mayer, 2014).

As we discussed in Chapter 2, the MBTI helps us understand how our conscious minds process information. The tendency of IT professionals to be introverted and to prefer working alone makes effective communications and motivation challenging. This introverted tendency impacts their ability to communicate with their team, peers, and leaders. We also discussed the Big Five Study in Chapter 2, which found that IT professionals scored low on visionary style and may have trouble thinking strategically, which is another core leadership requirement.

While the MBTI preferences may not change, the personality patterns can change as people adapt to their situations, choosing when to use their preferred behavior style and when to use one of their less preferred styles.

IT geeks can learn to adapt to the leadership mindset—to use their less-preferred extraverted preference, to establish and lead others to pursue a clear vision, to value teamwork and collaboration; IT geeks can learn leadership just as a programmer that prefers Visual Basic can learn to code in C#.

4.2.2 Internal Motivation

In 1943, Abraham Maslow developed his Hierarchy of Needs Theory to explain human motivation. Figure 4-1 depicts the Hierarchy of Needs. Maslow theorized that we are compelled to respond to five levels of needs: physiological, safety, and social needs (considered lower-order needs); and esteem and self-actualization needs (considered higher-order needs) (Maslow, 2012a).

Figure 4-1 is best read from the bottom up. Maslow's theory is that people are motivated to satisfy the lower-order needs—to obtain food, water, and shelter; to be safe and secure; and to love and be loved—before satisfying the higher-order needs. Once these lower-order needs have been satisfied, people are then compelled to satisfy their needs for esteem and self-actualization—to be the best they can be and to fulfill their purpose in life (Maslow, 2012b).

Human beings are constantly wanting, working toward the satisfaction of a need. The basic needs are arranged in order of power and influence over the human consciousness. When a need is somewhat satisfied, the next most powerful need emerges and dominates thinking and behavior. Lesser needs may be set aside, forgotten, or denied. Once a person feels the need to self-actualize, he or she may become anxious, on edge, tense, and overall restless (Maslow, 2012b). It is easy to tell when a person feels hungry, unsafe, unloved, or lacking self-esteem, but it is difficult to determine what will satisfy a person's need to self-actualize.

Self-leadership requires you to find internal motivation to achieve your leadership goals. External motivators, such as paying your mortgage or rent, passing an exam, or completing a project at work, are good positive motivators. But better motivators are those that help you achieve more, that help you to change

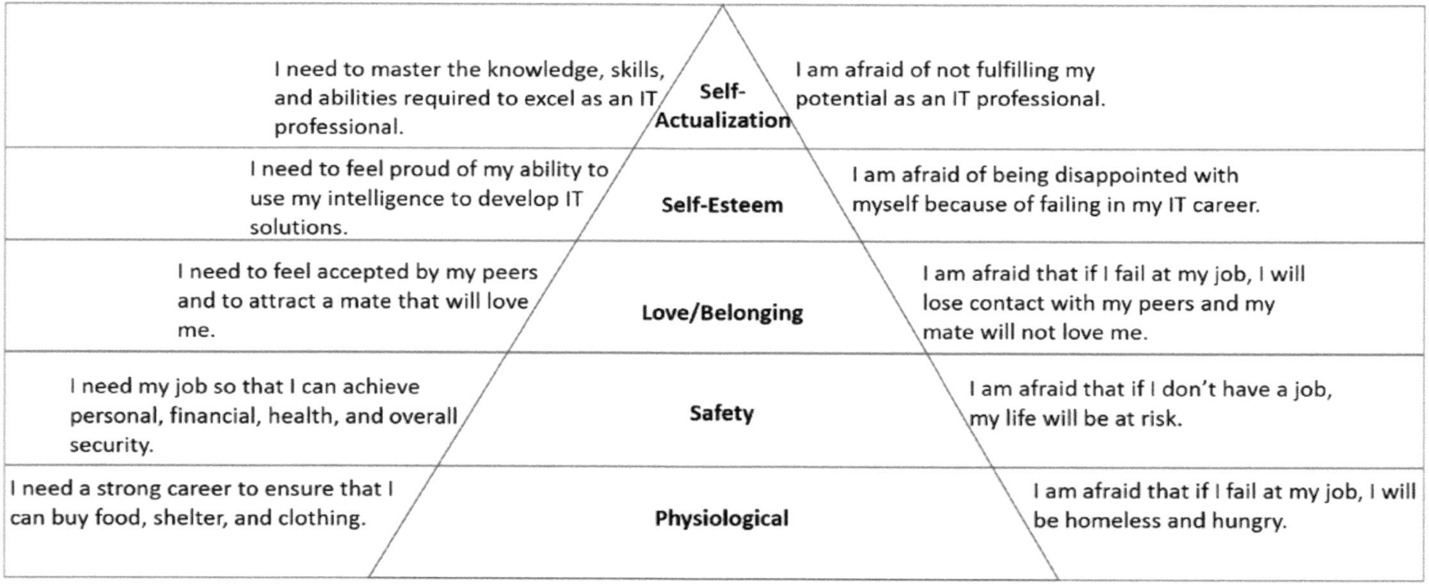

I need to master the knowledge, skills, and abilities required to excel as an IT professional.	**Self-Actualization**	I am afraid of not fulfilling my potential as an IT professional.
I need to feel proud of my ability to use my intelligence to develop IT solutions.	**Self-Esteem**	I am afraid of being disappointed with myself because of failing in my IT career.
I need to feel accepted by my peers and to attract a mate that will love me.	**Love/Belonging**	I am afraid that if I fail at my job, I will lose contact with my peers and my mate will not love me.
I need my job so that I can achieve personal, financial, health, and overall security.	**Safety**	I am afraid that if I don't have a job, my life will be at risk.
I need a strong career to ensure that I can buy food, shelter, and clothing.	**Physiological**	I am afraid that if I fail at my job, I will be homeless and hungry.

Figure 4-1 Maslow's Hierarchy of Needs.

for the better. Internal motivation does not require an outside stimulus; instead you have a sense of purpose, a determination to change yourself, if necessary, in order to self-actualize, to become all that you can become (Helmstetter, 1982).

Stephen Covey's Habit 2, "Begin with the End in Mind," is based on the principle that all things are created twice, first in the mind, and then, physically, in life (Covey, 1989). No one else knows your needs, goals, and desires like you do, so they cannot—should not—create in their mind what manifests in your life. No one else is responsible for or capable of setting a path for your future.

I have interviewed several people who did not know what they wanted to do. They were working in an area outside of their degree; they had changed jobs several times. They were actually very capable workers, but they didn't know if they were fulfilled because they did not set out to achieve a particular goal. They struggled to find a position that satisfied their self-esteem needs because they could not visualize or articulate what they were looking for. You don't have to be that way. You can commit yourself to becoming an IT leader. You can devote yourself to discovering where you are on Maslow's hierarchy and set out on a journey to self-actualize. Aristotle said, "Knowing yourself is the beginning of all wisdom" (Aristotle, 2012).

An IT geek that has made the commitment to become an IT leader faces such a challenge. You need to find not only external motivation, such as a promotion, but also internal motivation, a sense of purpose that is unique to you, the geek. "Real leaders are guided more by internal than external regulation" (Tice, 2005). Many psychologists believe that you cannot motivate anyone to become something they do not internally agree to become (Helmstetter, 1982). IT geek leaders need to have an emotional connection; a requirement to satisfy a physiological need, a safety need, a self-esteem need, or a need to self-actualize; a need to develop a sense of pride and accomplishment; a belief in themselves; and a fulfillment that comes from living in accordance with their values, beliefs, and expectations.

"You have beliefs and expectations that affect every aspect of your life," Tice writes, "what kind of person you are morally, socially, spiritually, intellectually. So, in a sense, you don't have just one self-image, you have thousands. For example, you have a belief about what kind of leader you are, and within that belief, you may have self-images. You may think, 'I'm a leader on my softball team and as a teacher at my school, but I'm not a leader in my community or church'" (Tice, 2005).

Your belief about your IT geek leadership ability follows the same principle. You may believe you are a leader, that you have a leadership mindset in your family or at school, but not on an IT project.

But you can change this self-image and become an IT geek leader. Taking responsibility for your team means first taking responsibility for your own self-leadership by motivating yourself to adapt, to don the leadership mindset required to succeed in your organization.

4.2.3 Rewriting Your Code

As discussed in Chapter 3, a schema is a framework into which we pour our experiences and the emotions associated with those experiences. If we limit ourselves to schemas from days gone by, we cannot grow. We have to live in the present. This is a new day, and we are facing new situations. The fears of the past are not relevant to today's situation. The constraints that once restricted us do not apply to the challenges we face today.

In Chapter 3, I introduced self-talk as the first element of the Talk Continuum. Self-talk is the voice in our minds that presents our thoughts and feelings in language. What we say to ourselves not only reflects our thoughts and feelings, but also influences our values, assumptions, beliefs, and expectations. What we say to ourselves influences the image we have of ourselves.

Changing your self-talk can change your life. When you begin to picture yourself as a leader, to use your imagination to sense how a leader thinks and feels, your brain builds neural pathways to help you "become" the new picture you create. Whenever you send the same message, or have the same thought, or have the same experience, your brain sends nutrition and energy along that neural pathway, and that pathway gets stronger (Helmstetter, 2013). Weight lifters develop a workout routine that builds muscles through repetition, and the body sends nutrients to those muscles so that they grow stronger and larger. The brain works in a similar fashion. In the brain, the action that builds new neural pathways is not weight lifting, but self-talk.

In 1998, I attended a seminar entitled "Investment in Excellence," presented by Louis Tice of the Pacific Institute. Lou, who died in 2012, was an outstanding motivational speaker who taught us techniques for visualization, constructive self-talk, setting and achieving goals, and building teams. Lou taught us to create positive, specific affirmations that we were to review every day, morning and night. In 1998, my goal was to earn a Microsoft Certified Systems Engineer (MCSE) certification to complement my MBA and my undergraduate degree in computer science. I wanted to be equally as good with technology as with management. Lou's techniques helped me accomplish this goal and many, many more. His techniques are recorded in his book, *Smart Talk for Achieving Your Potential* (Tice, 2005). I am using his techniques right now to imprint into my mind the goal for improving my speaking and writing abilities.

Your self-talk strongly influences your internal motivation. Olympic athletes use it to motivate themselves to perform at a world-class level. Scores of sports teams use it to increase the performance of their players (Helmstetter, 1982). Incidentally, Lou Tice honed his techniques while working as a football coach (Tice, 2005).

The brain builds neural pathways for both positive and negative self-talk. The environment you live and work in, your values, assumptions, beliefs, and expectations—everything you experience—impacts your self-talk (Helmstetter, 2013). You can decide if the neural pathways you create are poisonous weeds or nutritious vegetation. You can directly use self-talk to become what you want to become, including an IT geek leader.

Self-talk can help those who avoid leadership to learn to value good leadership. It can change your assumptions about yourself from "I can never lead" to "I am improving my leadership abilities every day." Self-talk can change your belief about your work style, drowning out the voice that says, "I'd rather work alone," with a louder voice that says, "I work very effectively in teams." It can change what you expect for yourself, transforming "I just do what I'm told" to "I establish and lead others to pursue a realistic vision."

4.2.4 Improving Your Self-Talk

You can take proactive steps to improve your self-talk. Figure 4-2 provides a high-level process for improving your self-talk.

Monitor Your Self-Talk

Monitoring your self-talk requires you to be mindful. You have to "think about what you are thinking about," as if you are a third person listening to the chatter going on inside your head. Accomplishing this step makes you self-aware.

Table 4-1 explains how to monitor your self-talk.

Edit Your Self-Talk

When you listen to your self-talk, you identify the negative thoughts about yourself that are detrimental to improving your leadership abilities. No one controls your thoughts but you, so you siphon out the poison, replacing the negative with positive.

Your new self-talk, replacing negative thoughts with positive thoughts, may not sound like you at first. However, repeating the processes provides your brain

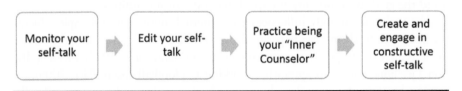

Figure 4-2   Self-talk improvement process.

Table 4-1 Monitor Your Self-Talk

Step	Instructions	Self-Talk
Monitor your self-talk	• Listen to everything you say or think. • Pay attention to the poisonous things you say about yourself that could work against you.	Listen for thoughts such as: • "I don't know what to say to senior leaders." • "No one listens to me." • "The customer makes me nervous." • "I will never understand the big picture." • "I never do well working with teams." • "I am not cut out for leadership."

Data derived from Helmstetter, S. (2013). *The Power of Neuroplasticity,* p. 161.

with new instructions, and your brain will do what you repeatedly tell it to do (Helmstetter, 2013). If you change the way you think, you will change the way you act. If you learn to think like a leader, you will become a leader.

Table 4-2 provides instructions for editing your self-talk.

Table 4-2 Practice Your "Inner Counselor"

Step	Instructions	Self-Talk
Edit your self-talk	• When you anticipate that you will say something negative to yourself, something that should not be imprinted into your mind, stop. • Instead of saying the negative phrase, replace it. Think your best and not your worst. Rewrite and reframe. • Choose a positive thought to record in your brain.	Sample self-talk changes: • "No one listens to me" becomes "Everyone respects my point of view." • "I can't talk to my senior leaders" becomes "Senior leaders value my input." • "I'm not comfortable delivering bad news" becomes "Leadership needs to hear the truth and they trust me to deliver it." • "I don't understand the customer" becomes "I'm the bridge between the customer and my technical team."

Data derived from Helmstetter, S. (2013). *The Power of Neuroplasticity,* p. 162.

Editing alone will not remove all of your negative programming, but it keeps you from getting more of the same.

Practice Being Your "Inner Counselor"

During this step, you take on the role of what you imagine to be your more enlightened self. You create an image of yourself that is your coach or mentor. This "Inner Counselor" provides you with inspiration and guidance for improving your leadership abilities.

Table 4-3 explains the role of the "Inner Counselor."

Of course, your "Inner Counselor" is no substitute for an actual counselor, but it supplements your experience with your coach, mentor, or professional counselor.

Table 4-3 The Role of the "Inner Counselor"

Step	Instructions	Self-Talk
Practice being your "Inner Counselor."	• Image your "Inner Counselor" to be a more enlightened form of yourself. • Give this image of yourself the authority to work with you to help you reduce fear and to identify and correct false notions. • Your "Inner Counselor" uses cognitive, inner dialogue to inject reality into your self-talk so that you focus on the current situation and not the irrelevant past where the negative thoughts originated. • Meet with your "Inner Counselor" daily in order to break old, negative habits and replace them with new, positive habits. • Speak to yourself in the second person, using "you" instead of "I."	Here is an example of an "Inner Counselor": "Alright, Tony. I know you're nervous about presenting the project schedule to the CIO. You need to calm down and relax. You and the team worked really hard to develop the schedule. You have already socialized it with the CIO's office—they know about the delays the vendor caused and your contingency plan. Your nervousness stems from that time five years ago when your presentation didn't go so well. You have learned much since then, and those people aren't even here—but you are! And you have had many successes since then! You've rehearsed and you know this project cold! You can do this!"

Data derived from Helmstetter, S. (2013). *The Power of Neuroplasticity*, p. 164.

Create and Engage in Constructive Self-Talk

Your creative subconscious mind enforces your behavior. It maintains your present version of reality, causing you to act like who you believe you are. When you wake up in the morning, you don't have to rediscover who you are. Your creative subconscious maintains this image and thereby allows you to maintain your sanity. It provides consistency for who you are (Tice, 2005).

Your creative subconscious always maintains your presently dominant self. This is the self that you present to the world, the self that everyone reacts to. Maintaining your idea of reality is more important than anything else—any ambition, drive, or goal that you set. Constructive self-talk, tempered by your inner counselor, tells your brain what reality is, changing the way you think and therefore changing the way you act (Tice, 2005). Table 4-4 provides instructions for creating and engaging in constructive self-talk.

Table 4-4 Create and Engage in Constructive Self-Talk

Step	Instructions	Self-Talk
Create and engage in constructive self-talk	• Create your self-talk in the present tense—"I am . . ." "It is . . .". • Create specific self-talk. Include the details, and don't be vague. • Avoid self-talk that produces unwanted side effects—pushing yourself too hard can cause stress and illness. • Keep your self-talk simple and easy to use. • Create self-talk that is practical and achievable. Plant your self-talk on solid ground, not on miracles. • Create self-talk that stretches you and demands the best of you.	Examples: • Present tense: "I really am a very special person." • Specific: "I accept responsibility for leading the Dillinger Software Development Team." • Avoid danger: "I will work 16 hours a day until I complete this project." • Simple: "I never worry." • Practical/achievable: "I read leadership books every day and I practice what I learn." • Stretch goals: "I can clearly see myself successfully leading a team of 20 software engineers and developers, delivering a critical project on time and within budget."

Data derived from Helmstetter, S. (2013). *The Power of Neuroplasticity.* Gulf Breeze, FL: Park Avenue Press; and Tice, L. (2005). *Smart Talk for Achieving Your Potential: 5 Steps to Get You from Here to There.* [Kindle Version].

My inspiration for the self-talk example provided above in the section Practice Being Your "Inner Counselor" came from a couple of my emotional experiences. I was a shift lead in an operations center as a 20-something US Air Force Airman. While I was in charge, a special operations event occurred that we had to respond to. I can't go into details concerning the event, but I can say that I was responsible for making sure the team followed procedures correctly and then reporting the results of our scientific analysis to higher headquarters. I remember how embarrassed I was because my voice was trembling and my hands were shaking. This was long before the Lou Tice seminar. I plowed through it, and we were successful, but I did not get any style points. I knew the bits and bytes cold, but I was not prepared to interact with senior leadership.

"If you want to be a leader, but believe yourself a follower, you will automatically act like you believe yourself to be when a crisis occurs," writes Lou Tice in *Smart Talk to Change Your Life.* "If you feel out of place, tension constricts your vocal chords so your voice changes. That's why, when someone gets up in front of a group of people and says in a squeaky, timid voice, 'I'm looking forward to this,' you sense they are lying" (Tice, 2005).

As that young shift lead, I hoped that we would not experience an event while I was in charge. I was certainly not looking forward to leading. My self-image was that of a programmer, as a technologist, as an IT geek. I was in a leadership position, but I did not have a leadership mindset.

I was working among the technical elite of Air Force enlisted personnel. We all needed high test scores to get accepted into our career field. I desperately wanted, needed, to be as good they were, to be as confident and accomplished as they were. However, during this operations event, I fell short of the mark, and I knew I had a lot of work to do.

Not long after this event, I took a speech class while in college. Then I earned an undergraduate degree, and after that, the Air Force sent me to leadership school with over 100 of my peers. Unlike a few others, I decided to apply myself at school because I needed to embrace what was taught in order to achieve my goals. At leadership school, I won the Communicator's Award as well as the Leadership Award, presented to the sole honor graduate. Next, I attended Officer Training School and Computer Officer Training School, where I was an honor graduate. Both of those schools required me to participate in communications training, both speaking and writing. Prior to departing from the Air Force, I attended the Lou Tice seminar, and I earned an MBA, which also provided extensive communications training.

After becoming a civilian IT project manager, I needed to make a presentation to the CIO of a large organization concerning the results of our analysis of a global workstation modernization requirement. I developed the presentation with the team, and I knew the material cold. But I did not rehearse, as I was taught to do for critical presentations. I thought I could "wing it." Although I was prepared, and although I had given many successful presentations up to that point, I was still haunted by my experience as a young shift lead, stumbling through leading our response to an operational event. I stumbled through the presentation—again, no style points.

When it comes to presentations, this geek is "hit and miss." The more I prepare the better I am. I joined Toastmasters so that I could constantly hone my presentation skills and so that I would have a fresh library—schemas—of recent successful presentations that I can now draw from for confidence. I am nervous almost every time, and Toastmasters allows me to practice handling that nervousness, channeling my nervous energy to a successful presentation. The more opportunities I get to practice overcoming nervousness, the better the outcome.

I have presided over hundreds of meetings for the dozens of projects and programs I have led. I have presented at seminars at churches and colleges in my area. I have received many compliments for my presentations at award ceremonies and the like. Why? Because now I am mindful and self-aware. I have worked hard to edit out previous failures and poisonous self-talk. I know what I need in order to be successful in this area, what I need to do and how I need to think. I have learned to rewrite my code. Since Lou Tice, and since my poor performance in front of the CIO, my daily self-talk has included, "I am an excellent public speaker and I am very comfortable in this role." Repeating this specific affirmation to myself before I speak, whether at Toastmasters or in a professional setting, gives me confidence, reminds me of my public speaking successes, and calms me down.

Now that you understand the power of self-talk, let's examine how self-talk can be combined with what I call the Self-Leadership Cycle to create and strengthen your IT geek leadership mindset.

4.3 The Self-Leadership Cycle

William Deming is known for the Plan-Do-Check-Act (PDCA) Cycle, a four-step model for carrying out change (isixsigma, n.d). Author Stephen Covey concludes the chapter "Habit 7: Sharpen the Saw," in *The 7 Habits of Highly Effective People,* with a description of an upward spiral, in which we learn, commit, and do activities that take us to increasingly higher levels of effectiveness in life (Covey, 1989). These two models inspired what I call the Self-Leadership Cycle, as depicted in Figure 4-3.

Let's take a closer look at the Self-Leadership Cycle in relation to improving IT geek leadership.

Figure 4-3   The Self-Leadership Cycle.

4.3.1 Commit

Have you ever made a vow to a country, an organization, or a person? When US military members make a vow to defend their country, they raise their right hands and say, "I solemnly swear to defend the Constitution of the United States against all enemies, foreign and domestic, so help me God." School children in the United States are taught to put their hands over our hearts and "Pledge allegiance to the flag of the United States of America." We make enduring commitments to our country and to our loved ones, but how about to ourselves? In the Commit phase, we make the same magnitude of commitment to ourselves to become IT leaders.

As an IT geek seeking to become a leader, your commitment begins with a choice. Commitment requires you to be mindful, "to pay attention to how you are paying attention" to the tasks and make the effort necessary to reach your goal of becoming an IT geek leader. You need to be mindfully aware of where you are and where you want to go as well as committed to changing your mental state so that you will first think like, then feel like, and finally behave like an IT leader.

The mindset you have as a team member is not the mindset required for leadership. You have to practice thinking like a leader. When I was a young Air Force Staff Sergeant, I dreamed of becoming a commissioned officer. I started to observe the officers around me, to listen to what they said and to watch how they behaved in order to understand how they thought. I would emulate how they approached situations, and then I would try to take the same approach to address challenges as I imagined an officer would. From my perspective, if I started with the academics first, understood the best practices and understood what schools were teaching about the subject matter related to the issue I was facing, and then applied those academics to the situation I faced, my approach would be as sound as the approaches of the officers around me. I thought about this goal every day and worked hard to adapt my mindset. Eventually, I got the opportunity to apply for Officer Training School, and I believe this thought process emulation exercise helped me successfully transition into the commissioned officer role.

There is power in the choices we make. Repeating the same choices again and again builds neural pathways in our brains that reinforce those choices. Positive choices build positive habits (Helmstetter, 2013). Choices concerning whether we will make the effort to be good communicators, to interact and collaborate with other team members, to develop and maintain relationships with our leaders and customers, to have an open mind and make the effort to use dialogue to understand the customer's requirements, to choose to pursue world-class solutions even when we don't agree with the requirements, to choose to courageously report bad news early and often—all of these choices determine how well we lead. As a self-leader, you need to understand where you are in these areas and make the commitment to form the positive habits to improve yourself in these areas. No one can make this commitment for you; only you can mindfully make this choice concerning your own thoughts, feelings, and behavior.

To transform yourself into an IT geek leader, choose to make the commitment to change your mindset. Learn to use self-talk to imprint this goal and build leadership habits, to create neural pathways for leadership that are stronger than the neural pathways for your current behavior.

When we make a commitment, we proactively take on responsibility for our own personal development. We take responsibility for developing a leadership mindset, for editing out what author Stephen Covey calls *reactive language* and replacing it with *proactive language*. According to Covey, reactive language absolves you from responsibility (Covey, 1989). As leaders, our team members, our peers, and our senior leaders depend on us to take proactive actions. This begins with proactive self-talk, editing out reactive language and replacing it with proactive, committed self-talk (see Table 4-5).

Covey said that there are two ways to put ourselves in control of our lives immediately. We can make a promise and keep it, or we can set a goal and work to achieve it (Covey, 1989). Both of these actions require commitment and build our credibility as a leader. As we make and keep even small commitments, according to Covey, we establish inner integrity that gives us the awareness of self-control.

Table 4-5 Reactive and Proactive Self-Talk

Replace Reactive Self-Talk	With Proactive Self-Talk
"I can't please this customer."	"I listen in order to understand the issues and take action to improve processes."
"He makes me so upset."	"I am in control of my feelings."
"They don't want to hear what is really happening."	"I choose to communicate the ground truth effectively."

We gain power—courage and strength to accept responsibility for our lives. We set an example for our subordinates to follow and our peers to emulate.

People in organizations are capable of change and growth. They can work toward progress, toward better teamwork and productivity. But they must first be committed to positive change.

4.3.2 Learn

IT geeks are a smart bunch. According to the US Census Bureau, in June of 2013, 68% of IT professionals in the US hold a bachelor's degree or higher, and an additional 24% had some college or an associate's degree (Department of Professional Employees, 2014). Many others have earned IT certifications and do not have any college.

We need our best and brightest IT professionals to lead IT projects, and many who have undergraduate and graduate degrees are doing just that all over the world. However, the Computer Science Curricula 2013, which is the curriculum guideline for undergraduate degree programs in computer science and information technology, does not include leadership in the body of knowledge (ACM/IEEE, 2013). The curriculum does, however, promote the principle for continuous learning, expounding, "Curricula must prepare students for lifelong learning and must include professional practice (e.g., communication skills, teamwork, and ethics) as components of the undergraduate experience."

To become an IT geek leader, you need to make a commitment to lifelong learning about leadership. During my leadership journey, I found that many IT professionals that I worked with avoided tasks that required them to write and to speak, and that they missed out on opportunities to present information to customers and to leadership. Because my peers avoided these job requirements, I knew that if I embraced speaking and writing, while remaining adept in technology, I'd have job security. Like a fireman that runs toward a fire instead of away from it, I made a conscious and continuous effort to overcome the fears that kept others in the shadows and on the sidelines.

You have the same choice. Your brain is a chemical organ that uses chemicals to develop neural pathways for your thoughts. Choosing to be mindful adds strength to those pathways, forming habits for activities that lead toward attainment of goals. Research has shown that concentrating for 10 to 15 seconds or more on a thought upgrades that thought from short-term memory storage to longer-term memory storage. You are in charge, not your brain, so you can mindfully instruct your brain that you are not just an IT geek, but an IT leader. And you can do this in a way that you enjoy; you are free to make yourself not only an IT geek leader, but an IT geek leader who enjoys his or her work (Helmstetter, 2013).

After you have made the commitment to change your thought processes about leadership, learn everything you can about how to be a strong leader. Take classes, buy books, go to the library, subscribe to periodicals, and read Internet sites. Create a "Smart-book"—a three-ring binder with articles, clippings, copies from library books, and the like that you can use as references.

I love how small, incremental steps can add up to something very substantial. Did you know that if you read 10 pages a day, a task that probably takes about 15 to 20 minutes, 10 pages a day every day for a year, you would read 3,650 pages in a year? Assuming the average book has less than 300 pages, you would read at least 12 books in a year. If you read 12 books about leadership in a year and apply what you learn, you will be a far better leader than your peers (and maybe even your bosses). In the Learn phase, you commit yourself to finding out whatever you need to know to become a great leader. Knowledge is power—commit yourself to becoming powerful!

This type of dedication to learning requires a growth mindset instead of a fixed mindset. Dr. Carol Dweck, a psychologist at Stanford University, defines a learner with a fixed mindset as someone who believes that intelligence is a fixed trait. People with fixed mindsets believe a person is either smart in a given area or not. People with a fixed mindset usually exert much less effort to learn material they believe is too difficult to grasp (Doyle and Zakrajsek, 2013).

In contrast, people with growth mindsets toward learning believe that intelligence grows as one obtains new knowledge and skills. Failure to them is a trigger that they need to work harder to overcome the challenges they face in order to succeed (Doyle and Zakrajsek, 2013).

A person can have a fixed mindset in one area and a growth mindset in another. For example, an IT professional can have a growth mindset toward software development and a fixed mindset toward leadership.

As discussed earlier, your brain is capable of developing new neural pathways based on your experiences. According to Jesper Mogensen, a psychologist at the University of Copenhagen, neurons in the brain grow new connections, build new neural pathways, when we learn. Our intelligence is not fixed (Doyle and Zakrajsek, 2013).

To become an IT geek leader, you have to overcome the fixed mindset toward learning to be a leader. You need a growth mindset; you need to believe that if you can learn the complexities of IT, you can learn anything, including leadership. A leadership mindset is a growth mindset focused on leadership.

Here are some daily self-talk suggestions that can help you overcome a fixed mindset about leadership and develop a growth mindset:

- "I am smart and creative. I continually increase my leadership knowledge."
- "I am a lifelong learner. I can learn anything I want to learn."
- "I accept the responsibility to learn to be a great leader."

4.3.3 Seek Mentorship

Proverbs 12:1 says, "If you love learning, you love the discipline that goes with it—how shortsighted to refuse correction!" While you are learning what you need to know to succeed, you are going to need guidance from someone who can keep you on track and help you make decisions.

No one knows everything. It's important to get guidance from someone you respect who has performed similar tasks or who has been on similar projects. Seeking mentorship allows you to create a dialogue with someone and get direction on where to find the information you need. A mentor can tell you what works and what doesn't, and what to look out for. A mentor can direct you to other people who can help you.

We see the world the way we are, not the way that the world is (Kehoe, 2011). Scotomas, blind spots, cause us to see what we expect to see, hear what we expect to hear, think what we expect to think (Tice, 2005). "I don't communicate well—I get too nervous." "I am not good with people; I have never been a people-person. I'd rather deal with computers." "I'm not the leadership type." Locking in such beliefs shackles you, prevents you from being anything other than what you tell yourself you are.

Your mentor can help you see yourself and what you are capable of from a different perspective. He or she can help you see the blind spots and unlock the shackles that prevent you from meeting your full potential.

You need a mentor who can show you the way. But don't wait for your mentor to find you—take the initiative to find a mentor. You can join organizations and clubs in your area of interest, such as the Project Management Institute and Toastmasters International. Seek mentorship, and you will find the direction and encouragement you need to become a strong leader.

4.3.4 Experiment

Management and psychology students generally learn about Abraham Maslow's Hierarchy of Needs Theory, discussed earlier. During the experiment phase, the goal is to mindfully pursue what Maslow defined as a *peak experience.* This is a profound moment of love, happiness, understanding, or rapture; an experience in which a person feels in harmony and balance with the world around him or her. A person who self-actualizes, who meets his or her full potential, has many peak experiences (Maslow, 2012a).

Now it's time to turn your commitment, your learning, and your mentorship into a planned peak experience. For example, the PMI® provides volunteer opportunities that will help you develop your leadership skills. The members of your local PMI® chapter can help you face and conquer your leadership challenges.

Because IT geeks are generally challenged when it comes to communications, I highly recommend Toastmasters International. Toastmasters provides opportunities for leadership as an officer in the Toastmasters club and during club meetings. Toastmasters will provide you with opportunities to develop and present speeches. Your fellow Toastmasters will gently evaluate your presentations. All of this mentorship occurs in a non-threatening environment that will help you grow as a communicator and a leader.

Experimenting with leadership in this way gives you the opportunity to visualize yourself committing, learning, being mentored, then planning and implementing a project. When you are successful, your self-esteem and belief in yourself as a leader will increase, and for a moment, you will self-actualize. It will be an experience you will not forget because you will develop a schema, as discussed in Chapter 3—a new neural pathway that you will draw on the next time you face a leadership challenge.

If you are taking on a leadership role for the first time, you may be nervous. You may fear failure. But if you have prepared yourself by studying and if you have a mentor to lean on for advice, you have the resources you need to be confident with your commitment. You have made a commitment to yourself to perform because you know you will be one step closer to becoming an IT geek leader. Experimenting allows you to make excellent contacts and to build a reputation for yourself as someone with outstanding character and determination.

I highly recommend keeping a Leadership Journal. This is just a notebook that you keep with you to write down and review your thoughts, feelings, plans, goals, and self-talk. It can help you stay focused and on track during your self-leadership journey.

Here are a few steps that can help you with your experiment:

Experimentation Exercises

1. Visualize yourself performing in a leadership role. Imagine what you will see, hear, and feel as you do lead. Think about situations you might encounter and how you will react. Rehearse presentations until you have them down cold.
2. Develop an action plan for the leadership tasks that you plan to perform. Ask your mentor and someone else on the project to review the plan and provide feedback.
3. Meet with all of the people involved in the project and communicate the plan. Get their feedback and address their issues.
4. Lead, communicate, correct, and encourage.
5. Follow up with your team members, your leadership, and your mentor. Keep everyone informed and keep the communications process flowing.
6. Thank everyone involved in the process. Consider showing your appreciation to those who helped you through this process with special gifts and recognition.
7. Write in your Leadership Journal any notes or observations you make along the way.

4.3.5 Review and Analyze

The last phase is Review and Analyze. Now it's time to take a step back and think about what you have learned.

As you consider your leadership experience, understand that you don't have to be perfect. Perfection is neither attainable nor required. No one is perfect, and no one expects you to be. Everyone has challenges, setbacks, and shortfalls.

Researchers have found that 77% of our mental programs are false, counterproductive, harmful, or work against us (Helmstetter, 2013). This means over three-fourths of our thoughts distract us from reaching our goals. You may have thoughts such as, "I am afraid of being in charge. What if I mess up? I will lose my job and get evicted. No one likes me and they are not going to follow me. No one listens to me. I am too nervous to lead my team. We failed when I was in charge of field day in high school, and if I am in charge, we will fail now. I am not a born leader like Tony is. I will never be as good as he is."

As much as we try to remain positive and focus on transforming our minds, we are distracted and interrupted by trips down mental pathways that lead in a different direction than the one we intended to follow.

In the Bible, the Apostle Paul finds himself in such a situation while trying to lead a righteous life. Romans 7:17–23 (The Message Translation) says, "But

I need something more! For if I know the law but still can't keep it, and if the power of sin within me keeps sabotaging my best intentions, I obviously need help! I realize that I don't have what it takes. I can will it, but I can't do it. I decide to do good, but I don't really do it; I decide not to do bad, but then I do it anyway. My decisions, such as they are, don't result in actions. Something has gone wrong deep within me and gets the better of me every time. It happens so regularly that it's predictable. The moment I decide to do good, sin is there to trip me up. I truly delight in God's commands, but it's pretty obvious that not all of me joins in that delight. Parts of me covertly rebel, and just when I least expect it, they take charge."

Paul struggled, as every leader does, but he never gave up. He became a great leader. He went on to establish several churches and to write thirteen letters that are included in the Bible. He was just a human being like you and me. He persevered and accomplished great things despite feeling he "did not have what it takes."

As a leader, when you make a mistake, commit yourself to recovering quickly. Your followers and the leaders in your organization will be watching you and paying attention to how you handle adversity. Tell yourself, "Next time, I will . . ." and proceed with instructions to yourself on how you will avoid making the same mistake in the future. In your plans, include time to recover and learn from your mistakes. The better you are at recovering, the more effective and respected a leader you will be.

After you have completed a leadership experiment, take some time to reflect on what you have learned. Are you taking your commitment seriously? Are you closer to reaching your goal of becoming a strong leader? What went well? What did not go so well and where do you need to improve? What additional help do you need? What is the next step? How have you grown? Are you closer to reaching your leadership goal? Do you need to modify your goal—perhaps make it more realistic, or perhaps speed up the deadline? Are you happy with your results, or disappointed, and why? Was your mentor helpful? Would you seek advice from him or her again? In your Leadership Journal, write down the following:

Leadership Journal Exercise

1. What went well in your experiment?

2. What did not go well or had unintended consequences?

3. If you had to complete the experiment again, what would you do differently?

4. What would you recommend, as a mentor, to others doing similar projects?

Now consider what you learned about yourself. Perform the following free-writing exercise:

1. On a clean page in your Leadership Journal, write the phase "If I could change one thing about myself . . ."
2. Complete the phrase and write non-stop for five minutes.
3. After five minutes, take a 10-minute walk.
4. Come back and read what you wrote. How do you feel about what you wrote?

Think about these things and consult with your mentor. Put a plan together and repeat the Self-Leadership Cycle. Over time, and with effort, you will become comfortable with leadership. You will build neural pathways that you can traverse during your next leadership challenge.

Like Tony in the "Things are Changing" use case, you can use self-talk to change your mindset, to don a leadership mindset, and to take on a leadership role with confidence. You can make a commitment to becoming a leader, to learning the discipline of leadership, to finding and trusting a mentor to guide you along the way, to engaging in leadership experiments, and to reviewing and analyzing your progress toward reaching your IT geek leadership goals. I'm a geek who overcame my communications weakness and embarked on a leadership journey. I've stumbled, but I've also found success. If I can find a leadership mindset that fits me, I'm sure you can find one that fits you.

Now that you understand more about self-leadership, let's move on to Chapter 5, where we will discuss what it means to be an effective follower and the relationship between effective leadership and effective followership.

Developing Your Leadership Mindset

The exercise below steps you through the Self-Leadership Cycle presented in this chapter in a manner that can help you develop a leadership mindset.

1. Take the Leadership Questionnaire at the end of Chapter 2.
2. In your Leadership Journal, list the areas in which you rated yourself with a 2 or below.
3. For each item you listed in Step 2:
   - Visualize yourself performing the task in a way that you would rate yourself a 3 or 4. Imagine how you would feel if you were to be successful at it.
   - Listen for poisonous self-talk concerning these items. What do you need to change in order to improve your self-image for performing this task?
   - Write down a constructive self-talk sentence for the item you need to change. Recite your new, positive self-talk every morning and every evening in the mirror. Record it and play it back to yourself each day.

4. Research what you need to learn in order to be successful in any area you listed in Step 2. What books can you read? What projects do you need to research at work? Who do you need to talk to at work who can help you understand the business goals and objectives and how they relate to your project? Create constructive self-talk for the areas in which you are working to improve.

5. Identify someone you trust at school, work, or your PMI® chapter who is successful at the tasks with which you need help. Seek out this person as a mentor. Ask him or her to help you refine your plan to improve in the areas in which you are challenged.

6. Identify opportunities to implement your new knowledge and initiatives on your project.

7. Speak with your mentor about your experience and plan your next iteration.

Chapter 5

Followership

A Google search on the word "leadership" produces 464,000,000 results, but a search on "followership" results in 1,780,000 results, over 260 times fewer. Yet, both leadership and followership are required for organizations and projects to succeed. We expect followers to naturally know how to follow, but I don't believe this is the case. Effective leaders set expectations of behavior and performance for their followers. Let's begin our examination of followership by defining what a follower is and exploring the follower mindset.

5.1 What Is a Follower?

You have probably seen different definitions of the word "follower." The simple definition of a follower is someone who has chosen a leader. This means the follower has accepted and supports the leader's vision and direction and will execute the plans that the leader creates. Leaders and followers have a symbiotic relationship. A leader cannot be effective without followers, and followers cannot succeed on their projects without effective leadership.

Ira Chaleff writes in *The Courageous Follower*, "Follower is not synonymous with subordinate. A subordinate reports to an individual of higher rank and may in practice be a supporter, an antagonist, or indifferent. A follower shares a common purpose with the leader, believes in what the organization is trying to accomplish, wants both the leader and the organization to succeed, and works energetically to this end" (Chaleff, 2009).

Have you ever worked with someone who is antagonistic or indifferent toward project goals, someone who only does the minimum amount of work to get by? Workers seek to perform tasks as documented in their position descriptions, objectives, or contracts. Followers are not limited to these written instructions. Not only do they accomplish the written instructions, but they also go beyond expectations to implement a project's vision. Their individual goals intersect with project goals. They seek to satisfy not only the written requirements but also the intent of the leader. They use their initiative to satisfy the spirit of project requirements.

In the IT industry, you can expect your team members to challenge your leadership. IT workers are generally not conscientious about dotting every *i* and crossing every *t*, as discussed in Chapter 2. Researchers have concluded that failure on IT projects is generally the result of neglect of the behavioral and social factors—influenced by management, the organization, and the culture—rather than the technology itself (Thite, 1999). Effective leaders influence behavioral and social factors through activities such as rewards, reprimands, training, and conflict resolution. Effective leaders connect with team members, motivating them by providing feedback and encouragement. Both IT geek project leaders and team members are responsible for paying attention to behavioral and social factors, for becoming more conscientious and building solid team member relationships, and for practicing effective followership rather than acting as mere workers—all in order to achieve success on IT projects.

Unfortunately, you will encounter some people on your team with the worker mindset instead of the follower mindset. They should be followers, but their mentality is that of a worker who shows up for work, does enough to meet minimum requirements, and then goes home. They do not respond to the effective leader's high performance and ethical standards. They do not take initiative for tasks or take ownership of outcomes. They negatively impact team morale and productivity. They are not loyal, either to the project leader or to the team. I have had to address IT workers who are antagonistic or indifferent through reprimands, coaching, and external motivation, but my inner circle—those who I relied on to get the job done—were the followers. Followers are internally motivated—they are believers in the project vision; the others are not.

It is a leader's responsibility to make sure followers understand the vision of a project. It is a leader's responsibility to inspire followers to have the self-confidence needed to take initiative when it is required, making sure followers understand project requirements and goals to ensure that any initiative a follower takes is in line with these requirements and goals. But most importantly, it is a leader's responsibility to make sure every team member is a follower and not just a worker. Your role is to challenge team members to set and maintain high standards of performance, empowering and encouraging them to achieve these levels. Through your dialogue with your team, through your actions and demeanor, your team members need to understand that you expect them to be followers rather than mere workers.

It is in your best interest to recruit team members who have a follower's mindset rather than team members who have a worker's mindset. In some organizations, it is very difficult to replace employees if it turns out they are not a good fit for the team. This means you need to develop skills for identifying, attracting, and cultivating talent. As a leader, you also need the courage to make the difficult decision to "release the worker to industry" if he or she is not willing and able to help you achieve the project vision.

This chapter will help you distinguish followers from workers. We will first take a look at the "Everything is Spinning" use case. Then, we will take a closer look at Effective Followership. Next, we will discuss the relationship between The Leader and the Effective Follower. On every project, there will be conflict, and we will next explore The Leader, the Followers, and Conflict. From here, we will explore Great Groups, then take a quick look at a technique I call Reverse Micromanagement, followed by concluding thoughts. At the end of this chapter, you will find a Followership Assessment that will help you examine your team and that can spark ideas on how to improve your team's followership ability.

5.2 Use Case: Everything Is Spinning

"Two final agenda items and we can get out of this conference room and get back to real work," said Terry at the weekly staff meeting, standing at the head of the table. "First, congratulations to Mark for developing an innovative solution for the authentication issue. That problem could have set us back for weeks."

"Thank you," said Mark, sitting with his fingers interlocked and his elbows on the table. "It was really no trouble at all," he continued, looking at the table, not at Terry.

"Second," Terry continued, "I almost forgot—everyone please welcome Tony, a new systems architect on Mark's team. Tony, we are all looking forward to working with you."

"Thank you," said Tony, waving at the other staff members. "I am excited to be here!"

"Have a great Monday!" Terry exclaims, ending the meeting.

Jack approached Tony in the corridor after the staff meeting. "I'm Jack," he said, "and I'm one of the engineers on Mark's team." "Nice to meet you," Tony replied as they shook hands.

"I have to go to an orientation meeting at headquarters," Tony said, "but can we get together later? Mark said you designed the cloud infrastructure and I'd like to talk to you about it."

"No problem, stop by my cube in the morning," Jack replied.

Then, Jack looked left, then right, then leaned toward Tony and lowered his voice, saying, "A word of caution about Mark. He will claim your work as his own. If you have a good idea, reveal it to Terry after you've worked it out and documented it. You know the solution to the authentication problem Terry credited to Mark? I discovered the problem and worked with the vendor to develop the fix. All Mark did was submit the change request—the change request that I wrote—and he put his name on it. Watch your back."

"Wow—OK," replied Tony, leaning back a little, brow furrowed, folding his arms in front of him. "I have to go," he said. "See you in the morning," replied Jack.

The next day, Mark called Tony into his office. As Tony entered, he noticed several framed training certificates, certifications, and diplomas proudly displayed on Mark's walls. *"Why would anyone still display an MCSE 4.0 certification?"* Tony thought. Mark's office was pristine, and he had a big, brown, plush leather chair that seemed out of place behind his rather ordinary office desk. Mark sat in his leather chair, and Tony sat in a chair in front of Mark's desk. *"Why is this chair so low?"* Tony thought.

"I don't want you talking to Terry," Mark said. "He has no idea what he's doing. He doesn't have a clue."

"What do you mean?" Tony asked.

"The requirements are all wrong, and he won't push the customer to change them. If I were running this program, I'd tell the customer that they don't understand what they're asking for and restart the requirements gathering process," Mark said.

"You'd start from scratch?" Tony asked incredulously. "Haven't we deployed Version 1?"

"The customer can afford to start over. They have deep pockets. They just need to be convinced. I'm going to get these requirements changed. Our revenue will double. I know what's best for them, and for the company, trust me. But I don't want you talking to Terry. Do you understand?" Mark asked, leaning forward, looking sternly at Tony.

"Yes sir," Tony replied.

On Wednesday morning, Tony arrived a few minutes early. As he walked by Mark's office to his cube, he notices Mark's lights were on, but that the room had been cleaned out. No certificates or diplomas on the walls, large leather chair gone. *"That's odd,"* Tony thought.

At his cube, Tony saw a sticky note on his monitor from Terry that said "Come see me." Tony headed to Terry's office, arriving at the same time as Jack.

"Good, you're both here early," Terry says. "C'mon in, have a seat."

Tony and Jack sat at the table, and Terry moved from behind his desk to a chair at the table. "Good morning," Tony said. "What's going on?" Jack asked.

"Well guys," Terry began, "Mark is no longer employed here."

"What happened?" Jack asked.

"You may not know this," Terry said, "but Mark's wife is a sales manager at CloudMatics. He's been lobbying to change the cloud services solution to CloudMatics Hosting Services instead of Nebula Services. Last night, he got into an altercation about this with Dr. Tanner, the deputy CIO and program sponsor, and he called Tanner an idiot. Tanner called me and directed me to remove Mark from the contract immediately."

"He called the program sponsor an idiot?" asked Jack, incredulous.

"Wow," said Tony. "What a first week. Everything is spinning around me."

"I'll be overseeing your work until we find a new project manager," said Terry. "This time, we will be more thorough in our recruiting effort and find the right fit. The PM not only needs to be a leader, he or she needs to be a team player and support the project vision and not go behind my back."

After a pause, Jack leaned back, looked at Terry, and said, "So can I get the big brown chair, or not?"

5.3 Effective Followership

Terry needed Mark to support the direction of the project whether he agreed with it or not, but Mark had other ideas. Followers need defined and shared goals that lead to the fulfillment of the organization's vision. Warren Bennis wrote in "The Secret to Great Groups," appearing in *Leader to Leader* in 1997, "All great teams—and all great organizations—are built around a shared dream or motivating purpose" (Bennis, 1997). Dr. Richard Steers and Dr. Lyman Porter, pioneers in goal psychology, describe four major goal functions: goals provide direction, define criteria for evaluation, lend legitimacy, and prescribe organizational structure (Porter and Steers, 1974). As an IT leader, defining and clarifying these goal functions, creating a unifying purpose, is a major element of our position.

5.3.1 Unifying Purpose

Followers are looking for leaders and causes they consider worthy of their commitment. As illustrated in Figure 5-1, they need a unifying purpose, vision, goal, or cause that can motivate them to contribute their best (Collins, 2013).

Followers need to feel that the efforts they put forth are not in vain, that they are making a difference. Contributing in this manner enhances their self-esteem and gives them a reason to get up in the morning. We spend more time when we are awake on our jobs than we do at home, with our loved ones. We

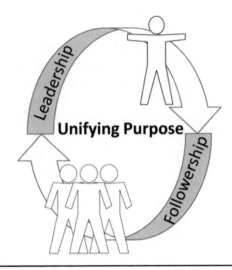

Figure 5-1   Unifying purpose.

want to spend this time in a meaningful way, a way that makes a difference, a way that is important.

Your challenge is to develop situations, when possible, in which the organization's goals and your follower's goals are in sync, as depicted in Figure 5-2.

Followers need to perform tasks that the leader cares about. The follower may do many things well, but if he or she does not accomplish what the leader needs accomplished in a way that satisfies the organization or project vision, the follower is not effective. As a 19-year-old working on my first technical job, I received this advice: *solve your boss's problems first.* Over 30 years later, I still apply this principle every workday.

Many followers have a burning desire to devote themselves to a common cause, to make a contribution, to be part of something bigger than themselves. Leaders are challenged to help these followers define this cause, to craft and project a vision that includes their likeness, to help them imagine themselves in action making the vision become a reality.

Followers who operate in this manner achieve their self-esteem and perhaps their self-actualization goals through followership, thereby satisfying their own inner motivation.

Your followers need opportunities to find success and happiness in their careers. They are looking for leaders who can provide opportunities to advance, make more money, and achieve their personal goals. They want to feel secure in their jobs so that they can pay their rent, purchase homes and cars, send their children to college, save for retirement, and take care of aging parents. Their reasons for being on your

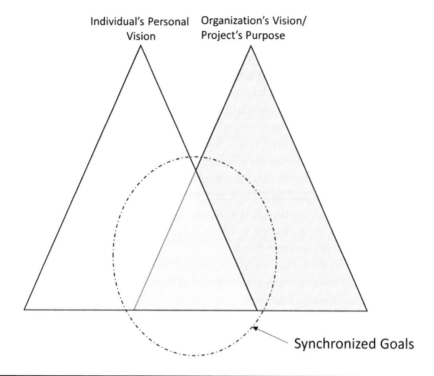

Figure 5-2   Individual and organizational goals.

team are personal, and they take their experience on your team and with your leadership personally.

Followers want to feel they are in control of their tasks and positions. They want you to provide them the authority to make decisions about how to perform their assigned tasks, and they want you to support their decisions. They look to their leaders to let them know why their tasks are important, and how their tasks fit into the overall vision and purpose of the organization; your response concerning the purpose of their tasks serves as a source of motivation. As their ability to pursue their own ideas during execution increases, so does their influence, and so does their job satisfaction. Once you empower your followers to make decisions on how to pursue project tasks, you should expect them to keep their commitments and to follow through on their decisions.

Your followers will react to your challenges; they need you to challenge them. Edwin Locke was professor of business and psychology at the University of Maryland in 1968. He found that goals cause behavior. His research found that hard goals produce a higher level of performance and that specific hard goals produce higher levels of performance than "make your best effort" goals (Maley and Varner, 1994). Give your team members specific challenges; set high standards and hold them accountable.

Your team members will be more effective and productive when you involve them in setting these high standards. Followers need to participate in goal setting in order to feel commitment and to have a sense of personal involvement—ownership—for the required tasks. Researchers have found that follower goal acceptance is a critical factor for follower performance (Porter and Steers, 1974). Followers need to feel that there is a high likelihood that they will be rewarded for attainment of a goal and must assign value to the reward in order to feel motivated to perform well. Goal acceptance and value assignment differ from person to person, so you need to know your team members as individuals to understand how to motivate them.

Like Terry and Mark, leadership and followership are ineffective if leaders and their team members are out of sync. Let's explore the relationship between the leader and effective followers.

5.4 The Leader and Effective Followers

Effective followers are not afraid to take responsibility, and you should not be afraid to give it to them. The more leaders empower their followers to act, take responsibility, and act as leaders in their own right, the greater the benefit to the organization. On one occasion, I recognized that a team lead had developed a system to recognize his top desktop support performers. He called it the "100 Plus Club," which pointed out team members who had solved 100 problems in a month while at the same time remaining compliant with service level agreements. This was exactly the type of motivation and recognition system needed for all teams in his division. The team lead's supervisor submitted him for our quarterly leadership award, and he won. He certainly got my vote!

I eventually promoted him to regional manager and challenged him to implement the 100 Plus Club concept for each team in his region. I made it known that I wanted the 100 Plus initiative implemented across the program. I was thrilled when I was notified that each team in his region had recognized 100 Plus Club members, but I was ecstatic when a regional manager from another region in the program did the same thing shortly afterwards! By giving the inventor of the 100 Plus Club more responsibility and empowering him to act, we transformed the organization. We motivated the technicians, stimulating their internal motivation, resulting in better service to the end user customer and achievement of our program goals.

5.4.1 Motivating Followers

In this section, we discuss what motivates followers. Your team members need your encouragement. When requirements are not clear, they need you to provide clarity. Many followers want to be associated with good leaders—leaders with the courage to protect their team members and the heart to care for and support them and show appreciation. Team members who feel appreciated take initiatives that lead to project success. These effective team members create and adhere to their own high standards. Reward these followers with training and development opportunities and give them feedback on their efforts, and you will find that their morale will increase and your organization will be more successful.

A leader's job includes encouraging team members, especially during discouraging situations. As a leader, your self-talk needs to include language that provides self-encouragement, such as "I am not easily discouraged." If you are discouraged, you will find it difficult to encourage others (Collins, 2013). Many followers are in search of a role model, someone they can emulate so that they can enjoy a long, successful career. They want someone they can imitate until they can find their own way. Such team members need your support and encouragement, so you need to stay positive as best you can.

Leaders need to delegate to followers, and followers need to feel empowered. To empower a follower, the leader delegates authority, giving the follower the right to take action and make decisions on the leader's behalf. This empowerment is a source of motivation for the follower, because the follower knows his or her actions directly contribute to the attainment of the vision of the organization or project. The follower needs to feel not only responsible, but also in control. The follower does not want to be responsible for any situation he or she cannot control, as this situation leads to failure.

However, IT leaders can only effectively empower experienced IT professionals. Researchers have found that IT leaders need to employ a leadership style that is contingent upon the professional maturity of their team members and the ambiguity of the task (Faraj and Sambamurthy, 2006). When the team has a high level of expertise and when there is a high level of task uncertainty, *empowering* leadership is more effective. Empowering leaders encourage active participation from team members, placing a premium on their involvement in the project. When the team has a low level of expertise and when there is low task uncertainty, *directive* leadership is more effective. Directive leaders are not looking for initiative from the team members. Instead, directive leaders provide the expertise, guidance, and control needed to meet project objectives. Your challenge as an IT leader is to recognize when to employ empowering leadership and when to employ directive leadership. Your team and your organization will be more successful when you find opportunities to grow your less experienced team members so that you can empower them instead of engaging in a directive leadership style.

Followers may have a desire to associate with leaders who increase their own personal credibility. If the leader is perceived to be great, if he or she has an excellent reputation in the IT industry, for example, then the followers' perceived stock is higher because of their association with this leader. Some of the "halo effect" of the leader is transmitted to the follower. Followers want leaders they can learn from. They want to become better, more capable people because of their association with the leader. They want to be part of something great, and they want to follow a leader who is pursuing something great. No one wants a "dead-end" job or a "dead-end" career. It is the leader's responsibility to provide meaning to the follower's position.

Followers do not want to work for people they consider lesser than themselves. They generally don't want to be involved in any unethical activities. They want leaders who will help them stay on the straight and narrow and avoid situations that can affect their reputation, bank account, career, or freedom (Collins, 2013). Instead of behaving like Mark, they need you, their leader, to uphold the highest ethical standards.

Followers need and appreciate leaders who motivate them, that push them to perform more and better than they think they can perform. I once had an impromptu meeting with our portal administrator. She was gathering requirements for a portal redesign, and she was having trouble reconciling the various requirements she gathered from different users. She was going down the path of creating meta-data requirements for users to follow when submitting documents so that others would quickly be able to find what the users posted.

I told her that my opinion was that her approach was academically correct, but in our environment, users posted documents on the portal to serve the needs of their own team. Users in our organization did not have a collaborative mindset, I told her, and getting them to follow meta-data rules would be very difficult. I recommended that she analyze portal search logs to find out what users were trying to find and incorporate that data into her solution. I also challenged her to define the benefits of collaboration and how the portal enables attainment of those benefits, then to work with our trainer to educate the staff on how our portal could help them realize those benefits in their everyday work. She appreciated the challenge and was motivated to improve the organization's ability to collaborate, which would be a tremendous accomplishment for her and benefit for the agency. Leaders need followers to invest their time and creative energy in worthy tasks, and this portal administrator was willing to do just that.

Allowing followers to use their own initiative to make positive changes is critical to realizing innovative solutions to problems. Good leaders allow and encourage their followers to do more than expected, to take risks that will lead

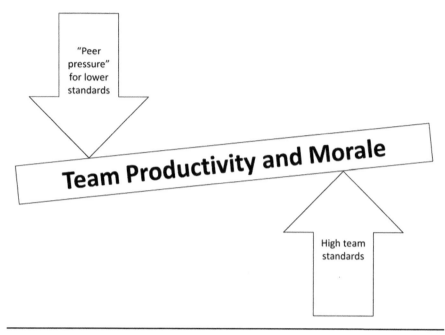

Figure 5-3 Team productivity and morale.

to novel, ground-breaking solutions. Good followers will test the limits of their authority, taking risks that will move the project or organization forward. Not all of their initiatives will lead to successful outcomes.

As a leader, provide your team members enough space to try, fail, and try again until success is reached. This is not always possible in every environment because of budget, schedule, and political constraints. Your challenge is to obtain space within the project environment for team members to take creative risks without penalty, risks that enable growth, recognizing that these initiative and innovation risks are necessary for positive changes that exceed customer expectations.

Figure 5-3 depicts the relationship between team productivity and morale. Leaders should empower and encourage followers to develop their own high standards of performance. The higher the group standard, the greater the quantity and quality of the group's work. Researchers have found that team members who reported high coworker standards also reported high levels of pride, cooperation, and teamwork (Maley and Varner, 1994). These team members felt recognized for their performance and were motivated to make their best contributions to their project and organization. Lower expectations of performance had the opposite effect. High leadership expectations were reduced significantly in the presence of "peer pressure" for lower standards.

Followers who establish and achieve high standards are preparing themselves to become leaders. Their leaders need to recognize and groom followers who show leadership potential and encourage them to take on more responsibility. In the IT industry, in which many team members are prone to introverted communication styles and rebellious behavior, team members who overcome these tendencies and demonstrate the ability to set a positive example for their peers should be encouraged to lead. They should be given the proper training and the opportunity to experiment as a leader, to build positive leadership schemas, and to make mistakes and learn from them.

Followers need leaders to invest in their training. This demonstrates that the leader is concerned about helping the follower reach his or her professional goals. Increasing knowledge increases self-esteem, resulting in increased follower commitment to the leader and to the organization. This training arms team members with the knowledge and skills needed to take initiatives and mitigate risks.

At the same time, followers have the responsibility to identify their own deficiencies, comparing the tasks that they are assigned to perform with their own skills and abilities, and then to find training solutions to bridge that gap. This directly impacts the follower's short-term success on the project and long-term success for his or her career.

The best performers on any team are those who practice self-leadership in order to be the best followers they can be. They treat their leaders as if they were customers, taking the initiative to understand the leader's needs and then taking actions to exceed those expectations. They are internally motivated to perform in this manner. They do not need to be enticed by external rewards or coerced by potential punishment in order to perform at a high level. They perform well by habit and instinct, not because they have to but because they *want* to.

Researchers have found that team member morale is directly related to feedback from their leaders (Maley and Varner, 1994). Committed team members want to hear from you on a frequent basis. This consistent feedback increases morale, and the more feedback, the higher the morale. Your team members want your leadership assistance when needed, and your praise and recognition when they feel they deserve it. They want constructive negative feedback, not a "chewing out," in order to be held accountable. Feedback on performance is the greatest motivator for team members. Leaders who provide this type of feedback produce productive, satisfied, and motivated team members.

5.4.2 Leaders Should Do What Only They Can Do

If you are a leader who has motivated followers, you are in a powerful position. If you have motivated, effective followers, they deserve a leader who will empower them. They need you to represent their ideas and initiatives in forums that you can access but they cannot. Leaders who support their followers in this manner deserve to be appreciated. In this section, we explore these ideas.

Great leaders typically desire to surround themselves with great people. They need people who can provide them with the support and advice they need to achieve the vision of their organization. They need people who can successfully execute the plans that they develop. Leaders need followers who are skilled in doing the tasks that the leader does not need to do, allowing the leader to empower his or her followers and focus on tasks that only the leader can do for the team.

While followers may want this empowerment from a leader, they may not know what the leader has to do to enable such a situation. The leader has to do the things only he or she can do for the project or organization, such as represent the team to senior leaders and to customers, fight to obtain resources, build goodwill with stakeholders, and promote and support team members' ideas and initiatives to stakeholders and board members.

Leaders spend time engaging with stakeholders to build support for team initiatives—including those spearheaded by followers—prior to acceptance and execution. If you are doing tasks that a team member could do, you are neglecting your leadership duties.

No one else speaks for the team. No one else integrates the work of each team member. No one else represents the team to senior management. No one else establishes the vision—the unifying purpose that brings everyone together and makes them feel like they are contributing to something important. While leaders focus on these important tasks that no one else is responsible for performing, team members can focus on their specialties with the assurance that the leader is bringing everything together (Collins, 2013).

How do you feel when a team member shows appreciation for your leadership efforts? I personally find this gratifying. Like followers, leaders also need encouragement. Leaders appreciate positive feedback from their followers. They want to know that their initiatives are making a difference. They want to know that their followers' lives are improved as a result of being part of the team. Good leaders make a sincere effort to take care of their followers, and they like to know those efforts are appreciated (Collins, 2013),

Regardless of how strong and mature your team is, there will be conflict, and your team members will look to you to resolve this conflict. In the next section, we discuss conflict management on project teams.

5.5 The Leader, the Followers, and Conflict

Followers don't always agree with their leader's direction and decisions. In such cases, they need the leader to allow them to express their perspective on the situation and to seriously consider their viewpoints. After their followers have been heard, leaders need them to avoid being discouraged, accept the final decision, and support the outcome. Disagreements need to be kept confidential so as to not give the appearance of disunity, which is a de-motivator. Followers lose confidence in the organization when they are exposed to strife. Conflicts can be misinterpreted and the source of uncertainty and rumors, but unity reassures followers that the organization is headed toward success. Unity builds momentum through motivation and creates positive feelings that lead to positive outcomes.

Leaders need followers who are willing to be strong critics of their plans and decisions (Collins, 2013). Leaders need these "devil's advocates" to point out their blind spots. These healthy conflicts lead to better decisions and approaches to solutions. Leaders need the ground truth. They need followers who are courageous enough to deliver bad news to their leaders when these leaders are considering options for the way forward. In order to obtain the feedback they need, leaders should cultivate an environment in which followers feel safe enough to provide negative feedback. Followers don't want to be considered complainers, and they don't want their negative feedback to lead to missed promotions and reduced raises.

If the leader does his or her part, and the followers do theirs, the team will be strong and capable.

Followers typically support good leadership and resist bad leadership. Followers who do not support their leaders or their vision may circumvent them and join with other followers, causing conflicts (Kellerman, 2008). I have seen this happen. Red flags go up on programs when committed team members request to be moved to another team. When this happens, I look for the tacit back story, the illusive ground truth about what is really happening on the team. As a leader, I often don't hear this story until it is too late make changes, to introduce a new narrative. I listen for it, but I don't always hear it.

Leaders and followers should never compete. This unnecessary competition is another source of conflict. Followers should not compete with their leaders, but should instead support them, accomplishing the tasks required to achieve the leader's vision. Good leaders reward followers who embrace their leadership, recognizing that followers who commit themselves to contributing to the realization of the vision do so voluntarily. Good leaders don't take such voluntary commitment for granted.

5.5.1 Loyalty and Submission

Years ago, I experienced a leadership change while working for a small company. I found myself under the supervision of a new boss and a new boss's boss. If you have never experienced anything like that before, I can tell you that it is very stressful. As a PM, I did not know if I would be replaced by someone that my boss or my boss's boss preferred for my position. During such volatile times, changes in key personnel are not unusual, and neither is the stress that stems from the uncertainty. I was challenged to first keep calm myself so that I could keep my staff calm. Yes, times were uncertain, but for most of us, there was no reason to panic. If we panicked, we would not be able to think clearly enough to navigate through the change.

Conscientious new leaders build relationships with their subordinates in order to be successful. Every leader has his or her own way of building these relationships. In my case, my boss's boss, let's call her Sandy, decided that the company should fire one of my senior managers because of her perceived leadership deficiencies. This leader, let's call her Jan, was effective, but not a rock star. Jan delivered, but not in a way that inspired her team members. Jan struggled at times, but not in an egregious manner, not in a manner that, in my opinion, should have put her on the chopping block. But Jan had reason to panic.

I did not agree with firing Jan, but I was unable to convince Sandy that Jan should stay. I did not know Sandy, and I felt as though she was testing me—perhaps this was her way of testing my obedience to her. I felt as though my job was on the line if I did not submit to Sandy's demand. I held my nose and carried out my assignment. Even as I write this, my stomach turns.

During this situation, I developed a cynical definition of loyalty: loyalty means you are willing to carry out your leadership's vendettas as if they were your own. Your leadership's resentment becomes your own resentment; you develop a need for vengeance that is married to your leader's need for vengeance, a need that is satisfied only when your leadership's vengeance is satisfied. I felt like I'd been inducted into the mob.

I had to prioritize my fears. I was afraid of losing my job, of being unable to take care of my family, pay my mortgage, and put food on the table. I was more afraid of not being able to fill my safety and physiological needs than my self-esteem needs.

You can learn something in almost any situation, and I learned how hard being a follower can be. I would never put any follower in such a position, and you should not either.

5.5.2 Ethical Conflict

Followers at all levels face tough decisions that impact their character and reputation. The follower's values, assumptions, beliefs, and expectations influence those decisions. Followers don't want to be put in positions in which they are asked to lie or break the rules on behalf of the leader or the organization. While working as a senior manager in a government contracting firm years ago, I was informed of a situation in which our contractors were directed to purchase items such as cell phones for the government customer and then to submit expense reports for those items, expense reports that the government customer approved. This action was done in such a way that we could not determine if the expenses were justified or not. Everything looked good on paper. But the employees knew. The government customer, in a leadership position, put the contractors—their followers—in a precarious position in which they had to make a choice: follow the direction of the government customer or risk being removed from the contract and losing their jobs. We experienced turnover, understandably. The contract ended and we did not win the renewal. While we missed having the business, I did not miss having to interact with an unethical customer.

If followers do not want to follow a leader, if they do not buy into the leader's vision, they will not be fulfilled, and they should follow someone else.

5.5.3 Influencing the Team

Followers working together as a team have a shared purpose—a purpose that the leader defines. The major influences on a team are team goals, team atmosphere, team communications, and team maturity.

Leaders must effectively communicate their goals to their team in order for the team to be productive. The team needs the ability to measure its progress toward reaching the defined goals.

Followers react to each other in accordance with their perception of the reaction of the rest of the team. This team atmosphere governs whether or not team members feel free to contribute to team activities that lead to attainment of team goals. The more freedom they have to participate in a democratic and inclusive manner, the higher the team motivation and morale are for both leaders and followers.

IT leaders need the courage to overcome any introverted tendencies and to find the assertiveness necessary to communicate. IT followers face the same issues. Leaders need followers to openly express themselves so that the leader has the information he or she needs to achieve the desired project outcome.

Followers need to feel they are receiving the information they need to perform as contributing members of the team. Leaders need to engage in face-to-face dialogue with followers whenever possible in order to facilitate authentic communications and to foster commitment for the individual. Followers need to see the body language of the leader. They need to connect both verbally and nonverbally so that they understand both the leader's stated intention and the spirit of his or her intention. They need the freedom to express to their leader how they feel, so that when the leader asks why the team member feels

Table 5-1 Gaining the Leader's Trust

Followers Gain Their Leader's Trust By:
• Demonstrating complete loyalty and respect for the leader
• Demonstrating professionalism in performance and emotional maturity in their approach to satisfying project and organization requirements
• Demonstrating support for the leader when publicly representing the project and the organization
• Demonstrating commitment to delivering on the leader's final decision regardless of any disagreements experienced during the decision-making process
• Demonstrating professional accountability for themselves, their growth, and their behavior
• Demonstrating the same concern and care for the leader as a person as the follower expects from the leader

Data derived from Maley and Varner, 1994. *Leadership: The Leader and the Group.* Maxwell AFB, AL: Air University Press.

the way he or she feels, the leader will discover ground truth. They need to have this communication with others on the team as well, building relationships and trust, comparing and contrasting each other's values, assumptions, beliefs, and expectations, as discussed in Chapter 2. The stronger the communications network among the team members, the more productive the team and the greater the likelihood that the leader can obtain the vital information he or she needs when needed. Table 5-1 lists follower behaviors that gain the leader's trust.

Followers who exhibit these qualities are worthy of their leader's trust. Leaders can delegate tasks to these followers, empowering them with the authority to carry out assignments on the leader's behalf.

5.5.4 Follower Maturity

Followers working in teams or groups relate to each other through increasing levels of maturity. Figure 5-4 depicts two models of group behavior: Cog's Ladder (Maley and Varner, 1994) and the Tuckman Model (Jensen and Tuckman, 1977).

Cog's Ladder

The Cog's Ladder Model has five steps: the Polite Stage, the Why are we here? Stage, the "Bid for Power" Stage, the Constructive Stage, and the Esprit Stage.

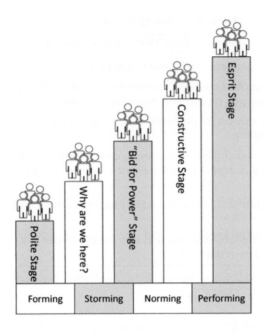

Figure 5-4   Cog's Ladder and the Tuckman Model.

1. In the first step, the *Polite Stage,* group members get acquainted, share values, participate in social interaction, and establish the group structure.
2. At the *Why are we here? Stage,* group members define and understand the objectives and goals of the group. To reach this stage, members risk the possibility of conflict and must deal with threatening topics.
3. The next step is the *"Bid for Power" Stage,* in which group members attempt to influence one another's ideas, values, and opinions. In this stage, members risk personal attacks from other members. Some members may be required to submit to a purpose they disagree with.
4. In the fourth step, the *Constructive Stage,* the team begins to take action. They become open-minded, engage in active listening, and respect one another's rights to different values and opinions. Some members may be required to cease defending their own views and accept the possibility that they may be wrong.
5. The last step is the *Esprit Stage.* Here, the group unifies and experiences mutual acceptance, high cohesiveness, and high spirits. Members have self-trust and trust other members.

The Bruce Tuckman Model

The Bruce Tuckman small group development model is based on his analysis of 55 articles on the stages of small group development. This model describes how group interactions change over time (Jensen and Tuckman, 1977). I have over-laid Cog's Ladder with the first four stages of the Tuckman Model in Figure 5-4.

1. In the *Forming Stage,* team members meet and are oriented to project goals. They learn the project and individual roles (Jensen and Tuckman, 1977). Team members need the opportunity to get acquainted. They need essential information about the content and context of the work expected, and they discover their individual values, assumptions, beliefs, and expectations. During this stage, the leader defines and clarifies the team vision and the goals to achieve the desired outcomes (Biech, 2008).

2. In the *Storming Stage,* the team seeks to understand the requirements, define an approach, and find consensus through collaboration. They respond emo-tionally to the required tasks at hand, potentially experiencing conflict (Jensen and Tuckman, 1977). In this stage, the team leader needs to assertively set parameters for the team. Team members need to listen attentively to all viewpoints and employ conflict management techniques such as mediation, negotiation, and arbitration if needed. During this stage, team members and team leaders explore alternative ways to view the problems they are facing (Biech, 2008).

3. Next, the team enters the *Norming Stage.* Here, the team members adjust to one another and experience an open exchange of relevant interpreta-tions of task requirements (Jensen and Tuckman, 1977). Here, the team leader is required to provide opportunities for all team members to be involved and to learn from and assist one another. The project leader needs to model and encourage supportive behavior, keeping communi-cation lines open. The team members need positive and corrective task-related feedback during this stage. Also during this stage, the successful team leader adds humor and fun to the team working environment (Biech, 2008).

4. The last stage, as depicted in Figure 5-4, is the *Performing Stage,* in which the team develops solutions, producing results and solving problems (Jensen and Tuckman, 1977). During this productive stage, team mem-bers need to be rewarded and recognized for their contributions to the project and the team's well-being. Team members participate in group problem solving, in setting future goals, and in shared decision-making opportunities. Team leaders delegate tasks to team members in this stage that foster their professional development (Biech, 2008).

5. The *Adjourning Stage* is not depicted in Figure 5-4. This stage was added to the model after the first four. Here, the group disbands after the project has ended (Jensen and Tuckman, 1977). During the separation process, the team leader provides evaluations and performance feedback. Team relationships and project success are celebrated, with an emphasis on fun and recognition (Biech, 2008).

5.5.5 Conflict Resolution

The team will traverse up and down Cog's Ladder, back and forth through Tuckman's Model, in a dynamic fashion as the team pursues its vision. Changes in requirements, leadership, and team members result in changes to the team's maturity level. Conflict is inevitable and normal. It is through this conflict that team leaders and team members learn and grow. Conflict builds character and maturity. Through these Cog and Tuckman stages, as a leader, you are expected to facilitate conflict resolution. Do it in a way that encourages your team members to learn and grow, and your team and organization will be stronger. You can influence the success not only of your team as a whole, but also your team members in a very personal way.

Psychotherapist Joyce Marter provides 10 Tips for Resolving Conflict, which I have adapted for your use, below (Marter, 2013):

1. Allow your team members time to pause and get grounded between the time of the conflict and your attempt to resolve it. When tempers are high—when team members are experiencing the "amygdala hijack" in which their cognitive unconscious minds are on overdrive—is not the time for conflict resolution. Team members need to use their mindful, intellectual selves during the conflict resolution process.

2. Help team members see the issue from a higher perspective. Help them imagine that they are a third party that is looking at the issue for the first time. Help them emotionally detach from the situation and think about the real, underlying issue. Are they angry about the current situation, or are they venting concerning some pent-up resentment over a past issue? Help team members avoid arguing about minutiae and focus on the real issues. Help team members see the big picture—the overall vision. Remind them of the noble motives of the project and how their roles relate to those motives.

3. Pay attention to nonverbal communication, your own and that of your team members. Be aware that your facial expressions, hand gestures, and body language may send messages that could be misinterpreted. If you

recognize nonverbal communication that could be misinterpreted, intervene immediately.

4. Set ground rules early concerning behaviors that are counterproductive to conflict resolution. Team members should not be permitted to physically or verbally abuse each other. They should avoid criticism and character attacks. They should avoid contemptuous behavior such as insults, eye rolling, stonewalling, and defensiveness.

5. Encourage team members to empathize with each other. Help them imagine themselves in the role of the other team members involved in the conflict, to imagine how it feels to face the challenges of being in their roles.

6. Encourage team members to take responsibility for themselves. Team members need to exercise honesty and integrity, owning up to their contributions to the conflict.

7. Encourage team members to be direct and assertive, not passive, aggressive, or passive-aggressive. If possible, communicate in person instead of over the phone. Avoid attempting to resolve conflicts through email, because this media is easily misunderstood and is often the very source of conflict.

8. Help team members to be active listeners by encouraging them to ask clarifying questions. Help them find common ground and "win-win" solutions.

9. As team lead, you can attempt to facilitate conflict resolution, but you cannot control how others will react. You can control your own behavior, so make sure your actions contribute to the resolution and do not make the conflict worse. Stay calm and help others stay calm. Apologize for any misinterpretations, setting a model for team members to emulate. Be fair in your judgments; do not show any favoritism.

10. Help team members to realize what they have learned through the experience of both the issue and the conflict resolution process. Encourage them to forgive and let go. Help the team members develop a positive path forward.

I used these guidelines to facilitate resolution of a conflict between one of my managers and one of his team members. The team member had become extremely upset because he perceived that the manager had disrespected him. He hastily resigned. The manager was upset with the team member because he felt he was insubordinate. I did not want to accept the team member's resignation until I understood the issue. I did not want him to resign over a simple misunderstanding. During the conflict resolution process, the team member explained that as English was his second language, sometimes he misinterpreted what he heard. The team member did not understand the criticality of performing the task that the manager directed him to perform, so I asked him to imagine how he would feel if he were in the manager's situation. He then understood the manager's frustration with his actions. The team member had interpreted the manager's direct manner of providing direction as "yelling" and felt disrespected. But he had never asked the manager why he reacted as he did, he just assumed the manager did not respect him as a person.

I asked the team member to take a pause the next time he felt the need to react emotionally with a team member or manager. Instead of reacting based on an emotional assumption, I encouraged him to take a break, calm down, and then ask the other person to clarify what he or she had said, then to react mindfully and intellectually, instead of emotionally.

During the conflict resolution process, the team member frequently pointed his finger at the manager when trying to explain himself. I stopped the team member, looked at him and said, "You don't realize what you just did, do you?" He stared at me blankly. I said, "When you pointed at *him*, *I* felt uncomfortable. *I* felt emotions build up inside of me when you pointed at *him* because your body language was offensive." The manager said, "That's right. I was getting angry because of your pointing." The team member said to him, "I did not realize I was making you feel that way! Why didn't you say something?" "Now you see my point," I said. "You did not intend to offend him with your pointing, but you did. In the same way, he did not intend to disrespect you. The next time you feel disrespected, take a break, calm down, and then ask the other person to clarify what he said so that you do not misinterpret the situation."

The team member decided not to resign, which was good for him because if he had not provided a two-week notice, we would not have been in a position to provide him with a positive referral for this next job. It was good for us because we did not have to recruit to find a replacement. The team member thanked me several times for intervening in this process. He said he had learned much from the experience, about himself and about the challenges of interpersonal communications.

Resolving conflicts faced during the team development process, traversing through the Cog and Tuckman Models, are one way of providing feedback to followers. Leaders also provide followers feedback through praise and reprimands. Followers need both of these in order to understand the behavior the leader expects in order to perform project tasks and to successfully interact with the team. Let's take a look at the processes for providing praise and reprimands.

5.5.6 Praise and Reprimands

I find myself in situations in which I have to make choices concerning personnel discipline, personnel salaries and raises, and the impact on the program budget

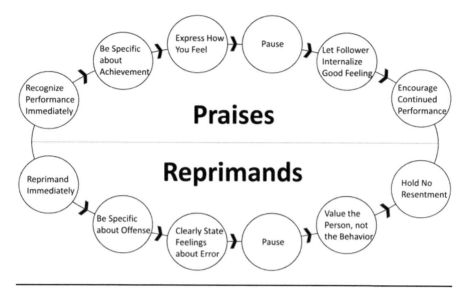

Figure 5-5   Praise and reprimands.

of bringing on new people. These decisions affect the performance as well the profitability and other financials of the program, and they affect the livelihood of the personnel involved. How I approach these decisions are a reflection of my character and impact my reputation.

Followers respect leaders who provide both praise and reprimands. Leaders should not recognize good performance and overlook poor performance, as this leads to a lack of team member accountability. Conversely, the leader should not overlook good performance and only pay attention to poor performance, as this leads to employee dissatisfaction and poor morale. Leaders who are disciplined in the application of both praise and reprimands set and reinforce standards of behavior, providing the team member the feedback needed to meet performance expectations and make positive contributions to the achievement of the team's purpose. Figure 5-5 shows the steps required to effectively provide praise and reprimands (Mayer and Varner, 1994).

A leader should praise followers by:

- Immediately recognizing positive performance.

- Being specific with the follower about what he or she has done right and how it impacts the project vision.

- Expressing his or her good feelings about the follower's good performance.

- Pausing to allow the follower to internalize how good it feels to receive praise—a feeling the follower will want to feel again—and how good the leader feels about the performance.
- Encouraging the follower to continue performing at a high level.

At the same time, a leader should reprimand followers by:

- Immediately addressing poor behavior.
- Being specific with the follower about what he or she did wrong.
- Expressing his or her feelings about the follower's poor performance.
- Pausing to allow the follower to internalize how bad it feels to be reprimanded—a feeling the follower will want to avoid in the future—and how bad the leader feels about the poor performance.
- Expressing that he or she values the follower as a person, showing that the leader means no harm and that his or her only intention is to help the follower perform at a high level. The leader should shake the follower's hand in order to express openness, warmth, and concern for the individual.
- Recognizing that the reprimand is over and holding no resentment toward the follower. Resentment is a poison that can destroy relationships between leaders and followers and that could lead to unnecessary vengeance.

5.5.7 Resentment

Followers who are forced to perform tasks they do not really want to do—things they do not agree with—may harbor negative emotions such as resentment and guilt. When asked if they will perform the task they disagree with, they may reluctantly say "yes" because they fear the consequences of saying "no." Good leaders don't put followers in such positions. The resentment caused by such demands builds up within organizations over time and is poisonous. Nelson Mandela said, "Resentment is like drinking poison and then hoping it will kill your enemies." Just as negative self-talk is poisonous to a person's self-image, resentment, guilt, and other negative feelings lead to grumbling and murmuring—poisonous self-talk that can debilitate an organization's morale and culture.

It is in the follower's best interest to make an effort to discover any resentment the leader has toward him or her and take action to assuage it. This is done through honest dialogue and through building trust verified by performance. Followers who get the job done within expected timeframes and at expected levels of quality earn their leader's trust.

5.5.8 Task Performance

Followers have the most at stake in the leader-follower relationship. It is easier for a leader to dismiss a follower, negatively impacting his or her career and livelihood, than for a follower to negatively impact the leader's career. The leader simply has more power and access. At the same time, leaders will not succeed unless their followers perform. The trust relationship between leaders and followers is critical, as both parties have much to gain and to lose.

Followers want to choose the problems that they commit themselves to solving. They are motivated by the challenge of understanding the project situation, identifying problems that impede achievement of the desired state, and developing solutions for those problems (Collins, 2013).

While it is important for team members to feel committed to identifying problems, performing tasks, and developing solutions that lead to achieving the desired state, leaders need to help followers avoid territorialism. I have encountered situations in which followers felt like they needed to protect their turf. For example, on one occasion, a systems backup administrator that was very good at his job refused to document the backup procedures he developed. He felt that anyone who came after him should have to figure out the procedures just as he had had to do. His attitude made the team weak. If he were to win the lottery, or leave the project for whatever reason, the team would be challenged to continue backup operations. As the leader, I had to motivate him to complete the documentation and then have another administrator validate his documentation in order to mitigate the risk.

Encourage your team members to solve their boss's problems first instead of exclusively performing the tasks they like. Solving your boss's problems first requires proactive communication on the part of the follower. The follower needs to clearly understand the critical success factors for the job—the expected quality level, the schedule, the do's and the don'ts. The follower should initiate conversations to determine these details, not wait for the busy leader to provide them. The leader may not know exactly what the follower needs to know, so the follower needs to ask questions until he or she sees the picture of what needs to be accomplished in the leader's mind. Then the follower can develop a win-win approach that allows him or her to perform at a high level, including accomplishing tasks that interest the follower as well as meet the leader's project requirements.

Leaders need followers to challenge ideas and approaches to problems. Leaders need "devil's advocates" in order to vet ideas and to facilitate critical thinking. Leaders need to consider all sides of issues and to analyze multiple alternatives to solving problems. Without engaged followers, the leader's ability to make critical decisions is diminished.

Followers have the responsibility to address conflict in order to improve situations for the sake of themselves, the team, and the team leader. Leaders should encourage and facilitate their followers' internal motivation and self-leadership, enabling and empowering them to enhance their working life experience, giving them the freedom to influence the morale and feeling of goodwill within the team.

5.6 Building Great Groups

Warner Bennis wrote in *The Secret to Great Groups,* "How do you get talented, self-absorbed, often arrogant, incredibly bright people to work together?" (Bennis, 1997). He was not writing about IT geeks in particular, but his article is in line with what we experience in the IT industry.

Bennis continued, "As they say, 'None of us is as smart as all of us.' That's good, because the problems we face are too complex to be solved by any one person or any one discipline. Our only chance is to bring people together from a variety of backgrounds and disciplines who can refract a problem through the prism of complementary minds allied in common purpose. I call such collections of talent Great Groups. The genius of Great Groups is that they get remarkable people—strong individual achievers—to work together to get results. But these groups serve a second and equally important function: they provide psychic support and personal fellowship. They help generate courage. Without a sounding board for outrageous ideas, without personal encouragement and perspective when we hit a roadblock, we'd all lose our way."

Bennis provides 10 Characteristics of Great Groups in Table 5-2.

In your Great Group, if you find a skilled IT team member who can naturally communicate, is naturally conscientious, is naturally trustworthy, and delivers, you have found a natural IT leader in the making. Groom this diamond in the rough for leadership; bring him or her into your inner circle; challenge him or her with leadership opportunities; position him or her as someone other team members should emulate. Develop this leader so that he or she can one day lead a Great Group. As an IT geek leader, no one else on your team can do this but you.

5.6.1 Team Charter

Dr. Ginger Levin and Allen Green developed a Team Charter that is an excellent way to set followership guidelines for your team (Levin and Green, 2014). A team charter is an agreement on the standards of performance and behavior for project team members. It formalizes team members' roles and responsibilities and provide guidelines for operations. IT geek project leaders can use the

Table 5-2 10 Characteristics of Great Groups

10 Characteristics of Great Groups
• *"At the heart of every Great Group is a shared dream."* IT geek leaders are responsible for crafting and articulating this shared vision or purpose, and IT geek team members need to buy into it.
• *"They manage conflict by abandoning individual egos in the pursuit of the dream."* IT geek leaders need to work with their team members to find the intersection of personal goals with project and organizational goals.
• *"They are protected from the 'suits.'"* The IT geek project leader's job is to be a firewall between the politics of senior leadership and daily project operations, giving team members the mental space to focus on achieving the project's vision.
• *"They have a real or invented enemy."* A common enemy bands the team together, motivates them to work together to defeat an adversary. This adversary may be another IT company or another development or operations team within the company.
• *"They view themselves as winning underdogs."* I have encountered many IT geeks who are achievement oriented and that are looking to make a name for themselves within their companies.
• *"Members pay a personal price."* Committed IT professionals in both technical and leadership roles are often required to work long hours, weekends, and holidays. Self-leadership activities such as developing and maintaining a personal IT lab at home or performing independent research require a sacrifice of personal time.
• *"Great Groups make strong leaders."* Groups that produce great results spawn leaders, followers who become leaders in their own right.
• *"Great Groups are the product of meticulous recruiting."* A common mantra among IT leaders is "hire for attitude and train for skill." A former boss of mine equated IT workers to athletes. "I can train a good athlete to play any sport," he said. But if it turns out that the athlete does not have the talent you need, don't try to work around the issue. Refine your recruiting process, and replace the poor talent with a better athlete. Your other, more talented team members will appreciate the opportunity to work with more talented teammates, and your team will be more productive in the long run.
• *"Great Groups are usually young."* Not young in age, but in spirit and energy.
• *"Real artists ship."* In the end, Great Groups produce tangible results.

Data derived from Bennis (1997). "The Secrets of Great Groups." *Leader to Leader*, 3(4).

team charter to set expectations for team member interaction. Tailor your team charter to include the characteristics of great groups, genetically engineering greatness into the DNA of your team. Table 5-3 provides suggested elements for the contents of an IT Project Team Charter.

Table 5-3 IT Project Team Charter

The IT Project Team Charter Contains:
• Project purpose statement
• Project scope and boundaries
• Project deliverables and assigned responsibilities
• Team member commitment statement
• Program/project sponsor role
• IT project leader role
• Client role
• End-user role
• Team member performance objectives
• Team member success measures
• Conflict management process
• Issue escalation process
• Decision-making process

Data derived from Levin, G. and Green, A. (2014). *Implementing Program Management*. [Kindle Version].

As an IT geek project leader, brief each team member on the project charter. Allow team members to ask clarifying questions and ensure that they understand the document even if they don't agree with it. Don't expect every team member to be receptive to the team charter. Require team members to sign an acknowledgment indicating that they have been briefed on the contents of the document, explaining that the acknowledgment does not signify agreement, only that they have been briefed. Explain to your team members that you expect the team to be great, and that the team charter is the roadmap for team greatness. Once you have done this, you can hold your team members accountable for meeting the standards you have established for your team and you have increased the likelihood that your IT project will be successful.

5.7 Reverse Micromanagement

Nearly every experience provides a learning opportunity, even the experience of working under poor leadership. Poor leaders teach followers how *not* to behave. If the followers are paying attention, they will recognize poor leadership and remember their experiences when it's their turn to lead, remember and behave differently, and thereby become better leaders.

In the IT industry, research has shown not only that more leadership is needed in order for projects to have a higher probability of success, but also that neglect of behavioral, social, and managerial factors attribute to project failure (Thite, 1999); so do not be surprised if you find yourself subordinate to someone who is a poor manager and leader. I have found myself in this situation more than once. I had a difficult time obtaining the leader's trust, and as a result, he overly involved himself in the details of the project. Each time this happened, I am sure the leader had valid reasons for his actions: high pressure from his superiors, a history of previous failures on similar projects, political conflicts and disagreements at his level and above, dependence on the success of the project for the leader's promotion or bonus—the list could go on.

Investopia.com provides a great definition of a micromanager: "A boss or manager who gives excessive supervision to employees. A micro manager, rather than telling an employee what task needs to be accomplished and by when, will watch the employee's actions closely and provide rapid criticism if the manager thinks it's necessary. Usually, the term has a negative connotation because an employee may feel that the micro manager is being condescending towards them [sic], due to a perceived lack of faith in the employee's competency. A micro manager may also avoid the delegation process when assigning duties and exaggerate the importance of minor details to subordinates" (Micro Manager, n.d.). I find it interesting that the subject of their definition is "a boss or manager" and not "a leader."

If you find yourself in a situation in which you are being micromanaged, my recommendation is that you employ something I call "reverse micromanagement." I don't mean to use this term in the pejorative sense. Reverse micromanagement as used here concerns communication. As communication is the foundation of program and project management, reverse micromanagement means providing your manager information about your project on a frequent basis. It simply means providing information and updates and asking for direction at frequent intervals, say every hour (or less). You, as the follower, initiate the communication whether the boss asks for information or not.

Only you can judge whether it is politically and socially safe to deploy such a technique. In the best case, your boss (say, for this example, Stephen) may be very happy to receive the information. You may build trust with him, establishing a solid relationship. You may convince him by your actions that he can delegate tasks to you without worry, that he can empower you without fear. In this case, let him tell you when he is receiving too much information. In this best case, your investment of time and energy to over communicate has paid off.

In the worst case, Stephen may be irritated by the frequent information updates. Be very careful in this case, because there may be an underlying reason that he does not want to hear from you, something political or personal, perhaps some type of hidden resentment. In this case, have a frank conversation with your boss and tell him how you feel. In this case, you are hemmed in, and there may be little you can do other than escape from your involvement with your boss.

In either case, if you pay attention, you will learn from the situation. You will gain experience to draw from, to build schemas that will help you determine the type of leader you want to be. You will understand how your followers perceive your actions, how and why they may interpret your style as micromanagement. Use this experience to gain self-awareness. Use self-leadership to become a "macromanager," someone who defines work in broad terms, builds trusting relationships with your followers, and then leaves them alone to do their work.

5.8 Conclusion

This chapter is about followership, which is another perspective on leadership. Now that you understand followership, you have an opportunity to be a successful IT geek project leader. You can do this by developing and encouraging your team members to be effective followers. You cannot neglect the behavioral and social factors of IT professionals—their tendency to be introverts who do not communicate well, their tendency to be somewhat rebellious against organization and project rules, norms, and values. Instead, clearly define the purpose of your project and capture it in a team charter. Identify and develop followers—team members that buy into the project's purpose and that will rally behind you as you lead them to achieve the goals of your IT project. Reprimand behavior that does not support the project's vision, and reward behavior that does. Empower and encourage mature performers who deliver so that less mature team members will want to emulate them. Be inclusive. Involve everyone in making project decisions when practical, even the most withdrawn members of your team. Earn your team's trust, and create opportunities for your team members to earn yours. Success is within your reach—be the leader your team members—your followers—and your customers expect and need you to be!

In the next chapter, Personal Credibility, we discuss proactive principles that geek leaders personify to earn a solid reputation, professional influence, and respect not only from followers, but also from peers and senior leaders.

Followership Assessment

The assessment below can help you think about your leadership effectiveness and the followership effectiveness of your team. You can use the results of your assessment to develop an action plan to improve your team's followership ability.

Use the following key for this assessment:

Not at all	Once in a while	Sometimes	Fairly often	Frequently, if not always
0	1	2	3	4

#		0	1	2	3	4
1	I apply direct leadership for team members who are inexperienced in performing their assigned tasks.					
2	I apply direct leadership when there is a high level of certainty concerning project requirements.					
3	I apply empowering leadership for team members who are experienced in performing their tasks.					
4	I apply empowering leadership when there is a high level of uncertainty concerning project requirements.					
5	I have developed and presented the unifying purpose for my team.					
6	I have earned my team members' trust.					
7	I identify and address team members who are withdrawn in order to encourage them to participate in team interactions.					
8	I identify and address team members who assert personal dominance and try to get their own way to the detriment of the team.					

(Continued on next page)

#		0	1	2	3	4
9	I identify and address team members who resist authority and who oppose the group.					
10	I identify or appoint "devil's advocates" in order to obtain an alternative viewpoint for project and team issues.					
11	I motivate team members to be committed members of the group.					
12	I offer decisions and conclusions after team discussions.					
13	I protect my team from the political environment in my organization so they can focus on achieving project goals and objectives.					
14	I provide encouragement to team members in order to establish and maintain a warm, friendly environment.					
15	I provide training opportunities for team members.					
16	I recognize and reward team members for their contributions to the team and the project.					
17	I reprimand team members who fail to meet project standards.					
18	I routinely pull together and summarize team suggestions and ideas.					
19	I seek consensus from team members on the approach to resolving project issues and meeting project requirements.					
20	I take action to foster commitment from each individual team member.					
21	I take action to keep communication channels open so that team members obtain the information they need when they need it and so that they are free to ask for information when they need it.					

#		0	1	2	3	4
22	I take action to resolve conflicts, reconcile disagreements, and reduce tension on the team.					
23	My team delivers the products and services the team was established to provide.					
24	My team members actively seek information and opinions concerning project tasks and issues.					
25	My team members can articulate the team's unifying purpose.					
26	My team members clarify and elaborate information in order to clear up confusion.					
27	My team members demonstrate that they care about my personal well-being.					
28	My team members freely provide relevant information concerning project tasks and issues.					
29	My team members have earned my trust.					
30	My team members practice self-leadership.					
31	My team members propose tasks and goals for the team.					
32	My team members recommend ideas and procedures for solving team problems.					
33	My team members seek training opportunities that will benefit the project and the team.					
34	My team members set and keep their own high standards.					
35	My team members trust one another.					

Chapter 6

Personal Credibility

Dale Carnegie wrote in *How to Win Friends and Influence People,* "Few people are logical. Most of us are prejudiced and biased. Most of us are blighted with preconceived notions, with jealousy, suspicion, fear, envy, and pride" (Carnegie, 1936). Sandy Allgeier, author of *The Credibility Factor,* wrote, "It can be very difficult to value others. Some 'others' are downright difficult people! A few are nasty, mean-spirited, and truly seem to enjoy hurting or harming others" (Allgeier, 2009). Brian Fitzpatrick and Ben Collins-Sussman used geek-speak to express a similar sentiment in *Team Geek,* in which they wrote, "People are basically a giant pile of intermittent bugs" (Fitzpatrick and Collins-Sussman, 2012). All of these authors recognized that people at every level—team members, colleagues, senior leaders, and stakeholders at large—are subject to human character frailties. These people make leadership challenging and sometimes perilous.

In Chapter 3, I discussed the importance of providing senior leaders with the ground truth concerning the actual circumstances of IT projects. The ground truth is unadulterated reality, delivered free of fear. The ground truth is what senior leaders need to know, not what others think they should know. It contains the facts in their purest form, not watered down by politics, misinformation, intentional ambiguity, or hidden agendas. Senior leaders with the ground truth have the facts and understanding they need to make decisions that lead to successful projects and organizations.

As project leaders, we may encounter another type of senior leader—those who who enjoy shooting the messenger. They are armed and dangerous, hunting the very people who everyone needs to deliver the ground truth. They load their quivers with arrows targeted at the truth-tellers and are eager to advance their contemptible agendas at the expense of the honest and the innocent.

Some might say that to expect leaders to lead is to expect too much. This puts program and project managers in a precarious position. We expect projects and programs to be successful as a result of sound processes and best practices, even in spite of poor leadership. IT project leaders are expected to achieve success regardless of organizational and political obstacles. They are expected to deliver the ground truth even at their own personal peril.

We can't make the mistake of assuming that those who operate in leadership positions actually do lead. We can't assume that those who have oversight responsibility are effective and responsible leaders who are concerned about your best interest and the best interest of the organization.

Leaders who lack personal credibility impede progress despite processes and practices. Personal credibility is the seed that yields a harvest of competent leadership and oversight. Zig Ziglar said, "Your children pay more attention to what you do than what you say." In the same way, team members expect their leaders' actions to be consistent with their words. Do you trust a leader whose words and actions are inconsistent? Are you willing to follow a leader who has demonstrated a lack of credibility? The leader may follow established processes, such as developing project management plans, but a leader who is not credible lacks the ability to effectively and consistently motivate team members to follow his or her plans and directions. Leaders without personal credibility are unable to inspire others to trust and believe in who they are and what they do, and this lack of trust becomes a barrier between leaders and team members (Allgeier, 2009).

Leadership and personal credibility are processes, not destinations. They are processes that require continuous improvement, like tending a garden. They are personal struggles with outcomes that have interpersonal and organizational consequences. Success is not measured by how far you've come or by how many miles or kilometers you have left to go. Instead, success is measured by the quality of the harvest—by how effective you are at obtaining the benefits and the valued and required outcomes that projects and programs are designed to achieve.

As IT leaders, our challenge is to persevere in spite of these challenges, to resist imitating incompetent or corrupt leaders, and instead to behave credibly and ethically in the face of clear and present danger, to improve our leadership acumen and deliver the ground truth without wavering or flinching. Equipping ourselves to perform in this manner requires stalwart personal credibility fueled by self-leadership. Most geeks are not interested in such pursuits. Researchers have found that IT professionals scored below the norm for conscientiousness, which includes dependability, reliability, trustworthiness, and the inclination to adhere to company norms, rules, and values (Lounsbury et al., n.d.). But those who are—those bold enough to break from the geek culture in pursuit of leadership with credibility—can expect to increase their value to their organization and reap rewards for taking such risks.

The personal credibility of IT leaders impacts the credibility of the organization and the credibility of the IT industry as a whole. As discussed earlier, the IT industry has a reputation for poor delivery of IT projects. Although several factors contribute to this issue, researchers have found that organizational and social factors, including leadership, have a profound impact (Thite, 1999). The credible IT geek leader can directly impact or influence these factors and, consequently, improve the success rate of IT projects and the credibility of the IT industry.

In this chapter, we begin with a case about a leader facing a personal credibility challenge. We then explore the concept of social styles, including the Driver, Expressive, Amiable, and Analytical styles. We examine the characters in the case to demonstrate how social styles can impact personal credibility. We then build on this knowledge of social styles as we discuss the Four Steps to Mindful Credibility: Know Yourself, Control Yourself, Know Others, and Do Something for Others. After the conclusion, there is a Leadership Assessment Questionnaire that can help you mindfully improve your personal credibility.

Let's begin with a case about a manager with an incredible reputation. This story was inspired by actual events.

6.1 The Incredible Craig

"Tony, you gave an excellent presentation this morning!" said Mr. Stamos.

"Thank you," Tony replied. Tony was an IT project manager at DICOM Solutions (Digital Imaging and Communications in Medicine), and Mr. Stamos was his customer and the project sponsor.

Tony was sitting next to Mr. Stamos, having lunch. There were several customers at the table with them at the Annual Medical Imaging Conference, where Tony was a guest speaker. "Lunch is great today!" exclaimed Tony. "This hotel never disappoints," replied Mr. Stamos.

"I need to talk to you about something," Mr. Stamos whispered to Tony, leaning toward him. "What can I do for you?" Tony replied. They rose from the table and walked together toward the ballroom, talking privately.

"I saw on your website that you're recruiting for a deputy project manager for our DICOM Data Repository project," said Mr. Stamos.

"Yes sir," said Tony. "Since we're ramping up deployments, I need management help."

"I may have just the guy for you—Craig Leonard," said Mr. Stamos.

"He's currently on your staff, correct?" Tony asked. "He's participated on several conference calls. Is he looking to move on from your staff?"

"His contract with us ends next month, and as you know we're facing a budget shortfall," replied Mr. Stamos.

"I understand. Please send me his résumé and we'll setup an interview," Tony said, shaking hands with Mr. Stamos.

"You'll have it tomorrow," replied Mr. Stamos.

Craig interviewed for the position, and Tony hired him. Tony spent two weeks training Craig, introducing him to everyone and helping him get acclimated to the company. Coming from the customer organization, Craig already knew much about the program. After it seemed that Craig had caught on, Tony assigned him to manage customer deployments.

One Monday morning, Tony heard a commotion in the engineering area and went over to investigate.

"What's wrong with you?" Jack screamed at Craig. Jack was a systems engineer on the deployment team. "How many times do I have to explain this to you?" he continued.

"What's going on here?" asked Tony, walking over to Jack's cubicle. "Craig told Mr. Jones at Walter Reed to order a switch for their data center," said Jack, flinging his arms (Mr. Jones was the IT Director at Walter Reed). "We are not responsible for the network," Jack continued. "We just tell the site how many Ethernet drops we need and they provide them. Now they expect us to configure the switch—that's out of scope!"

"He did what? Is this true, Craig?" asked Tony. "Well . . . ," Craig replied with a shrug. "I'll call Mr. Jones and clear this up," Tony said. "Maybe they can return the gear."

Jack followed Tony to his office. "One more thing," Jack said, closing Tony's door behind him. "On the kickoff conference call with Walter Reed yesterday, Craig was working from home while leading the call. Right in the middle of the call, he stopped everything, then came back and said 'Sorry, I had to let the cable guy in.'"

"He did what? Ohhh—that's not very professional," Tony said.

"Why did you hire him again?" asked Jack. "He knows the program, and he came highly recommended from Mr. Stamos, our customer." Tony said.

"Well, in my opinion, if he were any good, Stamos would have found a way to keep him," Jack replied.

"Of course I'll talk to him," Tony said. "Whenever someone new joins a team, the team goes through the forming, storming, norming, and performing phases all over again. We're storming right now, and that's normal. But every ship doesn't survive every storm. Let's see how this goes."

The next morning, Tony called Craig into his office. "Please, close the door and have a seat," Tony said to Craig. Tony sat behind his desk, Craig sat at a table in Tony's office.

"It seems you have had a rough start," Tony said. "I'm sorry about the cable guy incident," Craig said. "I don't know what I was thinking."

"You've been in this business a long time, Craig—longer than I have—and you come highly recommended by Mr. Stamos," Tony began, looking Craig in the eye. "We have high expectations for you. We expect you to be technically competent, to be professional at all times, and to inspire confidence."

Craig broke eye contact with Tony, looking down at the floor. "Our team members, like Jack, and our customers, Mr. Stamos and Mr. Jones, need to be able to trust you to deliver," Tony continued sternly. "I need to be able to trust you to represent me and DICOM Solutions with credibility. Right now, I'm concerned. Your personal credibility is on the line. As a leader in this company, your personal credibility directly impacts the company's credibility. You need to get your act together and you need to do it right now. Do you understand?"

"I do. I'll try harder," Craig replied, exhaling, never looking at Tony.

Two days later, Tony, Craig, and Jack were preparing for a conference call with Mr. Jones. The call was very important, because Craig had to review the deployment plan with Mr. Jones and the rest of the team to help them prepare for the deployment team's visit to the site two weeks later.

"I didn't see your draft deployment plan in my inbox this morning, Craig. Where is it?" Tony asked.

"I did not finish it," Craig said, softly. "Why not?" Tony asked. "We need to provide it to the customer twenty-four hours before the conference call to give them time to review it and prepare questions. I thought you were working on it yesterday."

"I got tired and I went home," Craig replied, again with a soft voice.

"You did what?" Tony asked incredulously. "Argh! Send me what you have and I'll finish it!" Tony yelled in frustration. "We don't have time for this. We're deploying three sites at a time, and the customer is depending on us to keep the schedule."

Tony and Jack completed the plan in Tony's office and sent it to Mr. Jones within minutes of the deadline. "Jack, you were right about Craig," Tony said. Jack raised his hands, tilted his head to the side, and shrugged his shoulders.

As Jack left Tony's office, Karen from Human Resources came in. "Good afternoon, Tony," she greeted him.

"Hey Karen, I was just about to come see you about Craig," Tony replied. "Interesting," Karen said. "He's the reason I'm here to see you. We completed Craig's background check and found that he lied about having a degree. We just fired him."

"He did what?" Tony exclaimed. "That guy's lack of credibility is ***incredible!***"

Each character in this story had his own way of interacting with others—his own social style. In the next section, let's examine social styles and their relationship to personal credibility.

6.2 Social Styles for Personal Credibility

In Chapter 2, you learned about the Myers Briggs Type Indicator (MBTI) tool, which is useful for identifying behavioral preferences. MBTI helps you understand your own psychological tendencies for extraversion and introversion, sensing and intuition, thinking and feeling, and judging and perceiving. The social styles model is also a very useful tool for your IT geek leadership toolbox. Your awareness, adaptability, and versatility with personal styles can enable you to increase your interpersonal effectiveness and improve your personal credibility with team members, peers, senior leaders, customers, and other project stakeholders.

Psychologists David Merrill and Roger Reid published their social styles model in *Personal Styles and Effective Performance* in 1981 (Merrill and Reid, 1981). They defined four behavioral profiles: Driver, Expressive, Amiable, and Analytical:

- *Driver.* Behavior characterized by "telling." Driver types "control" their feelings and are considered assertive and serious. They tell people what they think and require, and they usually do not display their feelings.
- *Expressive.* Behavior characterized by "telling." Expressive types "emote," showing their feelings, and are considered assertive.
- *Amiable.* Behavior characterized by "asking." Amiable types "emote," openly displaying their feelings, and are considered agreeable and cooperative.
- *Analytical.* Behavior characterized by "asking." Analytical types "control" their feelings. They are inquisitive. Their nature is to gather data and study information.

These social style profiles, and their associated Myers Briggs Type Indicators, are shown in Figure 6-1.

All social style profiles are equal; one is not better or worse than another. Each has its own advantages and disadvantages, and each can be effective.

Like MBTI, we all have a dominant, preferred style. We have parts of each style within us, and we are capable of demonstrating those styles when necessary. However, our preferred style requires the least energy and stress and is therefore dominant.

The basic difference between MBTI and social styles is that social styles are based on the perception of others while MBTI is based on self-perception. Together, those two tools provide a more detailed and complete view of a person (Mulqueen, n.d.). As a leader, if you understand both, you can better adapt your behavior to make the person you are engaging with more comfortable around you, a concept Merrill and Reid refer to as *versatility*. The more versatile you are,

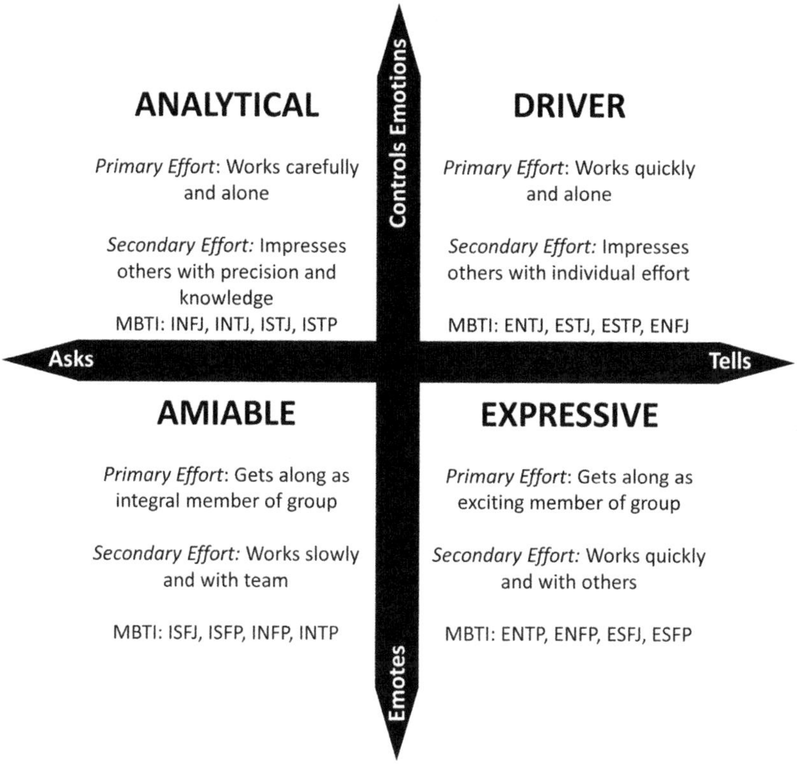

ANALYTICAL

Primary Effort: Works carefully and alone

Secondary Effort: Impresses others with precision and knowledge
MBTI: INFJ, INTJ, ISTJ, ISTP

DRIVER

Primary Effort: Works quickly and alone

Secondary Effort: Impresses others with individual effort

MBTI: ENTJ, ESTJ, ESTP, ENFJ

AMIABLE

Primary Effort: Gets along as integral member of group

Secondary Effort: Works slowly and with team

MBTI: ISFJ, ISFP, INFP, INTP

EXPRESSIVE

Primary Effort: Gets along as exciting member of group

Secondary Effort: Works quickly and with others

MBTI: ENTP, ENFP, ESFJ, ESFP

Controls Emotions — Asks — Tells — Emotes

Figure 6-1   Four personal styles.

the larger the audience of people who feel comfortable interacting with you, the better equipped you can be to handle conflict, the more people trust you, and the stronger is your personal credibility.

Our style does not define who we are, only our behavior patterns as perceived by others. Our styles do not define how we think or how we feel.

As we work together to achieve our shared vision, we still have different individual needs and goals. We communicate differently. We use time differently. Our style impacts how we make decisions and how we deal with conflict.

Let's take a closer look at each of the social styles.

6.2.1 Driver

People with the Driver pattern of behavior are action oriented. They are task specialists who seem to know what they want and where they're going. They

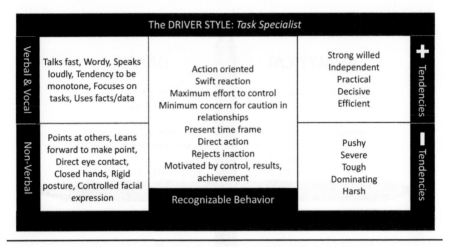

Figure 6-2   Driver style.

don't wait for someone else to initiate action. They are independent and may seem to work with other people only because they must, not because they enjoy it. Figure 6-2 describes the Driver style.

Those who display the Driver style prefer to respond quickly, and they prefer to be around others who do the same. They can be seen as impatient, getting things done in a hurry, even if rework is sometimes necessary. They take risks and decide quickly. They do not like being told what to do; instead, they would rather direct others (Merrill and Reid, 1981).

6.2.2 Expressive

Expressive people place a high value on power and politics. They seem to prefer to be around people who support their dreams and goals instead of those who compete with them. They are ambitious, yet warm and approachable. Figure 6-3 describes the Expressive style.

People who portray an Expressive style focus on the future and are undisciplined in their use of time. They may appear fickle, changing their course of action when a new direction seems to be more exciting. They do not spend enough time on a subject to delve into the details, and they make decisions using their own intuition. Expressive people are willing to take risks that they feel can hasten achievement of their goals and desires. They are creative, and they rely on personal opinion more than on logic (Merrill and Reid, 1981).

The EXPRESSIVE STYLE: *Social Recognition Specialist*
Verbal & Vocal
Talks fast, Wordy, Speaks loudly, Vocal inflection, People focus, Gives opinions/tells stories
Non-Verbal
Points at others, Leans forward to make point, Direct eye contact, Open hands, Casual posture, Animated expression
Intuition oriented
Rapid reaction
Maximum effort to involve
Minimum concern for routine
Future time frame
Acts impulsively
Rejects isolation
Motivated by excitement, personal approach, acceptance
Recognizable Behavior
+ Tendencies
Ambitious
Stimulating
Enthusiastic
Dramatic
Friendly
– Tendencies
Manipulative
Excitable
Undisciplined
Reacting
Egotistical

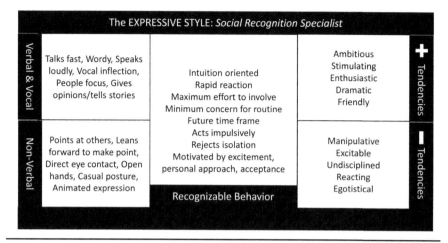

Figure 6-3 Expressive style.

6.2.3 Amiable

The Amiable person places a high value on relationships. They choose mutual understanding and respect over authority and force. They desire to be accepted. They make personal connections and pay attention to the personal motives and actions of others. Amiable people seek to bring joy and warmth to situations. Figure 6-4 describes the Amiable style.

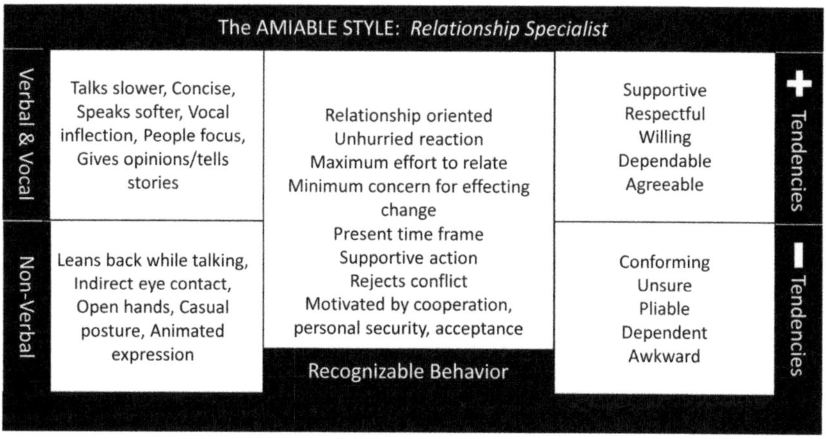

The AMIABLE STYLE: *Relationship Specialist*
Verbal & Vocal
Talks slower, Concise, Speaks softer, Vocal inflection, People focus, Gives opinions/tells stories
Non-Verbal
Leans back while talking, Indirect eye contact, Open hands, Casual posture, Animated expression
Relationship oriented
Unhurried reaction
Maximum effort to relate
Minimum concern for effecting change
Present time frame
Supportive action
Rejects conflict
Motivated by cooperation, personal security, acceptance
Recognizable Behavior
+ Tendencies
Supportive
Respectful
Willing
Dependable
Agreeable
– Tendencies
Conforming
Unsure
Pliable
Dependent
Awkward

Figure 6-4 Amiable style.

Amiable people enjoy socializing with others and may find it difficult to focus on work tasks. They enjoy taking time to share feelings and personal objectives. They appear to move slowly and to be undisciplined in their use of time because of their tendency to give social interactions a higher priority than work tasks.

Amiable people desire to have security and stability. They are slow to change, and they desire to have guarantees that the changes being planned will minimize risk and maximize promised benefits. They do not support changes that risk personal relationships. Amiable people place strong emphasis on their own personal opinions when considering change (Merrill and Reid, 1981).

6.2.4 Analytical

Analytical people think systematically and logically. They look for patterns with people and are reluctant to trust people—especially people with power—until they understand their patterns. Upon initial contact, they may seem to value logic and data over personal warmth and friendship, giving others the impression that they are cold and detached. They would rather get work done without involving other people if possible. They enjoy having the freedom to organize and can be cooperative with others once they feel organized. Figure 6-5 describes the Analytical style.

Analytical people like to take the time to analyze data, looking at historical patterns in order to understand the present and the future. They prefer a predictable, calm, and common sense approach to work, moving in a slow and

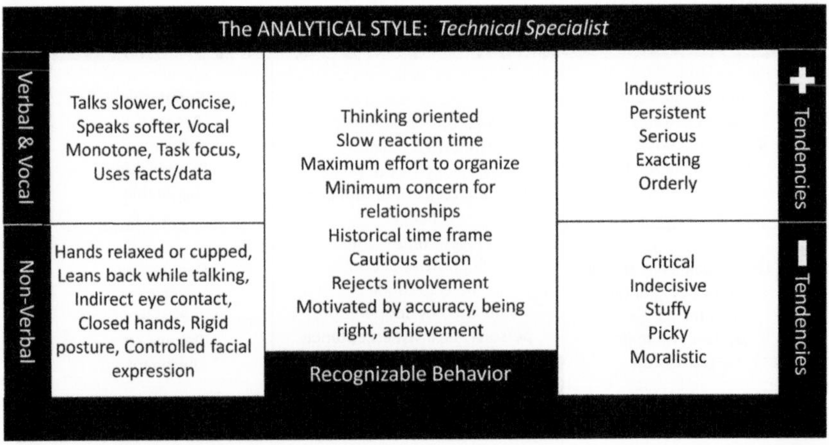

The ANALYTICAL STYLE: *Technical Specialist*			
Verbal & Vocal	Talks slower, Concise, Speaks softer, Vocal Monotone, Task focus, Uses facts/data	Thinking oriented Slow reaction time Maximum effort to organize Minimum concern for relationships	Industrious Persistent Serious Exacting Orderly	**+ Tendencies**
Non-Verbal	Hands relaxed or cupped, Leans back while talking, Indirect eye contact, Closed hands, Rigid posture, Controlled facial expression	Historical time frame Cautious action Rejects involvement Motivated by accuracy, being right, achievement	Critical Indecisive Stuffy Picky Moralistic	**– Tendencies**
		Recognizable Behavior		

Figure 6-5   Analytical style.

deliberate manner. Analytical people are risk-averse and make decisions based on facts and data instead of on the opinions of others. They desire to be right and to make decisions that last (Merrill and Reid, 1981).

All four styles—Driver, Expressive, Amiable, and Analytical—are part of the human experience and are necessary for a team to be effective. If one is only comfortable dealing with people with whom one shares a personal style, one may have a difficult time getting along with others. If one makes negative value judgments against people who have a different style, there can be tension within the work environment.

Let's take a look at the characters from "The Incredible Craig" through the lens of social styles.

6.3 Analysis of "The Incredible Craig"

Craig displayed Analytical tendencies. Mr. Stamos thought he was a good analyst who understood the program, and he thought he would be an asset to Tony's team. Having Craig, someone Mr. Stamos knew, on his vendor's team gave Mr. Stamos an advantage. But the qualities that made Craig a good analyst did not help him become a successful leader. Craig was a man of few words. Although Analytical types are generally inquisitive, Craig did not feel comfortable enough to ask Jack questions about the details of their deployment methodology that he did not understand, resulting in his providing the client with inaccurate information. Craig was more concerned about his own desire to have cable television than about being respectful of his client's and team members' time. Craig took his time to produce the deployment plan deliverable. He preferred to work on tasks alone and not ask for help. He was not concerned about the client's need to review the document before the conference call. He did not make the link between providing the document on time and his personal credibility. All of these behaviors are indicative of the Analytical social style. However, the lie Craig told about having a degree has nothing to do with social style. This behavior was unethical. It demonstrated a flaw in Craig's values and signified that he could not be trusted.

Tony demonstrated Driver tendencies. He was good at "telling" and did not mind presenting information to clients. He had no problem "chewing out" Craig when he felt his behavior did not meet standards. He was not concerned about how Craig felt about his position or the tasks he was assigned. He was not concerned about why Craig felt tired and decided to go home. Tony was only concerned about outcomes. He reacted quickly when there were client issues. He took direct action to correct the deployment plan deliverable in order to meet the client's deadline.

Neither Craig nor Tony displayed what Merrill and Reid refer to as *versatility*. Versatile people learn to control behavioral preferences when they create nonproductive tension in another person. Versatile people know how to communicate their words and intentions in a way that creates and maintains valuable interpersonal relationships. Versatile people interact with others in a way that makes them feel better about themselves. Others give versatile people endorsement, meaning people approve of their behavior and remain comfortable and non-defensive during encounters with them. No matter your social style, versatility is a skill that you can learn (Merrill and Reid, 1981).

Tony did not recognize Craig's Analytical style. He did not understand that his expectations for Craig's behavior were contrary to Craig's style. He wanted Craig to be more like him. Since he was not aware either of his own style or of Craig's style, he could not be versatile. He was unable to mentor Craig and help him learn to be versatile. While it is important to hold team members accountable, it is also necessary both to recognize where their style may cause them to be nonproductive and then to help them find ways to be effective in their roles using the strengths of their styles. Perhaps Tony could have facilitated collaboration between Jack and Craig in order to help Craig feel more comfortable about his relationship with Jack. Perhaps Tony could have involved Jack and Craig in team-building activities to help them understand each other. Perhaps he could have coached Craig to open up, helping him to understand that his inclination to work alone was not beneficial to the success of the team.

Versatile people monitor their behavior and adjust their actions to reduce tension in others, so that their actions do not interfere with their relationships with others. They share their feelings and thoughts about the messages they receive from others while also monitoring their own messages. They make an effort to understand what others are interested in and how they feel about situations. They seek to find common ground, asking good questions and providing good feedback (Merrill and Reid, 1981).

Craig did not engage in any of these versatile behaviors. As an Analytical person, he would have needed to exert some effort to gather the information he needed about the expectations for his leadership position. He would have had to operate outside of his comfort zone in order to collaborate with Tony and Jack to accomplish his assigned tasks. He would have had to demonstrate concern for how Tony and Jack felt about his performance, and he would have had to be willing to adapt his style in order to meet their expectations for his position.

The class I took on social styles included an exercise in which I had to identify my social style and deliver a presentation to the class on why I felt I identified with the style. "I am Analytical," I said. "I love to work alone. One of my favorite activities is to go into work on a Saturday when no one is there and write code all day. I can spend 12 hours writing code, and the time seems to go by extremely fast. I would much rather interface with a computer than to interact with someone else." The other people in the class with an IT background, who were also analytical, could relate. They saw me as dedicated and hardworking. The others could not understand how I could value a relationship with a computer over relationships with people. I had credibility with some of the class, but not with others, and that was fine with me. I was not concerned about what others thought of me. I was concerned about my own thoughts and actions, not about how my behavior might influence others.

In order to be successful in that business program, we all had to collaborate, working in small teams to complete class projects. We had to team up with people who were very different from us, who saw things from different perspectives.

Over time, I learned to appreciate the perspectives of others. I learned how our differences made us a stronger team. For example, I learned that if a team consists of members who are all Analytical types, the final result would most likely be an analytical one. When all four social styles are represented on a team, the team is in a position to analyze an opportunity or issue from various perspectives, providing a more complete result than if all of the team members had the same social style. Learning to appreciate—or at least tolerate—team members with a style that was not like mine took effort, but it turned out to be an investment with a high return. I learned to be versatile, and I learned that versatility leads to credibility.

Years after receiving this education in social styles, I was a program manager for a team deploying a large-scale hardware and software solution. One of the lead engineers on the team was very expressive. A conversation with him could be like the Seven Dwarfs Mine Train ride at Disney World: a strange, wild ride where you find yourself unsure of the direction you're going and how it will end. The other engineers on the team found his style annoying, but I went out of my way to keep him talking because he was very bright and had ideas that helped us solve customer problems. Many evenings, I'd be at my desk catching up on email or working on a deliverable, and he would call me. I'd close my door, put him on speaker, and continue to work. The conversations proceeded something like this: "Uh huh," I'd say, "Uh huh. Oh really? Oh, okay. Uh huh. Uh huh." But then a gold nugget would appear. He would say something really important, and I'd say, "Wait—what was that?" Then I would stop multitasking and ask questions, focusing intently on the issue or opportunity he mentioned, digging deep to mine the vein of gold. Sometimes the conversation resulted in a new contract with a customer, other times it resulted in a more efficient way to perform deployments. If I had found this engineer annoying and avoided him, the way other Analytical team members did, the project, the company, and the customer would not have experienced the full value of this bright engineer, and we would have missed out on important opportunities.

It is easy to identify a person's physical characteristics—whether he or she is short or tall, heavyset or thin, younger or older. A person's physical traits may be advantageous or disadvantageous depending on the situation. Groups such as sports teams and singing groups that have physical objectives take advantage of the physical characteristics of their members to accomplish their goals. In basketball, for example, a shorter person may not be able to dunk but can use his or her shooting, dribbling, and passing ability to contribute to the team. A taller team member may not be able to handle the basketball well but could be an accurate shooter when close to the basket. In a men's quartet, members have different voices: bass, baritone, first tenor, and second tenor. Individually, each may sing beautifully. Together, they can sing in harmony, producing a sound unique to their four blended voices, a sound that could make even the angels envious.

IT leaders need to recognize the mental characteristics and talents of their team members and stakeholders. If they understand who is amiable, who is analytical, who is a driver, and who is expressive, they can better assign team members to tasks that are compatible with their styles. IT leaders know when a task requires the team members to function outside of their comfort zones, and when they recognize this situation, they know to provide encouragement to help the team members feel comfortable and safe when performing their tasks. They know when the customer's style may be considered annoying or irksome to a team member, and they can then help the team member to learn to tolerate this difference in style, making the customer feel comfortable interacting with the team member, a comfortable feeling that leads to clearer and more complete requirements than might be obtained otherwise. As with different positions on a sports team, or different voices in a singing group, individuals with different social styles can accomplish more together than any of them could accomplish by themselves.

Next, let's explore Merrill and Reid's four-step process for improving your versatility, a process that can help you mindfully improve your personal credibility and IT leadership competence.

6.4 Mindful Credibility

David Gelles is a *New York Times* business reporter and the author of *Mindful at Work*. He provides the following great definition of being mindful: "Mindfulness is the ability to see what is going on inside our heads without getting carried away with it. It is the capacity to feel sensations—even painful ones—without letting them control us. Mindful means being aware of experiences, observing them without judgment, and responding from a place of clarity and compassion, rather than a place of fear, insecurity, or greed" (Gelles, 2015). This is exactly what we IT geeks need to exercise in order to achieve personal

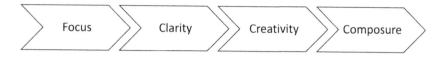

Figure 6-6 Characteristics of mindful leaders.

credibility. Because most of us IT geeks are introverts, we are very comfortable with living inside of our own heads. We think about what we say before we say it. We naturally try to connect the dots to solve problems.

Figure 6-6 depicts Gelles' characteristics of mindful leaders, which he developed after interviewing and mentoring several mindful leaders.

Allgeier wrote, "People with high credibility are able to roll over things in their minds, consider different perspectives, and stay neutral in their own positions while they do this. They have chosen neutrality as their first course" (Allgeier, 2009). This mindful approach enables them to focus on an issue without being emotional. It allows them to obtain clarity when others are experiencing amygdala hijackings. It allows them to think creatively to find third alternative solutions to conflicts. Mindful leaders are self-aware and can therefore control their speech and behavior to ensure that their actions will have the intended short-term and long-term effects. They remain composed, enabling them to anticipate the reactions of others and counter their emotional reactions calmly and thoughtfully. Leaders who can behave like this, who take a mindful approach to work, will develop and maintain personal credibility because others—team members, senior leaders, and stakeholders—can trust them to be a positive influence in any situation.

Figure 6-7 shows Merrill and Reid's four-step process for improving versatility, a process that can enable you to become a mindful leader.

Let's explore each step in greater detail.

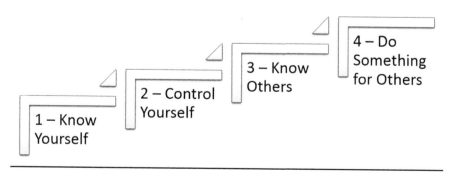

Figure 6-7 Four steps to mindful credibility.

6.4.1 Step One: Know Yourself

Knowing yourself requires you to be mindful of the impression you make on others because of your behavior preferences. You need to be mindful of how these behavior preferences cause tension. Your appearance, your competence, your oral presentation skills, and your feedback skills can all be sources of tension for others (Merrill and Reid, 1981).

Your Appearance

An important area in which many IT geeks have blind spots is their appearance. A senior customer told me, "I need your systems administrators to be more aware of and concerned about their appearance when providing desk-side support. Many of our users are important people, highly educated, and are involved in critical programs and operations. They dress a certain way, and they are accustomed to being around people who are dressed a certain way. When one of your systems administrators show up looking like they slept in their clothes, these users feel uncomfortable."

This sentiment is consistent with research. As discussed in Chapter 2, the Big Five study found that, in general, IT workers scored lower on "image management" than their peers in other occupations, meaning that they scored lower on the disposition to monitor, observe, regulate, and control the self-presentation and image they project during interactions with others (Lounsbury et al., n.d.). This presents a challenge for certain IT geeks' personal credibility. I have known many, many IT geeks who are extremely capable, trustworthy, and dependable, but would rather color their hair purple than wear a tie or a business suit.

According to Susan Bixler, author of *Professional Presence,* "Whenever we walk into a room, our clothing, manners, and mannerisms are on display. Others assess our self-confidence and our ability to present ourselves based on about five seconds of information. Each of us has our own signature of professional presence— an indelible statement that we make the instant we step into a room—that should afford us an opportunity to connect immediately" (Bixler, 1992).

People judge us IT geeks immediately based on how we present and carry ourselves. Many people feel tension when they perceive that others are dressed in a way that is socially unacceptable or that is different from what they are used to. Dress is associated with attitude, and people with a perceived attitude of social indifference can make others feel uncomfortable (Merrill and Reid, 1981). In order to have personal credibility, we have to be mindful not just about how our appearance makes *us* feel, but about how it makes *those around us* feel and how it influences our ability to effectively interact with them.

Your Competence

In Chapter 4, Self-Leadership, we discussed that leaders need to take responsibility for continuously learning, gaining more and more knowledge and understanding of what is required to be a successful IT project leader. Those who do this can gain credibility with their team members, peers, senior leaders, and customer stakeholders. As depicted in Table 6-1, there is always more to learn about IT leadership.

Your personal credibility increases when you demonstrate a commitment to learning. No one expects you to know it all, but others do respect and respond to a passion for learning. Your résumé may make you *look* credible, but by your demonstrating passion toward improving your knowledge, others *feel* your credibility. One of the best compliments I have ever received was when my CEO said, "When I know he is involved, I just get the feeling that everything will be fine."

Table 6-1 IT Project Leader Competence Areas

Technical Competence
• Software Engineering
• Software Development
• Graphic Design
• Network Engineering
• Network and Systems Administration
• Database Development
• Database Administration
Process Competence
• Agile
• Information Technology Infrastructure Library (ITIL)
• ISO 20000
• Capability Maturity Model Integration (CMMi)
Leadership and Management Competence
• Strategic Visioning
• Program/Project Management
• Human Resources Management
• Communications
• Environmental Awareness
• Organizational Behavior

Your Oral Presentation Skills

People constantly observe each other's character, most often subconsciously (Allgeier, 2009). We form thoughts, impressions, and opinions, and then we reform them. We observe each other's behavior, forming subliminal opinions of examined principles of right and wrong, honor and condemnation, and morality and corruption. Silently, as others observe us, the decisions we make about our behavior either strengthen our credibility or degrade it.

Have you ever gotten the sense that someone you know is not authentic? Perhaps they brag, exaggerating the truth about their accomplishments and credentials. Perhaps what they say is not in line with what they do. They give you the sense that they are not showing you their real selves. The image they portray of themselves seems to be out of sync with your perception of them.

People want to get to know the real you. They want to know that they are dealing with an authentic person, not someone pretending to be someone they are not. If you brag in an effort to make yourself seem more capable than you really are, or if you embellish the truth about yourself, you come across as phony. Others pick up cues from your nonverbal behavior and your voice inflections that give you away. They subconsciously try to determine if you are being real. People don't trust others when they sense they are hiding something, when they sense that the person they are engaging with is not demonstrating openness and transparency.

Introverts by nature are not open. They do not express their thoughts like extroverts do. This can cause others to be suspicious of them, because it is difficult to detect what they are thinking. For many geeks who are introverts, this presents a challenge, because people have a difficult time getting a sense of who the geek really is.

As a versatile geek leader, it is important to learn to communicate in a way that makes others feel comfortable about you. Those we engage with expect IT leaders to master the basics: speaking clearly, enunciating properly, using correct grammar and diction, avoiding vulgar or sexist language and slang. Geeks also have to make an effort to not use jargon but to explain technical concepts in terms the listener understands. As stated in Chapter 2, meanings are in people, not in words, so find a way to use words to connect to the people you are addressing.

The key is to be yourself; do not pretend you have a style that is different from your natural style. If you are naturally introverted, let everyone know that. Let them know that you are aware that you could be perceived as aloof or self-absorbed, but the reality is that you like to think about things before discussing them and that you need time to digest information before responding. Whatever your style is, help the person you are engaging with engage with you by being transparent about how your mind works. This simple demonstration of transparency and authenticity can help others understand you, reduce suspicion, and build trust.

Perfection is neither possible nor required. It's okay to show your warts, because doing so lets others know it's okay for them to show theirs. Just be honest about your imperfections while demonstrating commitment to working hard to achieve the vision and goals of your project, to taking responsibility for leading your team effectively, and for improving your leadership ability along the way.

Use of Feedback

In Chapter 2, we explored the importance of feedback and dialogue in the communications process. Mastering this skill is important for IT geeks to improve their credibility with stakeholders. Through feedback, we send verbal and nonverbal signals to help others understand the message we are communicating and to assist others in communicating with us. Versatile leaders share their feelings and thoughts about the messages they receive and are mindful of others' feelings about the messages they send. A versatile leader demonstrates personal credibility by using feedback and dialogue to mindfully reduce tensions in a conversation.

6.4.2 Step Two: Control Yourself

The next step of the Four-Step Process for Mindful Credibility is to control yourself. If you are mindful of your strengths and your weaknesses, such as those associated with your social style, you give yourself the opportunity to make the most of who you are, maximizing your strengths and minimizing your weaknesses. When you control yourself, you are mindful not only of others' reactions to your behavioral preferences, but also of your tolerance level for the behavioral preferences of others (Merrill and Reid, 1981). This requires you to be open, transparent, and patient with others, slow to judge and slow to react.

The credible leader is organized, a characteristic of the Analytical social style. The credible leader's transparency enables him or her to build trusted relationships and to face and overcome mistakes. Being patient, slow to judge, and slow to react requires composure. How can you obtain such skills? Gain them by using self-talk to shape your self-image and your behavior. Let's examine these ideas a little more closely.

The Organized Leader

Credible leaders are organized, which enables them to behave in a proactive manner. They don't have to "play catch up" because they make an effort to stay ahead. Others take notice of their organization and conclude that the leader is credible. Allgeier provides recommendations on how to get and stay organized in Table 6-2.

Table 6-2 Habits of Organized and Credible Leaders

Organization for Credibility
• Avoid over-commitment.
• Schedule daily "communication time."
• Keep time open between appointments.
• Arrive early.
• Keep your records in one place.
• Keep your email organized.
• Keep others informed if conditions change.

Overcoming Mistakes

Teresa Allen wrote in *Common Sense Service,* "Conflict often occurs not because of grievous error, but as the result of two individuals who meet on that somewhat stressful road of life. Small mistakes on such days can put us on dangerous ground. If, however, we are able to honestly admit our human weaknesses and mistakes, most customers will forgive us and move forward in a positive direction" (Allen, 2010).

This is the difference between perceived success and perceived failure. Successful people generally have the credibility to admit their mistakes; unsuccessful people generally do not. Successful people work with their stakeholders—their customers, leadership, and teammates—to overcome mistakes before they become failures. Unsuccessful people generally do not acknowledge their own mistakes; instead they blame others, blame the environment, blame leadership, and even blame the customer, instead of admitting their own faults and culpability and moving forward to correct problems. Many have a scotoma—a blind spot—to their own flaws. Either that or they know about them but choose not to face them.

If you and your team make too many mistakes, you put your credibility at risk. Consider the process in Figure 6-8 to maintain or repair your credibility.

During a conversation with a group of customer representatives for a large contract, I was leading a review of our continual service improvement plans. I went over my assessment of our quality management system and what I believed we needed to improve in order to enhance customer service and quality delivery. During this session, one of our customers said, "Your predecessor pretended everything was perfect. She never acknowledged having any concerns or problems, even though we clearly were not happy with the service provided."

Figure 6-8   Repairing and maintaining credibility.

"IT service management is like tending a garden," I said. "As soon as you think you have removed all of the weeds, new ones pop up out of nowhere, so you just have to keep at it." Everyone got it immediately. "I just rip out the garden and pour concrete," one of them joked. "Yes, but then I get cracks in the concrete and weeds grow in the cracks," another responded.

You can't keep your garden free of weeds unless you first acknowledge that you have them. Pretending you are perfect diminishes your credibility and the credibility of your team and organization. "So pity the poor perfectionist," wrote Dr. Adrian Furnham, professor of psychology at University College London and the Norwegian Business School. "They are driven by a fear of failure; a fear of making mistakes; and a fear of disapproval. They can easily self-destruct in a vicious cycle of their own making: 1) Set unreachable goals, 2) fail to reach them, 3) become depressed and lethargic, 4) have less energy and a deep sense of failure, 5) get lower self-esteem and high self-blame." This is not the behavior of a leader—not a person people want to follow, and not a person with credibility. "There is nothing wrong with setting high standards," Dr. Furnham continued, "but they need to be reachable with effort. It's all about being okay; human not super-human; among the best, if not *the* best" (Furnham, 2014).

Once you have taken ownership for the responsibility of removing the weeds from your garden, for acknowledging and correcting your mistakes and those of your team, you are in a position to coordinate with your stakeholders to determine the best next action. All of these stakeholders need to hear from you about the issues you are facing and what you are doing to resolve them. None of them are perfect; they have weeds in their gardens too. Reasonable stakeholders understand that your garden will have weeds, that mistakes will be made, but they need to know that you are tending your garden, because they are impacted by the harvest your garden produces.

Not all stakeholders are reasonable or understanding about your mistakes. You have to manage your expectations concerning how they respond. Develop your corrective action plan as quickly as possible, making sure it is as sound as possible and that you have as much consensus as possible. This puts you in a defensible position against those who intend to politically harm you and your team members.

After you have addressed a mistake, share what you have learned with others in your environment. Many organizations have "lessons learned" databases and knowledge management systems for documenting and sharing experiences that will help others avoid mistakes in the future. Taking ownership of your mistakes and sharing how you resolved them allows you to leave the situation in the past. It enables you and your organization to grow and be more successful. Your leadership in this area can produce IT projects that are more successful—and an IT industry that is more credible.

Maintaining Composure

David Gelles provides a formula that can help you put yourself in a mindful state that leads to an expression of the ground truth. Figure 6-9 depicts Gelles's advice for reacting mindfully to the situations you encounter as a leader, either at work or outside of work.

You cannot easily pick up subconscious cues from body language and tone of voice when you are talking. When you are listening deeply, focused, and open, you are more likely to obtain the information you need to make better decisions (Allgeier, 2008). You are more likely to avoid making mistakes that will lead to the failure of your IT project. Instead of engaging in heavy control talk, as described in the discussion of Talk Continuum in Chapter 3, engage in dialogue that enables you to obtain understanding of the ground truth and to collaboratively reach mutually beneficial solutions to problems.

Self-Talk to Improve Personal Credibility

Personal credibility is by definition personal. You cannot improve your personal credibility unless you take ownership of and responsibility for your attitude. You have to free yourself of excuses and of blaming others for your own credibility.

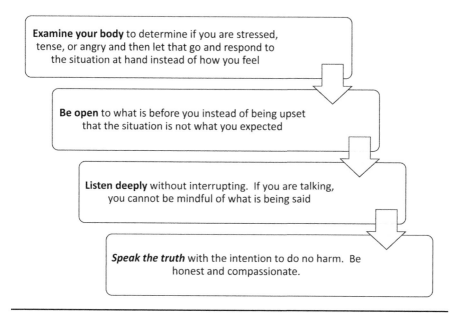

Examine your body to determine if you are stressed, tense, or angry and then let that go and respond to the situation at hand instead of how you feel

Be open to what is before you instead of being upset that the situation is not what you expected

Listen deeply without interrupting. If you are talking, you cannot be mindful of what is being said

Speak the truth with the intention to do no harm. Be honest and compassionate.

Figure 6-9   Reacting mindfully. [Adapted from: Gelles, D. (2015). *Mindful Work*. Boston: Houghton Mifflin Harcourt.]

You can directly and effectively improve your attitude toward personal credibility with your self-talk. Your self-talk—what you say about and believe about yourself—shapes your self-image, your behavior, and how others see you. It impacts your ability to influence the situations you are involved in. Positive self-talk leads to positive influence, which leads to improved personal credibility and leadership, which leads to accomplishment of project goals and objectives.

The scripts in Table 6-2 were inspired by the writings of Dr. S. Helmstetter (Helmstetter, 1982). Put into practice, these self-talk recommendations can help you improve your personal credibility.

By seeing yourself as a credible person, and by performing in a manner that is consistent with how you see yourself, you become a role model for others. Meditating on your self-talk makes you mindful of your own behavior and attitudes, allows you to control them, and prevents them from controlling you. It allows you to focus on adapting your behavior and attitudes to influence your team and your project.

Being mindful concerning your personal credibility through self-talk can set you apart from those difficult and nasty people everyone wants to avoid. Just as debugging tools can assist in resolving intermittent bugs in software applications, self-talk is a tool that can assist in resolving intermittent bugs in your

Table 6-2 Self-Talk for Leadership Credibility

What to say to yourself to improve your leadership credibility:
• I take full responsibility for everything about me—even the thoughts that I think. I am in control of the vast resources of my own mind.
• I alone am responsible for what I do and for what I tell myself about me. No one can share this responsibility with me.
• I enjoy being responsible. It puts me in charge of being me, and that is a challenge that I enjoy.
• I always meet the obligations that I accept. And I accept no obligations I cannot meet.
• I am trustworthy. I can be counted on. I have accepted responsibility for myself, and I always live up to the responsibilities I accept.
• I am versatile. I am aware of my style, I recognize others' styles, and I adapt my style to make others more comfortable.
• There is no "they" on whom I lay the blame, or with whom I share my personal responsibilities.
• I have no need to make excuses and no one needs to carry my responsibilities for me. I gladly carry my own weight, and I carry it well.
• Each day I acknowledge and accept responsibility not only for my own actions, but also for my emotions, my thoughts, and my attitudes.
• I exercise self-control, staying organized, overcoming mistakes, and maintaining my composure.

mental programming. Team members will see you not only as someone with position power, but as a role model—someone they want to emulate; and as a leader—someone they want to follow.

The next step of the Four-Steps to Mindful Credibility is to know others.

6.4.3 Step Three: Know Others

Mindfully building personal credibility requires looking outside of yourself and paying attention to others. If you pay attention, you can learn about the tension levels of the people you need to interact with in order to be successful. You can observe how they respond to your messages and what you can do to make their interaction with you more comfortable (Merrill and Reid, 1981).

If relationships are important for the success of your project, invest some time in observing your stakeholders to determine their social style. Pay attention to how their social style influences others in the environment. Use what you have learned in this chapter to minimize tensions when engaging with these key stakeholders, making them feel comfortable concerning their interactions with you and increasing your personal credibility.

This leads us to step four of the Four Steps to Mindful Credibility.

6.4.4 Step Four: Do Something for Others

Accommodating Preferences

After you have made the effort to know others, you are prepared to mindfully do something to accommodate their preferences (Merrill and Reid, 1981). For example, give Analytical types time and space to organize and prepare their thoughts concerning issues and solutions. Be a sounding board for Expressive types, allowing them to talk through issues to resolve problems. Change your attire so that you present an image that makes the person you are engaging with feel comfortable about engaging with you.

All of this may take significant effort on your part and may require you to sacrifice your comfort zone. You have to develop a tolerance for frustration. Only you can decide if this investment is worth it, if the relationship is important enough for the effort, and if the benefit outweighs the cost.

The more we practice this process, the more mindful versatility becomes a habit. We learn to adjust our behavior almost unconsciously to make others more comfortable (Merrill and Reid, 1981). To achieve this level, we have to be persistent, making the effort to gain experience and competence at being tolerant and accepting, steadily building our person credibility.

Credibility and Followers

As discussed in Chapter 5, the leaders' behavior, whether credible or not, influences their followers' behavior. Credible leaders are able to inspire others to trust them and believe in who they are and what they do (Allgeier, 2009). Bad leaders inspire poor follower behavior. "Bad leaders cultivate their in-groups with favors, and that makes it difficult for outsiders to identify bad leaders, or for followers to dislodge the leader from the position of power," wrote Dr. Ronald Riggio, Professor of Leadership and Organizational Psychology and former Director of the Kravis Leadership Institute at Claremont McKenna College. "The in-group followers defend the leader and work to keep him or her in power. Bad leaders often exist because their followers allow them to remain" (Riggio, 2009). Like poor parents setting bad examples for their children, I have known senior leaders who scream and yell at their "in-group" project leaders, and then I witnessed those project leaders scream and yell at their team members. I am sure you have witnessed similar events.

Most people do not want to follow this type of leader. They want to follow a leader who cares and who is involved, a leader who is not afraid to get his or her hands dirty. Leaders who do not ask followers to do anything that they would not do themselves build credibility (Allgeier, 2009).

Credibility is not connected to position or status (Allgeier, 2009). Credible leaders not only rely on their position to influence followers—leaders who have proven themselves to be credible inspire confidence in those around them. By delivering time and time again, by being accountable, and by remaining competent, a leader earns the trust of team members, senior leaders, and stakeholders. This leader's recommendations will be heard. By demonstrating respect and tolerance for the social styles of others, leaders earn the respect of their colleagues.

Respect for Others

No one has perfect personal credibility, but I find it especially hard to deal with those who are disingenuous, who intentionally present information out of context in order to attempt to gain an advantage and to further their own agenda. They knowingly revise history to suit their needs, exercising selective amnesia, remembering what they choose to remember and forgetting what they choose to forget. They paint misinformation the same color as the ground truth. They goad you into emotional reactions with personal attacks against you and your staff and take pleasure from their ability to use intimidation, agitation, and confusion to strengthen their position and weaken yours. These nasty people have no concern for ethics or personal accountability. They congregate together—the more senior ones hire those who are like them, and then they train the more junior ones to be like them.

In my first position as an IT manager, I was responsible for all of the information technology systems at a US Air Force facility. This was during the early 1990s, and the Air Force was just starting to deploy networks at all bases. The requirements grew faster than my staff, and we found ourselves working long hours to satisfy all of our customers. It was a labor of love, though, because it was all brand new and exciting. My boss saw everything we were doing and how we were trying to address all of the needs of the organization, from the lowest administrative assistant to the commander, every day. He came to the conclusion that I was "too nice." He felt that I was naïve and that people were taking advantage of me, making it difficult for me to prioritize my work. I did not feel that way, but I took this senior leader's advice to heart. Soon, an administrative assistant asked me for help, and then asked me to do a little more training than I normally provided, which would have taken more time. I don't remember what

I said in response, but I remember being mean. I don't even remember if what I said to her was true, but I do remember that my response upset her. I remember that it damaged our relationship. I was true to my boss and his advice, but I was not true to myself. This incident lasted less than 20 minutes, but it has haunted me for more than 20 years. I did not behave like the real me, and I diminished my personal credibility. I made up my mind after that incident to always make an effort be true to myself regardless of the advice from senior leaders.

You can be more respectful than I was. You can be successful as an IT leader without disrespecting others, inflicting emotional pain, and damaging your credibility. When you disrespect others, you may suffer the punishment of social isolation (Reynolds, 2012). You don't have to face the isolation that comes with this approach to life and work. All leaders have choices. Instead of choosing to be disingenuous, you can choose to be authentic. Instead of misrepresenting information, you can be honest and transparent. You can be ethical and credible, respecting others so that they will respect you. As a result, you will feel better about yourself and others will feel better about you.

Value Diversity

Respect for others includes respect for people in your organization with backgrounds and cultures different from your own. We live in a global, multicultural society in which people from different cultures and ethnicities frequently interact. In our IT projects, we are challenged to lead team members, follow senior leaders, and serve customers who are often of a different race, gender, age, or sexual orientation than our own.

Ethnocentrism is the tendency for people to put their own ethnic, racial, or cultural group at the center of their observation of the world. The ethnocentric person believes his or her own culture is superior to that of others. Ethnocentrism is a universal tendency that may include the failure to recognize the unique perspectives of others (Northouse, 2007).

Prejudice, closely related to ethnocentrism, is largely a fixed belief, attitude, or emotion a person holds toward another person or group that is based on faulty or unsubstantiated data. Prejudicial beliefs are generalizations that are resistant to change. These beliefs are judgments based on previous decisions or experiences with other people or groups (Northouse, 2007).

While we all hold ethnocentric attitudes and prejudices to some degree, these tendencies negatively impact our personal credibility and our ability to be effective leaders. A leader needs to recognize his or her own ethnocentrism and to understand and somewhat tolerate ethnocentrism in others. Leaders must balance the confidence they have in their own ways of doing things with recognizing that the ways of other cultures are also legitimate. Leaders must fight their personal prejudices and address the prejudices of their followers. They must address prejudices that followers have toward each other, toward stakeholders, and even toward the leader (Northouse, 2007).

Prejudice is sometime subtle. I was once one of two African-American project managers at an IT consulting firm. I would meet with my boss, a vice president, once a week to discuss my projects. One week, he told me about a situation with another client. My boss, the project manager for that client, and the company CEO had to visit the client to resolve a critical issue. After the meeting, my boss met privately with the CEO. "That was a close call," my boss said, "but everything seemed to work out fine." The CEO replied, "Yes it did, but the next project manager to fail will be Byron."

My boss told me he was astonished by the CEO's statement. He said my name had never come up in any discussion, and that the project that failed had absolutely nothing to do with me. He said he was aware of the status of all of my projects, and there were no issues. "The only reason that he would make that statement is because you are African-American," my boss said. I felt hurt and threatened, but not surprised. I had been told earlier that the senior leadership, including the CEO, had made racist remarks about a female African-American consultant the board had sent over for an audit.

I respected my boss for telling me the ground truth, but I lost all respect for corporate leadership. While I did not experience overt racism, corporate leadership created an atmosphere conducive to racial intolerance. I realized that I was not going to be promoted within that company. Even worse, I realized I was not secure in the position I held. By the grace of God, I was recruited for a program manager position in another company not long after that situation occurred.

Just as a leader needs to be tolerant of those with different social styles, he or she needs to be tolerant of those with different ethnic and cultural backgrounds. Leaders need to be mindfully honest with themselves about their own ethnocentric or prejuidicial attitudes and those of their team. The leader must make an effort to treat everyone with respect regardless of their cultural backgrounds. Others will endorse the leader who treats everyone equally, with compassion and empathy, as a versatile person, someone with personal credibility.

Delivering Bad News

Senior leaders, team members, and customers need to hear the ground truth from someone that they trust. However, delivering bad news can be extremely stressful. Many messengers have been shot, and some have never recovered from their wounds. Many executives who are poor leaders have inflected wounds on their IT managers when they attempted to deliver unfavorable information—information that the executives in fact needed in order to make the right decisions.

Where can the IT professional turn to learn how to deliver bad news? How about the medical profession? Every day physicians have to deliver bad news to patients. No one wants to hear that they have an incurable disease or that they are terminally ill. Yet, facing the stress of delivering this distressing information is one of the physician's occupational obligations.

Physicians use a process with the acronym "SPIKES" to deliver bad news to patients respectfully and compassionately (Baile et al., 2000). Bad news concerning IT projects is rarely a life-and-death matter, so if SPIKES works for physicians, it can work for IT leaders. The SPIKES process is depicted in Figure 6-10.

Let's explore some key activities in this process.

1. SET UP the Interview:
- Mentally rehearse the conversation.
- Expect to have negative feelings and to feel frustrated or responsible.
- Arrange for privacy.
- If possible, ensure that everyone is seated and in a relaxed position.
- Establish rapport by making eye contact.
- Choose a time when you will not be interrupted.

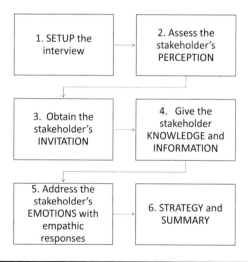

Figure 6-10 SPIKES process for delivering bad news. [Data derived from Baile et al. (2000). "SPIKES—A Six-Step Protocol for Delivering Bad News: Application to the Patient with Cancer." *The Oncologist*, 5(4): 302–311.]

2. Assess the Stakeholder's PERCEPTION:
- "Before you tell, ask." Ask relevant questions to understand the stakeholder's perception of the situation.
- Correct misinformation and misunderstandings.
- Address unrealistic expectations.

3. Obtain the Stakeholder's INVITATION:
- Determine how much detail the stakeholder needs about the situation.
- If possible and relevant, let the stakeholder know that more details are available in the future.

4. Give the Stakeholder KNOWLEDGE and INFORMATION:
- Warn the stakeholder that you are about to deliver bad news: "Unfortunately, I have some bad news for you," or "I'm sorry to tell you that . . .".
- Speak in terms of the stakeholder's vocabulary, in a way that you know he or she will understand. Avoid using unfamiliar jargon.
- Do not be excessively blunt.
- Give the information in small chunks.

5. Address the Stakeholder's EMOTIONS with Empathetic Responses:
- Understand that this is a very difficult part of the conversation.
- Observe and identify the stakeholder's emotion, naming it to yourself.
- Try to understand the reason for the emotion.
- Give the stakeholder time to express his or her feelings.
- Connect with the stakeholder's feelings: "I wish we did not have to face this situation."
- Continue the dialogue until the emotions clear.

6. STRATEGY and SUMMARY:
- Check the stakeholder's understanding of the situation.
- Explore options to address the issue going forward.

The SPIKES process helps you mindfully deliver bad news in a compassionate manner, providing the stakeholder with information he or she needs but does not want to hear while allowing you to keep your credibility intact. I have used this process during personnel layoffs, both for informing team members of the decision to lay them off and for explaining the situation to the remaining workforce. I made every effort to deliver the bad news mindfully and compassionately; however, not one of these conversations was easy or stress-free.

6.4.5 Conclusion

There is a relationship between your personal credibility and your leadership, your leadership and the success of your project, the success of your project and the success of your organization, and the success of your organization and the state of the IT industry. Figure 6-11 shows this relationship as an inverted pyramid.

Everyone in the information technology industry plays a role that impacts the industry's reputation. Personally, I want our industry to have a solid reputation. I want the public to have the same confidence that an IT project or program will be successful as they have that a highway construction program will be successful. In the same way that I don't want to be associated with a failed project, I don't want to be associated with an industry with a reputation for failure.

By accepting the responsibility for building and maintaining their personal credibility, IT geek leaders take an important step toward making this dream a reality. As a credible IT geek leader, you can become important to your organization. You can make your organization more valuable, and your leadership will place a higher value on you, putting you in a position to receive promotions and awards.

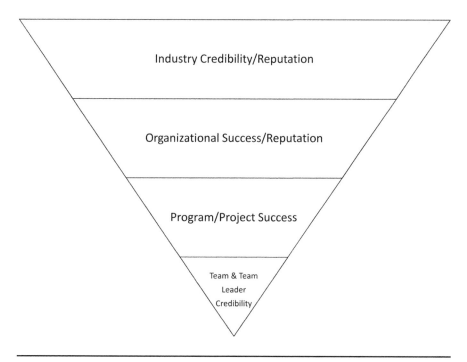

Figure 6-11   Credibility and the industry.

In Chapter 7, we explore leadership within the context of a quality management system that integrates leadership into standard IT project management practices. You will learn how to plan, implement, and maintain an effective leadership system that can enable you to deliver projects that meet stakeholder requirements.

Leadership Assessment Questionnaire

The statements in this questionnaire are designed to help you examine your personal credibility. This examination can help you identify and develop an action plan to improve your personal credibility.

Use the following key for this assessment:

Not at all	Once in a while	Sometimes	Fairly often	Frequently, if not always
0	1	2	3	4

#		0	1	2	3	4
1	I am mindful of the advantages and disadvantages of my social style.					
2	I am mindful of the social styles of key members on my team.					
3	I am mindful of the social styles of my senior leaders.					
4	I am mindful of the social styles of my key customers and stakeholders.					
5	I recognize when my social style causes tension in others.					
6	I adapt my behavior to make others comfortable and reduce tension.					
7	I share my feelings and thoughts about issues and opportunities with key team members, leaders, and stakeholders.					
8	I make an effort to find common ground and consensus with stakeholders.					

#		0	1	2	3	4
9	I tolerate the behavior of those who have a personal style that is different than mine.					
10	I am mindful of how my appearance impacts how others feel and impacts my personal credibility.					
11	I take action to continuously improve my competence with people, IT processes, leadership, and management.					
12	I take action to improve my oral presentation skills					
13	I provide feedback by sharing my thoughts and feelings with other people—people with whom I am investing the effort to establish and maintain a relationship.					
14	I organize my life in a manner that enables me to be an effective leader.					
15	I acknowledge the mistakes I make with others and take ownership with those that are impacted by those mistakes.					
16	I maintain my composure in a manner that enables me to reduce tension and speak the truth.					
17	My self-talk includes statements that help me improve and maintain my personal credibility.					
18	I am willing to do the tasks that I ask my followers to do.					
19	I am mindful of how others feel about my effectiveness in treating them with respect.					
20	I value and appreciate people in my organization who have backgrounds and cultures different from my own.					
21	I deliver bad news to stakeholders in an honest, courageous, and compassionate manner.					

Chapter 7

Project Leadership Integration

Disaster loomed. No one knew the full scope of the software deployment project, and no one would admit their ignorance. There was no budget, just a rough-order-of-magnitude cost estimate. There was no schedule, just something that resembled a high-level project roadmap. The project team worked frantically, like bees in a hive. One worker bee, Tom, was responsible for configuring the hardware security module to provide the encryption solution, but he was having trouble. "I can't figure this out," he thought, "but I doubt those idiots on the testing team will realize it's not fully operational until after I start my new job." Tom did not tell anyone he was struggling, and no one asked how he was doing, not even the project manager. Tom did not mention the problem or his plans to resign.

Independently, the team members created many artifacts, but unlike bees, together they produced nothing useful. The project sponsor reluctantly told the steering committee the project was on track and that the setbacks were minor. He sensed the project manager's fear, but he did not know how to address it. He did not realize the high level of discord among the project team members—discord that was not registered in the risk log and that impeded their efforts to deliver a secure, high-quality solution.

Project managers frequently face this type of chaos. Situations like this require not only adherence to project management best practices, but also leadership to standardize, educate, promote, and enforce best practices. A project leader is responsible for bringing order to chaos, leading the introduction of structure, and adhering to structure. A successful project leader observes and evaluates chaotic situations; develops a vision of harmony, cooperation, and project achievement; and then sets out on a mission to influence and lead people out of the chaos and into effective performance. Project management standards such as the Project Management Institute (PMI®)'s *Project Management Body of Knowledge (PMBOK®)*, the American Academy of Project Management project management standards, and the standard that supports CompTIA's Project+ certification are all excellent sources of structure for IT projects, but leadership is required for these standards to be effective within organizations. Leadership is required to confront and address stakeholder and team member resistance, negative attitudes, and hidden agendas.

7.1 CompTIA Project+ Project Domains

The CompTIA Project+ exam is designed to certify project managers and team members on the skills required to perform in every phase of the IT project management life cycle. I earned my CompTIA Project+ cert in 2002 before I obtained the PMI®'s Project Management Professional (PMP®) certification in 2004. I was attracted to Project+ because it had an IT focus in addition to its business focus, and because I found it to be a stepping stone to the PMP®. In this chapter, we will explore how to integrate leadership into the CompTIA Project+ management methodology for IT systems.

Figure 7-1 provides an overview of CompTIA Project+ concepts using a project management life cycle model.

CompTIA Project+ promotes the five project management domains that are very similar to the *PMBOK®*'s process groups: Initiation/Pre-Project Setup, Planning, Execution and Delivery, Change Control and Communications, and Closing.

Let's take a closer look at each of these process domains.

7.1.1 Initiation/Pre-Project Setup

The project is defined and authorized during this initial phase. Projects produce unique products or services and are temporary, with a defined start and end date. During initiation, stakeholders are identified, the project manager is assigned, and the organization commits resources to the project—resources that include personnel, equipment, supplies, and facilities. The project sponsor works with the project management team to develop the business case, feasibility studies, assumptions analysis, stakeholder analysis, and other artifacts to

Pre-Project Setup/Initiating	Project Planning	Project Execution and Delivery	Change Control and Communication	Project Closure
Identify & validate project and organizational structure	Prepare scope document, Work Breakdown Structure, schedule, and resource requirements	Coordinate human resources (assemble project team and management conflict resolution)	Implement change management process, evaluating impact to schedule, cost, quality & scope	Confirm & document status of meeting objectives, provide historical information for future projects
Validate project business case	Define change management process & plan	Execute project kickoff meeting	Perform qualitative and quantitative risk analysis	Perform post-project review & close contracts
Identify & analyze stakeholders	Develop communications plan	Comply with internal and external standards	Perform resource leveling & smoothing	Document standards compliance status
Define project charter components (deliverables, cost, approach, assumptions & constraints, risks, objectives)	Develop risk management plan: (initial risk assessment, risk matrix, risk register, & stakeholder risk tolerance)	Provide decision oversight & approval of deliverables at phase gates	Ensure quality of deliverables, monitoring performance & variances, managing change requests	Develop lessons learned, perform post-mortem analysis, develop transition plan & closure report
Define project and product/service lifecycle	Develop quality, cost, procurement, staffing management, & transition plans	Manage scope risks, issues, quality, costs, budget, & communications	Implement communications plan & information distribution processes	Perform final individual performance appraisal & release resources
Project Charter Approval	Project Plan Approval	Project Performance Reporting	Project Acceptance	Project Closure
Gate Review	*Gate Review*	*Gate Review*	*Gate Review*	*Gate Review*

Figure 7-1 CompTIA Project+ domain descriptions. [*Source:* Heldman, K. and Heldman, W. (2010). *CompTIA Project+ Study Guide.* Indianapolis, IN: Wiley Publishing. See Disclaimer page xix.]

document project requirements and customer expectations. This analysis is an effort to justify the investment the organization must make to execute the project and produce the required outcome (Heldman and Heldman, 2010).

The goal of the Initiation/Pre-Project Setup phase is to establish the project's foundation and direction and to give the project manager the authority required to lead the project effort. The project manager produces the Project Charter. This charter is submitted to the organization—either the program under which the project falls or another governing body within the organization—for approval (Heldman and Heldman, 2010).

7.1.2 Project Planning

Once the organization approves the Project Charter, project planning formally commences. The IT project manager works with team members and coordinates with stakeholders to thoroughly plan the project. Planning involves developing an approach to manage project scope, cost, schedule, quality, communications, risk, human resources and staffing, procurement, stakeholder engagement. Planning begins in this phase but occurs throughout the project. The project manager's task is to anticipate changes in scope, schedule, budget, and resources and then to control these changes in a manner that enables the project to be delivered on time, within budget, and at an acceptable level of quality and customer satisfaction (Heldman and Heldman, 2010).

Product Life Cycles

Planning occurs not only for the project management life cycle, but also for the product life cycle. A life cycle is the series of stages through which a system passes (Walden et al., 2015). While the *project management life cycle* includes the Initiation/Pre-Project Setup, Planning, Execution and Delivery, Change Control and Communications, and Closure domains, the *product life cycle* for IT products include phases such as Requirements Analysis, Design, Implementation, and Testing. The project management life cycle includes management and control activities for meeting schedule, performance, and cost requirements. The product life cycle includes stages for manufacturing articles (software and systems) for customers. The product life cycle is executed within the project management life cycle.

Information technologies are developed using a systems development life cycle. Life cycles for product development in use in industry include the Waterfall, Iterative, Incremental, and Agile models. Table 7-1 provides a description of these models.

Table 7-1 Product Development Life Cycles

Model	Description
Waterfall	Uses well-defined, linear stages for systems development that include requirements analysis, design and detailed design, code and implementation, integration, and testing (Schwalbe, 2000)
Iterative/ Spiral	A refinement of the Waterfall model in which software is developed using an Iterative or Spiral approach instead of a linear approach, including determining objectives, alternatives, constraints; evaluating alternatives; identifying and resolving risks; systems development, verification, and planning for the next phase (Vohra and Singh, 2013)
Incremental	Progressive development of operational software, with each release providing added capabilities (Schwalbe, 2000)
Agile	An iterative and change-driven software development approach that combines the activities of analysis, design, implementation, and testing, delivering small, progressive releases throughout the software development process (Vohra and Singh, 2013)

IT project leaders need to be well versed in the systems development model their projects use to develop IT products and deliver IT solutions. Failure to properly implement a systems development model can have grave consequences. In the US, the massive Office of Personnel Management (OPM) security breach in the spring of 2015 provides a fitting example. Hackers stole the personal security data of over 21.5 million government employees, costing the OPM $133 million to protect the victims from identity theft (Fingas, 2015).

After investigating, the Inspector General (IG) suggested that the agency should follow industry best practices for systems development. The OPM rejected the IG's suggestion, proclaiming that the agency followed the OPM Systems Development Life Cycle. The IG was neither convinced nor impressed. "The practices are applicable to any organization, private or public sector, involved in project management activities," the IG said. "At any rate, based on documentation we have reviewed, we have determined that OPM is not in compliance with either best practices or its own policy" (Ogrysko, 2015).

7.1.3 Project Execution and Delivery

Once the organization approves the project plan, typically at a phase gate review, project execution and delivery begins. During this phase, IT project leaders build their teams, beginning the process of interacting with them and directing team activities. Project leaders are responsible for organizing and leading a project kickoff meeting, during which they set the expectations and tone of the project, providing detailed information concerning the scope, schedule, quality requirements, budget, risks, and other Project Management Plan elements. This important meeting provides an opportunity for team members and stakeholders to ask questions and receive clarification concerning project requirements, stakeholder expectations, and roles and responsibilities. As team members progress in project execution, project leaders provide oversight and decision support, coordinate with team members and the organizational governance body, and take actions to ensure that the project performs in a manner that will produce the required deliverables on time, within budget, at acceptable quality levels, and in compliance with organizational standards and delivery processes. Project leaders and their team members provide stakeholders with the agreed-upon project performance reports, ensure that they are informed on the status of the project, and monitor compliance with established standards and performance metrics (Heldman and Heldman, 2010).

7.1.4 Change Control and Communications

Project leaders understand that change is inevitable on a project. They are responsible for implementing processes to keep changes to scope, schedule, costs, and quality under control in order to ensure that the project produces the deliverables that the stakeholders expect and require. The Change Control and Communications domain has an iterative relationship with the Project Execution and Delivery domain described above. This domain includes the performance of qualitative and quantitative risk analysis, quality control activities, and the management of change requests for work performed during execution and delivery. The project team communicates with stakeholders in accordance with the communications plan, which includes meetings, reports, presentations, and briefings that are provided to the specified stakeholders in the expected format at the expected time (Heldman and Heldman, 2010).

7.1.5 Project Closure

At the end of the Project Execution and Delivery and Change Control and Communications phases, the stakeholders requiring the project deliverables—which may be internal customers or external clients or organizations—decide if the project's outputs are acceptable. After project acceptance, the IT project leader is responsible for closing the project. The IT project leader documents the final status of the project and performs a post-project review. If the project is canceled without acceptance, the IT project leader performs a post-mortem review to analyze and document the cause. Whether the project completed successfully or was cancelled prior to completion, the IT project leader is responsible for coordinating lessons learned sessions and documenting lessons learned to enable the organization to capture knowledge gained through the project experience and to facilitate continuous process improvement. The IT project leader leads the process to close contracts associated with the project and to release personnel, facilities, funding, and material resources to the organization. This release may include transitioning resources and information to operational groups or to other projects or programs. The project leader performs a final performance appraisal of personnel resources and produces a final project closure report (Heldman and Heldman, 2010).

7.2 Leadership Integration

The CompTIA Project+ project management life cycle is sound and proven. It is based on best practices that can produce successful projects when followed correctly. However, the processes and practices are implemented by people—IT people with a tendency to be less conscientious concerning following processes and procedures. As discussed earlier, researchers have found that failure of IT projects is generally the result of neglect of the behavioral and social factors—influenced by management, the organization, and culture—rather than the technology itself (Thite, 1999).

This propensity of IT geeks to behave in a less-than-conscientious manner introduces challenging human factors and presents a risk to IT projects and a threat to the delivery of quality project outcomes. For example, several systems administrators that were on my teams vehemently resisted documenting procedures for critical tasks, such as performing system backups and restores. Some resisted providing training for other team members. Their attitude was, "Since I figured this out on my own, so should they"—a selfish, less-than-conscientious attitude that could put projects at risk. Strong leadership is necessary to positively influence the human factors and mitigate these risks. The quality of the IT project leader's performance needs to be assessed throughout the project, with corrective action taken as necessary to ensure that his or her leadership produces the required team performance results.

As discussed in Chapter 3, the IT project leader needs to be mindful of his or her team members' mental states throughout the project management life cycle, communicating with emotional intelligence in order to gain an understanding of their values, beliefs, assumptions, and expectations to enable the IT geek leader to tailor interactions with team members and stakeholders accordingly. Introverted IT geek project leaders need to be mindful of how this propensity can impede their ability to communicate effectively and how it can create psychological noise that distorts their messages. Detail-minded IT geek leaders need to be especially self-aware. They need to understand that, as leaders, they should work hard to see the big picture, crafting a vision for their projects and programs, and communicating this vision in order to motivate their team members and to inform and inspire project stakeholders.

The self-leadership techniques presented in Chapter 4 can help IT geek leaders add the leadership tools to their mental tool boxes that can enable them to be visionary, communicative, and inspiring. Using positive self-talk helps IT geek leaders believe in their own leadership ability. IT geek leaders can teach themselves to monitor their own behavior, mindfully making adjustments in their communications and actions that set positive examples for their team members. IT geek leaders who take the time and effort to understand themselves, their own personal styles—as presented in Chapter 6—and the personal styles of their teammates are better equipped to make the proper behavioral adjustments. The IT geek leaders' awareness of self and awareness of others enables versatility— the ability to interact effectively with people, making efforts to tolerate people with styles that are different from their own. This enhanced awareness and versatile behavior builds credibility with others, distinguishing IT geek leaders from their peers, enabling them to stand out as leaders.

Organizations supporting IT projects need to provide IT geek leaders the support required to overcome the tendencies that can hinder their ability to effectively lead their projects and that can thwart their ability to produce intended project outcomes. Industry standards such as ISO/IEC 20000 provide principles that can be tailored to develop a structure and environment for planning, monitoring, and assessing IT project leadership.

The ISO/IEC 20000 Service Management Standard is the internationally recognized standard in IT service management. It was first published by the International Organization for Standardization (ISO) and the International Electrotechnical Commission (IEC) in 2005 and revised in 2011. The standard addresses the need to audit the skills and abilities of IT personnel performing in their respective roles. ISO/IEC 20000 specifies that all people who have a management role have the correct skills to deliver effective results (Kunas, 2012). Figure 7-2 represents ISO/IEC 20000 guidance for assessing personnel skills and abilities.

These skills include leadership skills. The required leadership skills need to be identified and training provided. The application of these skills needs to be monitored, assessed, and continually improved in pursuit of leadership excellence. Leadership needs the same level of focus as risk management, quality

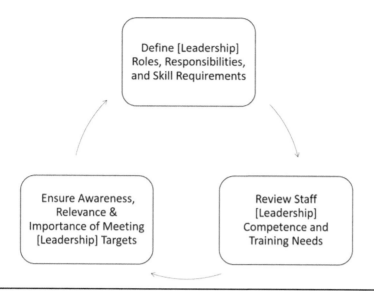

Figure 7-2   ISO/IEC 20000 Resource Management. [Data derived from Kunas, M. (2013). *Implementing Service Quality Based on ISO/IEC 20000*. Ashland, OH: ITGP.]

management, change management, communications management, and other critical project management processes.

In the case of quality management, ISO/IEC 20000 provides standards for delivering quality IT services. Quality planning specifies the quality standards that are important to a project. The organization develops quality standards and determines how they are to be applied within projects. Quality assurance deals with evaluating overall performance throughout the project management life cycle. Quality control activities monitor project results to determine compliance with prescribed standards and identifies ways to improve quality (Schwalbe, 2000).

Quality assessments can be both *quantitative* and *qualitative*. Quantitative assessments refer to performance metrics that can be measured and can be expressed in numbers. Examples of quantitative measurements include network response time and mean time between failure. Qualitative measures are subjective and are expressed in words. These measurements include stakeholders' opinions, beliefs, feelings, and attitudes about the entity or subject matter being measured. Qualitative measurements are taken using surveys, interviews, observation, and document content analysis (Westcott, 2006).

Quality assessments are useful not only for measurement of project deliverables, but also for assessing and evaluating leadership performance. IT project leaders require a qualitative review, which is subjective in nature. It measures the senior leader's impressions of the IT project leader's consistency and adherence to leadership standards established within the organization, or if absent from the organization, established within the project.

Figure 7-3 shows the CompTIA Project+ domains with integrated leadership assessments and control mechanisms.

This new integrated leadership assessment and control strategy ensures that not only schedule, budget, and quality performance metrics are reviewed, but also leadership performance metrics. Consistent with ISO/IEC 20000, it enables definition of leadership roles, responsibilities, and skill requirements; review of leadership competence and training needs; and promotion of the awareness, relevance, and importance of meeting leadership targets.

During the Initiation/Pre-Project Setup phase, the organization's leadership defines the leadership standards for the IT project leader and references those standards in the Project Charter. The project sponsor briefs the IT project leader on the standards during the project initiation gate review, stressing the importance of adhering to the standards throughout the project management life cycle, setting expectations for the IT project leader's performance. The standards need to include expectations for the IT project leader to establish a project vision, to follow project management standards, to build and maintain relationships, to communicate effectively—delivering bad news early—and to adhere to the leadership principles provided in Chapter 2.

Next, during the Project Planning phase, IT project leaders develop the Project Management Plan for the project. This plan needs to include a Leadership Integration Plan that explains the project leader's approach to adhering to the leadership standards, the qualitative performance metrics used to assess leadership performance, and the schedule for these assessments. The assessment includes a leadership self-assessment, as presented at the end of Chapter 2. The IT project leaders coordinate with the project sponsor to develop an approach to a leadership audit and include this approach in the Leadership Integration Plan. IT project leaders and project sponsors should assess the leadership training needs for the IT project leader and team leads, making preparations to provide the required training.

Finally, because effective followership is required for effective leadership, IT project managers develop a Team Charter, as discussed in Chapter 5, which is closely aligned with the staffing management plan, describing the roles, responsibilities, and processes for team member participation on the project. The Leadership Integration Plan should reference the staffing management plan's approach to rewarding excellent performers, coaching challenged performers, and disciplining non-performers. The Leadership Integration Plan integrates the staffing management plan, the Team Charter, and qualitative quality management processes across the project management life cycle. The organization's

Pre-Project Setup/Initiating	Project Planning	Project Execution and Delivery	Change Control and Communication	Project Closure
Identify & validate project and organizational structure	Prepare scope document, Work Breakdown Structure, schedule, and resource requirements	Coordinate human resources (assemble project team and management conflict resolution)	Implement change management process, evaluating impact to schedule, cost, quality, & scope	Confirm & document status of meeting objectives, provide historical information for future projects
Validate project business case	Define change management process & plan	Execute project kickoff meeting	Perform qualitative and quantitative risk analysis	Perform post-project review & close contracts
Identify & analyze stakeholders	Develop communications plan	Comply with internal and external standards	Perform resource leveling & smoothing	Document standards compliance status
Define project charter components (deliverables, cost, approach, assumptions & constraints, risks, objectives)	Develop risk management plan: (initial risk assessment, risk matrix, risk register, & stakeholder risk tolerance)	Provide decision oversight & approval of deliverables at phase gates	Ensure quality of deliverables, monitoring performance & variances, managing change requests	Develop lessons learned, perform post-mortem analysis, develop transition plan & closure report
Define project and product/service lifecycle	Develop quality, cost, procurement, staffing management, & transition plans	Manage scope risks, issues, quality, costs, budget, & communications	Implement communications plan & information distribution processes	Perform final individual performance appraisal & release resources
Define leadership standards	Develop leadership integration plan with performance measures & team charter	Lead team in accordance with leadership integration plan	Perform leadership self-assessments & audits	Document leadership lessons learned
Project Charter Approval	Project Plan Approval	Project Performance Reporting	Project Acceptance	Project Closure
Gate Review	Gate Review	Gate Review	Gate Review	Gate Review

Figure 7-3 CompTIA Project+ domains with integrated leadership assessment and control mechanisms. [Source: Heldman, K. and Heldman, W. (2010). *CompTIA Project+ Study Guide.* Indianapolis, IN: Wiley Publishing. See Disclaimer page xix.]

governance body approves the Leadership Integration Plan as a component of the Project Management Plan at the end of the Project Planning phase.

During the next phase, Project Execution and Delivery, IT project leaders present the Team Charter to the team during the kickoff meeting. Each member of the team signs the charter and receives a copy. IT project leaders enter into dialogue with each of their team members, using emotionally intelligent communications to ensure that each team member understands performance expectations. IT project leaders monitor the performance of their team members to ensure that they are in compliance with the Team Charter. They take corrective action for non-compliance with performance requirements and they reward, coach, and discipline team members as required. It is important that IT project leaders establish relationships with each team member in order to learn what motivates him or her, and then find ways to nurture this motivation.

During the Change Control and Communications phase, the IT project leader performs a leadership self-assessment, and the project sponsor performs his or her leadership assessment. The IT project leader and the project sponsor should meet to discuss the results of the assessments to determine if any corrective actions to the IT project leader's approach are required. This gives IT project leaders the feedback they need to improve their leadership effectiveness.

At the senior leader's discretion, the organization provides resources to perform a leadership audit. The audit includes an evaluation of IT project leader performance with respect to the Leadership Integration Plan and team performance with respect to the Team Charter.

These assessments and audits should take place whenever the organization or the project sponsor feels they are necessary, not just as scheduled in the Leadership Integration Plan. These assessments do not replace annual performance reviews, but instead the results of the assessments should feed the annual performance reviews. There should be several performance assessments and audits conducted throughout the year, not just one evaluation at performance appraisal time.

Finally, during the Project Closure phase, IT project leaders should perform the final performance appraisals for their team members, providing needed feedback that can help them improve their performance. They should also document lessons learned about their own leadership effectiveness and the effectiveness of the Leadership Integration Plan. Project sponsors and IT project leaders should discuss the lessons learned and develop a plan for the IT project leaders to make leadership improvements prior to the commencement of their next projects.

If the organization has not established leadership standards, project leaders should establish their own and perform their own leadership self-assessments and continuous improvements. This is the honorable and responsible course of action and is the mark of an ambitious and exceptional project leader. As discussed in the Chapter 5, Followership, good followers create and adhere to their own high standards. This principle also applies to the IT project leader serving in the role of follower in a larger program or organization.

7.2.1 Best Practice: US Air Force Airman Comprehensive Assessment (ACA)

The US Air Force integrates leadership assessments and feedback into their evaluation process for officers and enlisted personnel in every discipline. The leadership integration principles presented in this chapter for IT project leaders is consistent with those of the US Air Force:

- The USAF defines standards for leadership and trains members on those standards.
- The USAF established a mandatory process, the Airman Comprehensive Assessment (ACA), designed to provide periodic performance feedback on leadership, primary duties, followership, and training for officers and enlisted personnel.
- The ACA feedback sessions must take place within 60 days of initial supervision, at the midterm of the performance review period, and within 60 days of the annual performance review.
- Team members can request ACA feedback from their supervisors.
- The USAF encourages supervisors to perform ACAs face to face with their team members in order to facilitate dialogue and open communications, encouraging supervisors to get to know their Airmen (US Air Force, 2013).

After serving 21 years in the US Air Force, with experience as an enlisted member, an officer, an active duty member, and a reservist, I have intimate knowledge of the US Air Force's ability to build leaders in every discipline, including information technology. In the civilian world, as a consultant, I have had the honor of providing services to the US Air Force, gaining yet another perspective on their operational and leadership practices. Integrating leadership assessment and monitoring into current IT industry project management practices, in the same spirit as that applied in the US Air Force, can improve IT project leader performance across the industry.

7.3 Conclusion

In conclusion, a project leader uses standards to introduce and maintain structure in IT projects, providing the organization with communications necessary to prevent chaos and facilitate successful delivery of IT solutions. Industry standards such as CompTIA Project+ are excellent structural frameworks when properly implemented. Leadership is required to overcome the organizational and human factor challenges faced when implementing these standards.

The CompTIA Project+ project management life cycle consists of the Initiation/ Pre-Project, Project Planning, Project Execution and Delivery, Change Control and Communication, and Project Closure domains. Gate reviews between these domains provide stakeholders the opportunity to approve project artifacts and deliverables, such as the Project Charter and the Project Management Plan, and to provide authorization for the project to proceed from one domain to the next.

IT projects produce IT products using a product life cycle. The purpose of the product, or systems development, life cycle is to organize the stages a product passes through from conception to implementation. Examples of systems development life cycles include the Waterfall, Spiral, Incremental, and Agile Models. There is an iterative relationship between the project management life cycle and the product life cycle. IT leaders need to understand not only the project management life cycle, but also the product life cycles required to successfully execute their projects.

Project management is a challenging discipline, and IT projects are especially challenging. Researchers have found that while technology is complex, IT projects more often fail because of neglect of behavioral and social factors, and that IT personnel are generally not diligent about following processes and procedures (Thite, 1999). Leadership is required to address these human factors in order to ensure that project management standards are implemented effectively and that projects produce the outcomes stakeholders expect.

Leadership needs to be integrated into the IT project management life cycle in order to address the human factor challenges facing IT projects. The Leadership Integration Plan defines leadership standards, documents leadership performance metrics and the Team Charter, guides leadership execution, specifies leadership self-assessments and audits, and prescribes documentation of leadership lessons learned. The Leadership Integration Plan enables organizations to define, monitor, and assess leadership execution using processes similar to those of quality management.

The development of project manager leadership competencies is a recognized industry challenge (American Academy of Project Management, 2006). As an example, in July of 2015, the "Ashley Madison hack" scored world-wide headlines when hackers accessed sensitive customer credit card and sexual interest information stored in an unencrypted text file on an inadequately protected server. The Ashley Madison hack not only prevented AshleyMadison.com—a scandalous company with a business model based on adultery enablement— from going public, it also demonstrated what happens when geeks within a company fail to lead, regardless of the company's moral standards. The geeks in that company not only needed to think tactically, taking actions to keep the servers up and running, but they also needed to think strategically, taking leadership actions to ensure that a single mistake would not be fatal for the business (Paciullo, 2015). Management acumen is needed to establish project management and IT systems best practices in an organization, but leadership is required in order for those practices to be implemented effectively. Effective implementation requires vision, drive, motivation, communications, and accountability.

It has been said that "what gets measured, gets done." If IT leadership is not measured, it may not be effective. But if organizations integrate leadership planning, monitoring, and assessment into the IT project management life cycle, IT leadership can get done.

7.4 Leadership Integration Plan Template

The Leadership Integration Plan Template below can help the IT project leader inject leadership monitoring and assessments into the IT project management life cycle. Senior leaders and organizational governance boards can use this template to hold IT project leaders accountable for planning and implementing leadership initiatives within their projects.

Leadership Integration Plan Template

Section	Description
Leadership Policy	• State the leadership policy of the organization. If the organization does not have a leadership policy, establish one for your project or program. • *Example:* All project managers and team leads will make every effort to practice transformational leadership (see Chapter 2).
Leadership Standard	• Briefly describe the leadership standard mandated in the leadership policy. • *Example:* The transformational leadership model requires the leader to identify the needed change, create a vision to guide the team and the organization through the change with inspiration, and execute the change with the commitment of members of the group (see Chapter 2).
Team Charter	• Develop a Team Charter as described in Chapter 5. • Include the Charter as a section in this plan or create a separate Team Charter document and reference it in this plan.

(Continued on next page)

Leadership Integration Plan Template *(Continued)*

Section	Description
Leadership Training	• Identify leadership training requirements for the IT project leader and the team leads. • Determine what training will be provided, who will receive the training, when the training will take place, and the cost of the training. • Include the training schedule and costs in the project schedule and budget.
Leadership Assessments	• *Leadership Self-Assessments:* Develop a Leadership Self-Assessment tool that assesses compliance with this plan (see Chapter 2). This activity should also include an assessment of the team's compliance with the Team Charter. Schedule time for leadership self-assessments in the project schedule. • *Senior Leadership Assessment:* Coordinate with senior leadership to develop an assessment process. This activity includes an assessment of both the IT project leader's compliance with this plan and the team's compliance with the Team Charter. Document the process in this plan. Schedule time for senior leadership assessments in the project schedule. • *Leadership Audits:* If required and supported by senior management, develop and describe a process for a third-party entity to perform a leadership audit.
Leadership Lessons Learned	• Describe the process for developing, reviewing, communicating, implementing, and archiving leadership lessons learned for the IT project leader, team leaders, and team members.
Leadership Performance Improvement Plan	• Describe the process for developing, reviewing, communicating, and implementing a leadership performance improvement plan in accordance with the lessons learned analysis.

Chapter 8

Closeout

In previous chapters, I used business fables to illustrate the positive and negative impacts of an IT leader's behavior on projects. Business fables and stories are useful for training and transmitting knowledge, boosting morale, and even resolving conflict (Neile, 2015). In this last chapter, I leave you with one last business fable about a CEO's struggle to transform the leadership mindset within his company's culture. Janice Glover-Jones, CIO of the Defense Intelligence Agency, said in an August, 2015, speech that she was facing a similar challenge.

"This is why we're focusing on employee development. Our budget was reduced greater than 30%, but I doubled our training budget. This training program is focusing on developing leadership and soft skills like collaboration, critical thinking, active listening, to name a few, and finally to improve our technical acumen. We must optimize the productivity of our current staff and leverage their talent, recruit and retrain personnel with relevant skills, or we will fail in our effort to support the mission." The story that follows addresses many of these important points. I hope this story and the others I have told help you visualize and understand how IT geek leadership can result in successful projects when applied effectively.

8.1 Sidelined

"The customer seemed really upset with you at the closeout meeting, Dad," Jonathan said to Saul. Saul and Jonathan both worked for JTS Security Systems, a small security systems firm. Saul had an unkempt, scruffy beard and wore a dingy white dress shirt and a blue tie that seemed too short for his large build. Jonathan was clean-shaven, with an athletic build, and wore a dark green polo shirt neatly tucked into his khakis.

Saul was the CIO and managed major deployment projects. Jonathan was a project manager in the Project Management Office. He did not work directly for Saul, but he produced deliverables to support JTS projects. They were having lunch together after the customer closeout meeting.

"I think they were robbed last week," Saul said as the waiter brought his cheeseburger and fries. "We would have delivered the system three weeks ago, but Joab screwed up the testing schedule." Joab was the testing team lead on Saul's project.

"What did Joab say about that?" asked Jonathan, cutting into his salmon Caesar salad.

"I see you're eating that rabbit food again," Saul said. "You are definitely your mother's child. Anyway, Joab said there was a customer conflict with the testing schedule. Maybe if the customer was more responsive, or if Joab were a better team lead, if he weren't such a fool, we would have delivered on time. It was just unfortunate timing. Oh well. They'll pay the invoice, and that's all that matters to me."

Saul planned to retire in three years. He recruited Jonathan from an IT company a year earlier, promising to promote him to Senior Project Manager. Jonathan had an undergraduate degree in computer science and was Project Management Institute (PMI®) Project Management Professional (PMP®) certified. Saul wanted to groom Jonathan to replace him after he retired.

8.1.1 Gold Plating

It was a late meeting in the large conference room, scheduled after normal business hours because there was no time during the day. Alva, the PMO director and Jonathan's boss, insisted on conducting a lessons learned session at the conclusion of each major project.

Alva had been with JTS since the company started, as had Saul. She wore a dark pantsuit and kept her hair cut short. She took her leadership role in the company seriously, and she dressed the part.

Saul's project was complex and taxing for JTS, and Alva felt there was much to be learned. Although the JTS had delivered the solution to the customer, project closeout activities still remained undone, and reviewing lessons was one of those activities.

Samuel, the JTS CEO, arrived early and chatted with Alva. Samuel had just returned from a customer meeting. He wore a dark three-piece suit with a white shirt and a red tie.

"I think you'll find the case Jonathan submitted very interesting," Alva told Samuel, removing her jacket to get comfortable for a long meeting. Samuel did the same. "He identified an issue that would have made the project come in much later and further over budget than it did."

"I've heard good things about Jonathan and his performance," replied Samuel. "I'm curious about what he found, and I want to see how he handles himself."

Saul and Jonathan arrived together, at the same time that the pizza arrived. Saul wore a wrinkled blue dress shirt and black jeans. Jonathan wore a neatly pressed green polo shirt and khakis. Other staff members filed in and greeted each other. Everyone picked up a slice and took a seat at the conference table.

"Ok, let's start," Alva said. She then took them through the agenda, reviewing each lessons learned case submitted, allowed for questions, and provided instructions to the note taker for the meeting minutes.

Jonathan's case was last. "Jonathan discovered an interesting case of gold plating," Alva said, about an hour into the meeting. "Jonathan, please explain your findings."

"I was performing an impact analysis for a change request per our normal process," Jonathan began. "As I reviewed the preliminary design document, I noticed a section on an interesting feature that I didn't remember from the Statement of Work or the requirements document. It was a very detailed design for a physical access monitoring system module. It enabled the security manager to receive an alert every time a person of interest badged into specific rooms. It included a management console where the security manager could designate which doors to monitor for specific badged employees. The design did not use the directory in our access control system. Instead, it used a custom cloud-based light directory access protocol interface to integrate with the client's directory service."

"Ok, ok," interrupted Samuel, "Your inner geek is shining through, which is good, but what does this mean? It sounds advanced, but what problem does the feature solve?"

"Let's say the security manager suspected an employee was stealing," Jonathan replied. "She could monitor the specific *doors* the employee entered and exited, instead of which *zone* he entered and exited, as our current system is designed to do. She could also block access to specific doors, instead of blocking an entire zone, as with the current system. Because the new module was integrated with their directory and not just the directory in our system, her staff could develop applications to integrate with their HR system. When the employee was fired, for example, HR could flag his personnel record in the HR system, which would automatically disable his access badge in the security system."

"That's pretty slick," said Samuel.

"I like the way his geek glows," said Alva, getting a laugh from the room.

"The problem is, the customer did not pay for this," Jonathan said as the laughter subsided. "This is a classic case of gold plating. The new module was dangerous to the project because it made the solution more complex. It introduced a new source of security risks that would need to be mitigated. JTS would be liable if the customer's employee directory was hacked through the custom interface or if a hacker used it to gain control of the security system. The module needed extensive testing and documentation. Tasks to properly complete the module were not in the work breakdown structure. There was no budget, schedule, or resources to complete the module before the deadline."

"The enemy of efficiency is complexity," Samuel said. "And this customer was adamant about staying within their budget. In fact, we removed features during negotiations to reduce complexity and lower the price." Samuel turned to Saul. "Did you know about this new module, Saul?"

"I did," Saul replied, "But I didn't understand how complex it was until Jonathan submitted a change request to remove it from the design."

"Why did the engineer create this design?" Samuel asked Saul.

"He thought it would look cool on his résumé," said Saul.

"He was more concerned about his résumé than about following procedures?" Samuel asked.

"Where have you been?" Saul replied. "Most of our engineers think like that."

"I applaud the innovation and I don't want to discourage creativity," Samuel said. "But we have to follow our processes so the business is not put at risk. The engineer should have submitted a change request before designing the module."

"The board approved Jonathan's change request to remove the module from the design and praised him for the discovery," Alva said. "They also approved Jonathan's recommendation to include the design in future solutions."

"And no one caught this when the preliminary design was approved?" said Samuel, shaking his head back and forth. "What would it cost to fully develop the module?" he asked.

"My initial estimate is $100K," Jonathan replied.

"That would be for the engineering effort, but there are legal costs, too," Samuel replied. "We need to protect this intellectual property. Jonathan, I want you to work with the legal team to evaluate patent and trademark opportunities. Saul, you need to talk to your engineers about gold plating and about adhering to our processes."

"I'll make sure all of this is captured in the minutes and included in the final report," Alva said.

Alva adjourned the meeting. Jonathan and Alva were the last to leave.

"Samuel is impressed with you," Alva said. "As you know, I've known him a long time, and I can tell. You did a great job!"

"Thank you," said Jonathan. "I was really nervous."

"Well, no one noticed. In fact, I think Samuel has plans for you," said Alva, nodding her head slightly.

Samuel stopped Saul in the parking lot as they left for the day. "Jonathan is more articulate than I realized," Samuel said, "and he thinks strategically, not just tactically."

"I think it's time that you make good on that promotion we discussed when we hired him," said Saul, getting into his car.

"I agree," said Samuel.

Jonathan went home and found himself exhausted from a long day and an exciting new experience. This was the first time he had briefed Samuel. He felt proud of his work. He wanted to learn more about how the business worked, and he looked forward to working with the legal team. "Maybe I'll get that promotion," he thought as he fell asleep.

8.1.2 Let's Do This Another Way

Rock music rattled the multipurpose room at JTS after work, and drinks flowed freely. "Why we're celebrating a late and over-budget project is beyond me," Samuel said to Jonathan. Earlier that day, Samuel had sent Jonathan an email requesting that he stop by his office before the party. They met in Samuel's office just as the party started.

It was dress-down Friday, but Samuel was wearing a monogramed dress shirt with gold cuff-links and a red tie. He was a tall man with a large frame. His office was big and immaculate, with dark European furniture, paintings, small sculptures, and his Harvard MBA diploma hung prominently. He sat behind a grand, dark oak antique desk. When he looked out the window behind his desk, he could see his large luxury car parked in his private space.

"Saul and I have worked together since before you were born," Samuel told Jonathan. "He has never consistently met profitability targets, and his personnel turnover rate is too high. I asked him to improve his leadership performance, but he won't change." Jonathan squirmed in his seat after hearing Samuel's candid criticism about his father's performance.

"But there would be no JTS if it weren't for Saul," Samuel continued. Samuel leaned forward in his chair, put his cigar in the ashtray, picked up his glass of cognac, acknowledging to himself that his internecine battle with Saul was dangerous for the company.

"I have a small but important project for you, Jonathan," Samuel said, leaning back in his chair. Jonathan leaned forward.

"You want me to lead a project?" Jonathan asked. "Saul has led all of the projects since I've been here. I've always been behind the scenes."

"In order for you to become a senior project manager, you need to lead projects," Samuel said. "We have a contract to install a new IP surveillance system at the Kaplan Motors dealership that maintains my cars. Complete it successfully, within budget and on time, and I'll give you that promotion."

"Works for me!" Jonathan said.

"Don't get too excited," Samuel said. "We're going to do this my way, not Saul's way. We're going to develop our team members."

"What does that mean?" Jonathan asked, leaning back, brow furrowed, with his hand on his chin.

"I'm going to mentor you through the project." Samuel said. "Execution needs to start in two months, and we need to complete the initiation and planning phases during that time. We'll meet every week for the next few weeks on developing and implementing a Leadership Integration Plan."

"Leadership Integration Plan?" Jonathan asked. "I don't remember that artifact."

"Saul thought it was BS," Samuel said, looking down, shaking his head slowly. "He doesn't believe in empowerment. Classic Theory X. But we need to standardize on it. We're going to pilot the use of this plan in your project. If successful, it will become a standard artifact for the company's projects. You did an impressive job with Saul's project management plan," he continued, looking Jonathan in the eyes, "and I'm sure you'll do well with this."

"Thank you, sir," Jonathan said with a smile.

"Go enjoy the party, and be back here Monday at 8 AM," Samuel said.

8.1.3 You Are No Steve Jobs

It was Sunday evening, and Samuel's mobile phone rang. He saw that it was Saul. "What now?" he thought. "Good evening, Saul," he answered. "What's wrong now?"

"What's this I hear about you mentoring Jonathan?" Saul snorted. "What's this 'Leadership Integration Plan' nonsense? I told you that empowerment crap will never work here!"

"Saul, you have the emotional intelligence of a toad," Samuel replied.

"What's that supposed to mean?" asked Samuel.

"The Steve Jobs style of leadership may have produced some incredible products at Apple and may have made Jobs very wealthy, but you are no Steve Jobs," Saul answered. "Your way has failed too many times. We're going to do things differently." Then he hung up.

8.1.4 I Can Handle the Truth

Jonathan was excited yet nervous about the opportunity. He could hardly sleep on Sunday night before his first session with Samuel. Jonathan had led small teams, but he had never led projects.

Jonathan reported to Samuel's office at exactly 8 AM on Monday morning.

"Come on in and have a seat," Samuel said, sitting at the table in his office. As Jonathan sat down, Samuel slid a printout of a Leadership Integration Plan template over to Jonathan.

"This is the leadership framework we spoke about last week," Samuel said. "I want you to integrate it into our standard initiation and planning phase activities that you're already very familiar with."

"Looks easy enough," Jonathan said. "I see here that the plan requires that we adhere to the corporate leadership policy. What is that policy?" Jonathan asked.

"Our policy is that all project managers and team leads will lead performance of project activities in accordance with a leadership model that best fits the project," Samuel said. "The project manager will coordinate with the CEO to determine the appropriate leadership standard."

"If you don't mind me saying, sir, that sounds ambitious and complicated," Jonathan said. "Wouldn't it be better to have one leadership standard across the company? This would allow us to have a common language and would reduce training costs."

"That's one of the things I like about you, Jonathan," Samuel said. "You're not afraid to tell the truth as you see it. You've just earned a homework assignment. I want to you to research the myriad leadership models out there and come back to me next week with a recommendation. We'll develop and publish our policy based on our next conversation. I wanted Saul to work on this with me, but he's not interested. I think you and I can get this done."

"No problem, sir," Jonathan said.

8.1.5 A Not-So-Simple Requirement

Samuel sent Jonathan an email the next day instructing him talk to Joab about a technical work breakdown structure. He wanted to get a head start on developing the design, and he wanted Joab to be the architect for the Kaplan Motors (KM) project.

"Joab has been in the test lead role for a long time," Samuel said in the email. "He's ready to move into the lead architect role, and this project is small enough to allow him to safely cut his teeth. I've spoken to Joab, and he's waiting for you to contact him."

Jonathan arranged a meeting with Joab to discuss the design for the customer's solution. As he sat at the table in the conference room waiting for Joab to arrive, he heard his father's loud voice.

"Your stupidity cost me my bonus!" Saul yelled at Joab, following him down the corridor. "You're not going to get away with this! I can't believe you're still working here!"

Joab did not say a word. He simply entered the conference room, sat down with his back to Saul, and stared blankly towards Jonathan.

"What are you doing here?" Saul said, hands on his hips, looking at Jonathan with squinted eyes.

"Samuel assigned Joab the architect role on my project," Jonathan said. "We're meeting about the design."

"Then Samuel is dumber than this guy," said Saul as he stormed off.

"Did you read the Statement of Work I sent you?" asked Jonathan, eager to move things along.

"I . . . ah . . . did," said Joab slowly, voice quivering. Joab had a slim build and wore an untucked gray polo shirt and blue jeans. "It's a . . . ah . . . simple requirement. We deployed dozens of these systems, and we did a . . . ah . . . site visit a few weeks ago before we submitted the proposal, so we know the work. But there have been issues with the . . . ah . . . IPM network module. The vendor is supposed to replace it, but there's a production issue."

"Now how would *you* know that?" Jonathan asked, tilting his head to the right.

Feeling insulted, Joab delayed his response. He made a fist with both hands as they rested on the table, looked at Jonathan and said, "It's my job to know. I guess you don't trust me, either."

Joab held Jonathan's stare for a few seconds. "I have a good design template for this system," Joab said as he got up to leave. "I'll send the design document in a week."

"This is going to be harder than I thought," Jonathan said out loud to himself. "So much tension!"

8.1.6 Creating the Leadership Standard

The rest of the week disintegrated, then Monday suddenly appeared. Jonathan found himself sitting in Samuel's office for the weekly mentoring session. He had spent all weekend researching leadership models.

"Here are three leadership standards I think we should consider," said Jonathan, sliding a report across the table to Samuel. (These standards are summarized in Table 8-1.)

"Great work!" said Samuel. "I see common themes here concerning creating a vision, goal setting, communicating effectively, modeling expected behaviors,

Table 8-1 Leadership Model Summaries

Leadership Model	Summary
Exemplary Leadership Model	Consists of 5 practices: *Model the Way.* Leader is clear about own values; finds own voice and expresses it; sets personal example for others. *Inspire a Shared Vision.* Create a compelling vision that guides people's behavior; visualize and communicate positive outcomes; listen to and encourage the dreams of others. *Challenge the Process.* Leader has the courage to change the status quo; leader experiments, takes risks, and learns from them. *Enable Others to Act.* Leader builds trust with others and promotes collaboration; values teamwork and cooperation; treats others with dignity and respect; listens to diverse points of view. *Encourage the Heart.* Reward and recognize others; use authentic celebrations to show appreciation and encouragement.
Situational Leadership Model	Consists of Directive behaviors: one-way communications about who, what, how, and when to perform tasks; and Supportive behaviors: two-way communications that show social and emotional support, solving problems through collaboration and information sharing. Consists of four categories of behaviors: *Style S1, Directive.* High directive, low supportive. Leader focuses on goal achievement and less on supportive behaviors, giving instructions and supervising carefully. *Style S2, Coaching.* High directive, high supportive. Leader focuses on goal achievement and meeting socioemotional needs. Leader makes decisions but solicits subordinate support. *Style S3, Supporting.* High supportive, low directive. Leader brings out employee's skills around required tasks. Leader asks for input, listens, praises, and provides feedback. *Style S4, Delegating.* Low supportive, low directive. Leader offers less task input and social support. Leader is less involved in planning, control of details, and goal clarification. There are four levels of development, D1 through D4, representing low development through high development for particular tasks. Leaders use Style S1 for D1 employees, S2 for D2, S3 for D3, and S4 for D4, depending on the situation.

(Continued on next page)

Table 8-1 Leadership Model Summaries *(Continued)*

Leadership Model	Summary
Team Leadership Model	Model provides the leader a mental road map that assists in diagnosing problems and taking the appropriate actions:
	Leadership decisions: Monitor situation or take action, task or relational response, internal or external leadership actions.
	For Internal Task requirements, leaders focus on goals by clarifying, getting agreement, performing process improvement, guiding the decision-making process, and providing training.
	For Internal Relationship requirements, leaders coach team members, collaborate with team members, manage conflict, build commitment and *esprit de corps*, model expected behavior.
	For External Environmental requirements, leaders network to increase influence and gather information, advocate to represent the team, provide recognition, and share information.
	Satisfying above requirements results in high performance through development and maintenance functions.

Data derived from Northouse, P. (2007). *Leadership Theory and Practice*. London: Sage.

and providing encouragement and support for team members. I did a little homework myself. Take a look at this *Harvard Business Review* article." Samuel gave Jonathan a copy of "How Google Sold Its Engineers on Management," which is summarized in Table 8-2.

"This article seems consistent with what I found," said Jonathan. "Google runs on analytics, and they have the data to back up their findings."

"OK, this works," Samuel said. "I want to you write up a draft JTS leadership policy based on the Exemplary Leadership Model, which is really a Transformational Leadership Model. This fits because we're trying to transform our leadership culture, and we'll do this through visioning, role modeling, and empowering. It's not going to be easy, but it is necessary."

8.1.7 Creating a Schedule

"Got it," said Jonathan. "Did you get the draft schedule for the initiation and planning phases that I sent last week?" (The schedule is provided in Table 8-3.)

"Yes, I did," said Samuel. "I think we're in good shape. You included leadership policy and standard development in the Initiation and Setup phases and

Table 8-2 Google's Characteristics of a Good Manager

#	Characteristic	Key Qualitative Question
1	Good coach	Does the project leader effectively coach his or her team members in a manner that improves performance?
2	Empowers team members	Does the project leader empower his or her team and avoid being a micromanager?
3	Expresses concern	Does the project leader express interest in and concern for team members' success and personal well-being?
4	Gets results	Is the project leader productive and results oriented?
5	Good communicator	Is the project leader a good communicator who listens and shares information?
6	Develops team members	Does the project leader help team members with career development?
7	Establishes a clear vision	Does the project leader have a clear vision and strategy for the team?
8	Technically skilled	Does the project leader have key technical skills that help him or her advise the team?

Data derived from Garvin, D. (2013). How Google Sold Its Engineers on Management. *Harvard Business Review* (December).

fully developed the plan in the Planning phase. Good. Also, make sure you include standard weekly meetings beginning in execution and running through closeout. You need to establish a consistent 'battle rhythm' for communications. Saul didn't keep his meetings, and that cost him on his last project."

"Got it," said Jonathan.

8.1.8 Are You Practicing What You Preach?

"Now you need to practice what you're preaching about leadership."

"Sir?" said Jonathan.

"Think about the experience you and Saul had with Joab last week," Samuel continued, looking Jonathan in the eye.

"You heard about that, huh?" Jonathan said, leaning back and exhaling.

"Saul has never been concerned about Joab's personal development," Samuel said. "He never did anything but berate him in front of others. He blamed Joab

Table 8-3 Initiation and Planning Schedule

ID	Task Name	Duration	Start	Finish	Predecessors
1	**Kaplan Motors Dealership IP Surveillance—Initiation and Planning**	**39 days**	**2/1**	**3/24**	
2	**Pre-Project Setup/Initiating**	**14 days**	**2/1**	**2/18**	
3	Identify and validate project and organizational structure	1 day	2/1	2/1	
4	**Validate project business case**	**3 days**	**2/2**	**2/4**	**3**
5	Review Statement of Work	2 days	2/2	2/3	
6	Develop draft Statement of Success	1 day	2/4	2/4	5
7	**Identify and analyze stakeholders**	**6 days**	**2/5**	**2/12**	
8	Initial coordination with internal legal, contracting, accounting, and HR	3 days	2/5	2/9	6
9	Initial coordination with customers, vendors, suppliers	3 days	2/10	2/12	8
10	**Define project charter components (deliverables, cost, approach, assumptions and constraints, risks, objectives)**	**3 days**	**2/15**	**2/17**	**7**
11	Define project and product/service life cycle	1 day	2/15	2/15	
12	**Define leadership standards**	**2 days**	**2/16**	**2/17**	
13	Leadership Policy	1 day	2/16	2/16	11
14	Leadership Standard	1 day	2/17	2/17	13
15	Project Governance Review	1 day	2/18	2/18	10
16	**Project Charter Approval**	**0 days**	**2/18**	**2/18**	**15**

ID	Task Name	Duration	Start	Finish	Predecessors
17	**Develop Project Management Plan**	**25 days**	**2/19**	**3/24**	
18	Prepare scope document, Work Breakdown Structure, schedule, and resource requirements	3 days	2/19	2/23	16
19	Define change management process and plan	2 days	2/24	2/25	18
20	Develop communications plan	2 days	2/26	2/29	19
21	Develop risk management plan: (initial risk assessment, risk matrix, risk register, and stakeholder risk tolerance)	3 days	3/1	3/3	20
22	Develop quality, cost, procurement, staffing management, and transition plans	5 days	3/4	3/10	21
23	**Complete Leadership Integration Plan**	**9 days**	**3/11**	**3/23**	
24	Team Charter	2 days	3/11	3/14	12,22
25	Leadership Training	3 days	3/15	3/17	24
26	Leadership Assessments	2 days	3/18	3/21	25
27	Leadership Lessons Learned Planning	1 day	3/22	3/22	26
28	Leadership Performance Improvement Planning	1 day	3/23	3/23	27
29	Project Governance Review	1 day	3/24	3/24	23
30	**Project Plan Approval**	**0 days**	**3/24**	**3/24**	29

for the issues that caused the last project to slip, and he never took any responsibility himself. Saul led the project; he had overall responsibility for the outcome, yet he blamed Joab and the customer. Saul could have taken proactive action to prevent the problem. He could have provided better project oversight, communications, and control. But instead, he threw Joab under the bus. Behavior like this builds resentment, and employees get their vengeance by leaving the company. And then you reinforced Saul's poor leadership when you didn't trust Joab's advice about the IPM network module."

Jonathan looked down at the floor, thinking more about the knot in his stomach than about how to respond.

"How do you feel?" asked Samuel.

"I feel horrible that I treated Joab the way I did," Jonathan said. "I assumed, based on Saul's attitude, that Joab was a loser. I didn't even give him a chance. We're obviously not following best practices for leadership. What if Joab leaves? How will that impact our business? I've never had to deal with these issues. The stakes are high for the business."

"I share your concerns," said Samuel. "We have to shift our focus. We have to be more collaborative and empowering. We have to take care of our people, both personally and professionally."

"How do I approach this?" Jonathan asked. "All of this is new to me."

"Everyone either has been through something, is going through something, or is about to go through something," Samuel said. "You have to talk to your people, have a dialogue where you ask questions and listen to find out what that something is. Once you know their story, you can help them. This will help us develop a culture where we authentically treat our employees as well as we treat our customers."

"I don't feel comfortable talking to Joab about these issues," Jonathan said. "I just want him to do the job. I'm not good at helping people with their issues."

"But if you were able to help people, you could not only lead projects to successful outcomes, you could also inspire team members like Joab," Samuel said. "You can give them encouragement that builds confidence, confidence that can help them be successful long after your project is over."

Jonathan sat silently, looking down at the table.

"You see, your mind is like fertile soil that will grow whatever you plant," Samuel continued. "The same soil that can grow delicious blueberries can also grow poisonous baneberries. You will reap the self-talk that you sow. You are responsible for planting positive thoughts in your own mind, thoughts that can result in positive outcomes. If you believe you're not able to help people with their issues, you're planting poisonous thoughts, and you'll never help anyone. If you keep thinking like that, you won't reach your leadership potential."

"What should I do?" asked Jonathan. "What do you recommend?"

"Change your self-talk," Samuel said. "Instead of saying 'I don't know how to help people with their issues,' say 'I care enough about my team members to listen to their feelings and to have a dialogue about their concerns.' Say this to yourself in the morning and at night, every day; tweak your attitude so that you feel comfortable with this simple change in your point of view. If you *believe* you can make this change, you *can* make it. People in the company look up to you. I think it's a small but worthy investment you can make in yourself."

"OK," Jonathan said. "I'm willing to try."

"That's the first step to becoming a leader instead of being just a manager," Samuel said. "I want you to have a conversation with Joab. Find out what he's going through right now. Figure out how to motivate him. Also, I'm going to send you material to read on Myers-Briggs Type Indicators, emotionally intelligent communications, personal credibility, self-leadership, and followership. You may not understand it all right away, but you need to start the journey."

8.1.9 Anxious and Uncomfortable, but Not Alone

After meeting with Samuel, Jonathan's day seemed to drag on like a flatbed trailer with a flat tire. He felt like going dark. He did not feel like talking to anyone who sat near him, and he barely answered email. The voicemail indicator on his phone was a solid red. All he could think about was his conversation with Samuel. Could Samuel be so right and Saul, his father, be so wrong?

Lunch hour came, and instead of eating or going to the gym, Jonathan went for a walk in the park near the JTS office. It was a cloudy fall day, but it was warm enough to be outside. As he neared an empty bench, he felt his phone vibrate. He checked the indicator, and it was an email from Daniel at Torch Systems, his former boss. It read, "Jonathan, we won a new contract to deploy an identity management system for the county government, and we want you to come back and lead the project. Give me a call!"

Reading the message made Jonathan's heart beat a little faster. He had to sit down on the bench. As he sat, he stared in the direction of people walking through the park, but he did not see them. He took deep, calming breaths, and sank into his thoughts.

"I could go back to Torch Systems, and Joab would be someone else's problem," he thought. Then he had a realization. *"The Torch Systems job requires leadership, too. Instead of having to deal with Joab, I may have to deal with an even more difficult situation."* He pondered a bit more. *"Others are thinking of me as a leader,"* Jonathan thought, *"But am I ready? I'm not comfortable dealing with other people's problems."*

Jonathan sat for a few more minutes, and then realized he needed to go back to work. He stopped at a convenience store and picked up a sandwich and a drink, eating and thinking as he walked back to JTS.

After arriving at his desk, Jonathan logged in and checked his email. He had received a message from Samuel with the reading material he promised. "I highly recommend that you read the self-leadership material first," Samuel wrote in the message. Jonathan spent the rest of the day reading that material. Right before he went home for the day, he finally checked his voicemail. It was not urgent; just a vendor trying to schedule a meeting. Jonathan got up from his desk to leave for the day, feeling relieved that he had not missed an important call.

It was about 6 PM, and the sun was setting as Jonathan left the parking lot. He turned off the radio so that he could hear himself think as he drove to his apartment. His car used to be his mother's. After she and Saul divorced five years prior, she gave it to Jonathan and then took an assignment in Germany. Since she'd left, he video chatted with her about once a month. *"I used to hate it when those two fought,"* Jonathan thought while waiting at a stop light. As he entered the highway, he remembered the last Thanksgiving when they were all together. In his mind's eye, he could see Saul following her down the hall; he could hear Saul screaming at her about one thing or another. *"He screamed at Joab the same way,"* he thought.

The rain started as Jonathan arrived at his apartment complex. He parked his car and went upstairs. Once inside his apartment, he decided to cook himself a stir fry dinner. He did not turn on the television as he usually did. The only light he turned on was the one over the stove. As he prepared his meal, his mobile phone buzzed, and Chrissy's picture appeared on the device. Chrissy was his girlfriend. He cared for her deeply, yet did not feel like talking to her, so he let her call go to voicemail.

As Jonathan sat down to eat, he thought about his mother again. Light from the stove, still the only light on in the apartment, streamed over the breakfast bar onto the dining room table where he ate. *"Maybe I should call her and ask her what to do,"* he thought. His mind flashed to a memory of the last time he was with his mother. It was at the airport before her flight to Germany. *"Be a better man than your father,"* she had said.

All of a sudden, Jonathan felt guilty about not taking Chrissy's call. He called her and apologized for not answering. "I have a lot on my mind and I need to think," he said. "Everything is fine, but can we talk tomorrow?" Chrissy was concerned, but she said she understood, and they hung up.

"Be a better man than your father." Jonathan thought of his father as smart and successful. He considered him to be strong. But he understood what his mother said that day now more than ever. *"I love my dad,"* Jonathan thought,

"*but Samuel was right. Dad lost control of that project and he did not take respon-sibility for everything that happened.*"

Jonathan finished his dinner, went into the kitchen, and started washing the dishes. He enjoyed washing dishes; he found the task to be therapeutic. "*When I'm older, I'd rather be more like Samuel than like Saul,*" Jonathan admitted to himself. He thought about all of the conversations he had had with Samuel and the information Samuel had sent him.

After finishing the dishes, Jonathan sat down at his dining room table and opened up his laptop. He was about to connect with his mother on video chat, but he changed his mind. "*I can handle this myself,*" he thought.

Then he reviewed the information Samuel had sent him. "*A good manager effectively coaches his team, empowers his team members, and expresses concern for their personal well-being,*" Jonathan read. "*That is certainly not Saul, but that's Mom. And it's Samuel, too.*"

Jonathan then reviewed the self-leadership material Samuel had sent him earlier in the day. "*I keep telling myself that I'm not good at helping people with their issues,*" Jonathan thought. "*But that's part of leadership. Every leader, from Little League coaches to elected officials, are responsible for taking care of people. Samuel is taking care of me. No other leader in my career has taken the time to help me understand leadership like Samuel has.*"

"*I can do this,*" Jonathan thought. "*I'm anxious and uncomfortable, but I'm not alone. Samuel is helping me. I can do this.*"

Jonathan scrolled through the self-leadership document. "*How do I change my negative self-talk?*" he thought. "*Ah, here it is. 'Instead of saying the negative phrase, replace it. Think your best and not your worst. Rewrite and reframe. Choose a positive thought to record in your brain.' So 'I'm not comfortable helping people with their issues' becomes . . .*" His mind raced as he searched for a positive self-talk phrase to replace his negative thought.

After a few minutes, he wrote this positive affirmation on a sticky note: "*I'm a problem solver. I'm a good listener and everyone respects my point of view.*" He went into the bathroom and taped the note to the mirror so that he would be reminded of the new attitude he was forming every night and every morning.

Jonathan went into his living room and turned on his television and his game console. "*Just what I need to take my mind off everything,*" he thought as he put on his headset. A few of his friends were online and he joined them in a game for a few hours, and then he prepared for bed. As he brushed his teeth, he read his note—"*I'm a problem solver. I'm a good listener and everyone respects my point of view*"—and he thought about this as he got into bed. The sound of rain on the roof of the building and on his windows was like a lullaby, and Jonathan drifted off to sleep.

The next morning, Jonathan woke up and looked out of the window. The rain had passed and the sun was coming up. He took a shower, got dressed for work, and went to the sink to brush his teeth. There was that note again, reminding him of his new attitude: *"I'm a problem solver. I'm a good listener and everyone respects my point of view."*

Jonathan went downstairs and got into his car to drive to work. *"I'm going to get promoted at JTS and I'm going to buy a new car,"* he thought. *"And I'm going to start saving for house."* Before he started the car, he picked up his smart phone and replied to the email he'd received from Daniel at Torch Systems. *"Thanks for thinking of me, Daniel,"* he wrote, *"but I'm fine where I am. Good luck with the new project!"* Then he called Chrissy and made a dinner date for Friday night.

Morning and night, Jonathan read his affirmation, *"I'm a problem solver. I'm a good listener and everyone respects my point of view."* He thought about it during the day, and found himself analyzing his own thoughts when he interacted with people. He found himself being more attentive to people around him who were having issues. He did not intervene, but he imagined how he would and he felt he could make a positive difference for some of the situations he observed.

8.1.10 Leadership in Action

A week later, Jonathan and Joab met in the small conference room to discuss the design document.

"How are you today?" Jonathan asked with a smile.

"I'm . . . ah . . . OK," Joab responded.

"The design document you sent me looks great," Jonathan said. "And you were right about the IPM network module. We received an email from the vendor explaining how they will rectify this problem."

"Thanks," said Joab with a slight smile. "I'm friends with one of the vendor engineers, and he told me what's going on."

"If you don't mind me asking," Jonathan said, "what happened on Saul's project? Why does he blame you for the testing schedule slippage? You seem to be on top of your game, and I'm looking forward to working with you, but I need to make sure we avoid problems like that on this project."

"I tried to tell Saul about the schedule risk," Joab said. "I notified him about the risk, expecting him to update the risk register per our policy, but he said I was responsible for coordinating with the customer to convince them to open the facility on the day we scheduled for testing. The customer had another event scheduled for that week, so I escalated the issue to Saul to resolve. I want to be a team player, but they were not going to listen to me—they needed to hear from him."

"I see," Jonathan said, nodding in agreement.

"There is . . . ah . . . something else, too," Joab said. "Ever since the day Saul saw me leaving my place of worship, he's treated me differently. I think he does not like me because I'm . . ."

"It doesn't matter what religion you are," Jonathan said, cutting him off. "Or your race, gender, or who you love. Everyone deserves to be treated with dignity and respect. I've learned a lot from Samuel over the past few weeks, and one of the things I've learned is that we have to be tolerant of one another. We can't expect you to be productive if you're feeling disrespected. The way Saul treated you was wrong, and I'm sorry for misjudging you. I'm sorry for letting how he treated you influence my behavior."

"Thank you," Joab said. "You're not like your father. He never asked me how I felt. He certainly never apologized. He just yells. Samuel is the only one around here who listens."

"You can talk to me, too." Jonathan said. "And I have a feeling that Samuel will deal with Saul."

8.1.11 A Leadership Opportunity

Joab joined Jonathan and Samuel at the next mentoring session. "I asked Joab to join us this morning to talk about the way forward," Samuel said. "The PMO approved the project charter out of cycle, but I want you two to brief the project management plan and the design at the Steering Committee meeting."

"Saul usually briefs both of those," said Jonathan.

"It's another process improvement," Samuel said, "and it's a leadership opportunity for both of you."

"Saul will be there," Joab said. "And the PMO is going to, ah, eat us alive."

"No they won't," Jonathan said with confidence. "I know those guys. We have time, and we'll be ready."

"I love it," Samuel said. "I want you guys wearing suits for your presentation. And make sure you both attend the leadership training HR emailed you about before execution starts."

8.1.12 Stay Out of the Way

Two weeks later, Joab and Jonathan attended the Steering Committee meeting to brief their project.

"What's this?" Alva asked, looking at Jonathan's and Joab's suits. "You guys look great!"

"What's Joab doing here?" asked Saul.

"Don't you worry about it," said Samuel. "Come out in the hallway with me. I need to talk to you."

"What's this all about?" Saul said, standing outside the conference room.

"Saul, I appreciate everything you've done for JTS," Samuel said, looking at the floor. "All the sacrifice, the late hours. You made the company a lot of money."

Samuel looked up at Saul and continued. "But we need to change our leadership culture to be successful in the long term. We can't keep losing good people and barely breaking even. You're not going to drive Joab away, and you're not going to diminish Jonathan's potential."

"What do *you* know about Jonathan?" Saul said. "He's MY son!"

"Then be a better example, Saul! You're sidelined when it comes to Jonathan's KM project," Samuel said, pointing his finger at Saul. "Stay out of the way."

Samuel turned and walked into the conference room. Saul frowned, but followed him.

Samuel walked to the head of the conference table and addressed the group. "One of my favorite proverbs is, 'Like the horizons for breadth and the ocean for depth, the understanding of a good leader is broad and deep,'" he said. "Project managers and leaders bring their full human experiences to their craft. We manage processes and activities, but we lead people. This requires connecting with people's hearts so that they choose to follow us. An IT project leader needs a broad, and sometimes deep, understanding of technology, management, psychology, and communications to connect with and positively influence people from diverse backgrounds, people who are team members and stakeholders.

"Gaining this understanding is not easy, but it is possible. It is a breadth and depth of understanding we gain over time through experience and continuous learning, expressed and demonstrated through our writing, speaking, and the example we set by how we behave and how we treat others. At JTS, we will learn to develop and support our employees, especially those with leadership potential. We will learn to treat our employees as well as we treat our customers. Those who lead the company to success will enjoy recognition and prosperity.

"Today, Jonathan and Joab will brief you on their project for the first time, taking an important step on their IT leadership journeys. I expect you to give them your full support, to help them improve and be successful, and to give them the same respect that you give me. Does anyone object to anything I've said?"

Applause erupted like a volcano, and Saul sat silent and red-faced.

8.1.13 The Final Deliverable

As discussed in Chapter 2, Erika Andersen wrote for Forbes.com, "Most folks who start out with a modicum of innate leadership capability can actually become very good, even great leaders" (Andersen, 2012b). Samuel recognized innate leadership abilities in Jonathan, including his ability to think strategically and his mastery of project management methodologies. Although Jonathan was technical, a geek at heart, Samuel recognized that he had the courage to speak up when necessary. Samuel loved JTS and wanted the future of the company to rest in the hands of people like Jonathan, not people like Saul. Samuel demonstrated his commitment to his vision for JTS by investing the time to mentor Jonathan.

Following the Leadership Integration Plan, Samuel performed leadership assessments as part of the health checks and milestone reviews for the Kaplan Motors project. This enabled him to continue mentoring Jonathan throughout the execution, controlling, and closeout phases of the project. Samuel provided his assessments to Alva and worked with her to make the Leadership Integration Plan a standard JTS project management artifact. The assessments ensured that Jonathan had established a dialogue with the team members assigned to the team as the project progressed—a dialogue that resulted in an improved flow of information between the team and Jonathan, enabling Jonathan and the Steering Committee to make timelier and higher-quality decisions.

As Jonathan encountered new challenges, he found himself creating new daily affirmations, using self-talk to help him focus and to propel himself to take the actions needed to correct course. Jonathan was an analytical person, an introvert. He had to expend significant energy to perform all of the communications required to be a successful leader. It would have been easy for him to revert to his normal, reticent pattern. But Jonathan utilized his affirmations and the feedback from the leadership assessments to stay focused on the leadership requirements for his position.

The Kaplan Motors project finished on time and within budget. Both the customer and the Steering Committee were happy with the results. Did Jonathan get the promotion? Yes, and he bought that new car, too. He satisfied his external motivations. However, his real fulfillment came from the satisfaction of an internal motivation, a motivation he did not know he had. Jonathan was motivated by the positive experience of helping team members such as Joab contribute to JTS in new and significant ways. Within the context of Maslow's Hierarchy of Needs, Jonathan self-actualized when he developed a leadership mindset, when he helped others improve their self-esteem.

Saul was happy for his son, Jonathan, although Saul fought the leadership assessments for his own projects like a barbarian. When Jonathan video chatted with his mother and told her about it all, she was neither surprised at Saul's stubbornness nor at Jonathan's success. Most of all, she was proud that her son had become a better man than his father.

References

"A Commentary of Wiio's Laws of Communication." (2015, January 15). Tampere University of Technology. Retrieved on February 15, 2015, from http://www.cs.tut. fi/~jkorpela/wiio.html

Academy of Achievement (2010, March 17). "Interview: Bill Gates." Achievement.org. Retrieved December 6, 2014, from http://www.achievement.org/autodoc/print member/gat0int1

ACM and IEEE. (2013, December 20). *Computer Science Curricula 2013*. Retrieved April 13, 2015, from https://www.acm.org/education/CS2013-final-report.pdf

Allen, T. (2014). *Common Sense Service*. Success Solutions.

Allgeier, S. (2009). *The Personal Credibility Factor*. Upper Saddle River, NJ: FT Press.

American Academy of Project Management (AAPM). (2006). *Master Project Manager, Certified International Project Manager, and Project Manager E-Business AAPM Handbook and Study Guide*. Retrieved September 25, 2015, from http://www.theiafm. org/publications/1_project_management_handbook.pdf

Andersen, E. (2012a). *Leading So People Will Follow*. Hoboken, NJ: Jossey-Bass/John Wiley & Sons.

Andersen, E. (2012b). "Are Leaders Born or Made?" Forbes.com. Retrieved December 5, 2014, from http://www.forbes.com/sites/erikaandersen/2012/11/21/are-leaders-born-or-made/#7e0cec682ba2

Andrews, P. and Manes, S. (2013). *Gates: How Microsoft's Mogul Reinvented an Industry and Made Himself the Richest Man in America*, 20th Anniversary Ed. Seattle, WA: Cadwallader & Stern.

Aristotle, A. (2012). *Success and Happiness—Quotes to Motivate, Inspire, and Live By* [Kindle Version]. Retrieved from http://www.amazon.com

Assumptions. (n.d.) Psychologydictionary.org. Retrieved February 7, 2015, from http://psychologydictionary.org/assumption/

Baile, W. F., Buckman, R., Lenzi, R., Glober, G., Beale, E. A., and Kudelka, A. P. (2000). "SPIKES—A Six-Step Protocol for Delivering Bad News: Application to the Patient with Cancer." *The Oncologist,* 5(4): 302–311. Accessed from http://theoncologist.alphamedpress.org/content/5/4/302.full

Belief. (n.d.) Psychologydictionary.org. Retrieved February 7, 2015, from http://psychologydictionary.org/belief-system/

Bennis, W. (1997). "The Secrets of Great Groups." *Leader to Leader,* vol. 3(4).

Berman, S. (2001). *Words, Meaning, and People.* Concord, CA: International Society for General Semantics. (Original work published 1982.)

Biech, E. (2008). *The Pfeiffer Book of Successful Team-Building.* San Francisco, CA: Pfeiffer.

Bixler, S. (1992). *Professional Presence.* New York, NY: Perigee Books.

Bradberry, T. and Greaves, J. (2012). *Leadership 2.0.* San Diego, CA: TalentSmart.

Carnegie, D. (2010). *How to Win Friends and Influence People.* New York, NY: Simon & Schuster. (Original work published 1937.)

Cha, A. and Sun, L. (2013, October 24). "What Went Wrong with HeathCare.gov." Washingtonpost.com. Retrieved December 21, 2014, from http://www.washingtonpost.com/national/health-science/what-went-wrong-with-healthcaregov/2013/10/24/400e68de-3d07-11e3-b7ba-503fb5822c3e_graphic.html

Chaleff, I. (2009). *The Courageous Follower.* San Francisco, CA: Berrett-Koehler.

Chandomba, L. (2014). *Secrets of Success from the Story of Bill Gates.* London, UK: Raising Champions.

Chopra, D. and Tanzi, R. (2012). *Super Brain.* New York, NY: Random House Publishing.

Clarke (2014). "Australian IT Project Failures Spark New ICT Governance Standard." Theage.com.au. Retrieved May 17, 2014, from http://www.theage.com.au/it-pro/business-it/australian-it-project-failures-spark-new-ict-governance-standard-20140112-hv88k.html

Collins, J. (2013). *Creative Followership.* Decatur, GA: Looking Glass Books, Inc.

Conclusions. (n.d.) Psychologydictionary.org. Retrieved February 7, 2015, from http://psychologydictionary.org/conclusion/

Covey, S. (1989). *The 7 Habits of Highly Effective People.* New York, NY: Fireside.

Defense Mechanisms. (n.d.). Psychologydictionary.org. Retrieved February 7, 2015, from http://psychologydictionary.org/defense-mechanism/

Department of Professional Employees (DPE), AFL-CIO. (2014, November). "The Professional Computer Workforce." Retrieved April 13, 2015, from http://dpeaflcio.org/professionals/professionals-in-the-workplace/the-professional-computer-work-force/

Doyle, T. and Zakrajsek, T. (2013). *The New Science of Learning.* Sterling, VA: Stylus Publishing.

Ellis, A. and Harper, R. (1997). *A Guide to Rational Living.* Chatsworth, CA: Melvin Powers Wilshire Book Company.

Expectations. (n.d.). Psychologydictionary.org. Retrieved February 7, 2015, from http://psychologydictionary.org/expectation/

Faraj, S. and Sambamurthy, V. (2006). Leadership of Information Systems Development Projects. *IEEE Transactions on Engineering Management*, 53(2), 238–249.

Fingas, J. (2015). "US Will Pay over $133 Million to Protect OPM Data Breach Victims." Retrieved September 26, 2015, from http://www.engadget.com/2015/09/02/opm-data-breach-identity-theft-protection/

Fitzpatrick, B. and Collins-Sussman, B. (2012). *Team Geek.* Sebastopol, CA: O'Reilly Media.

Fogel, S. (2014). *Your Mind Is What Your Brain Does for a Living.* Austin, TX: Greenleaf Book Group Press.

Furnham, A. (2014). "The Curse of Perfectionism." Psychologytoday.com. Retrieved October 24, 2015, from https://www.psychologytoday.com/blog/sideways-view/201402/the-curse-perfectionism

GAO (2015). "High-Risk Series: An Update." Government Accounting Office. Retrieved 2/16/2015, from http://www.gao.gov/assets/670/668415.pdf

Garvin D. (2013). "How Google Sold Its Engineers on Management." *Harvard Business Review* (December). Retrieved October 1, 2015, from https://hbr.org/2013/12/how-google-sold-its-engineers-on-management

Gelles, D. (2015). *Mindful Work.* Boston, MA: Houghton Mifflin Harcourt.

Goatham, R. (2009). "The Story Behind the High Failure Rates in the IT Sector." Calleam.com. Retrieved December 21, 2014, from http://calleam.com/WTPF/wp-content/uploads/articles/Whatmakes.pdf

Goldsmith (2014). "BBC faces damning criticism over failed $170 mln digital project." news trust.org. Retrieved May 17, 2014, from http://news.trust.org//item/20140128160405-1h4zj?view=print

Heldman, K. and Heldman, W. (2010). *CompTIA Project+ Study Guide.* Indianapolis, IN: Wiley Publishing.

Helmstetter, S. (1982). *What to Say When You Talk to Yourself.* New York, NY: Pocket Books.

Helmstetter, S. (2013). *The Power of Neuroplasticity.* Gulf Breeze, FL: Park Avenue Press. [Kindle Version]. Retrieved from http://www.amazon.com

Hewertson, R. (2015). *Lead Like It Matters . . . Because it Does.* New York, NY: McGraw Hill.

Institute for Management Excellence. (2003, July). "Differences between 'Computer' Folks and the General Population." Institute for Management Excellence. Retrieved October 11, 2014, from http://www.itstime.com/print/jul2003p.htm

(ISC)². (2010). "Code of Ethics." The International Information Systems Security Certification Consortium. Retrieved May 9, 2015, from https://www.isc2.org /uploadedfiles/%28isc%292_public_content/code_of_ethics/isc2-code-of-ethics.pdf

ISixSigma.com. (n.d.). "Deming Cycle, PDCA." Retrieved May 2, 2015, from http:// www.isixsigma.com/ dictionary/deming-cycle-pdca/

Jensen, M. and Tuckman, B. (1977). "Stages of Small-Group Development, Revised." Retrieved June 9, 2015, from http://www.freewebs.com/group-management/Bruce Tuckman(1).pdf

Kehoe, D. (2011). *Effective Communication Skills.* Chantilly, VA: The Great Courses.

Kellerman, B. (2008). *Followership: How Followers Are Creating Change and Changing Leaders.* Boston, MA: Harvard Business Press.

Kouzes, J. M. and Posner, B. Z. (2010). *The Five Practices of Exemplary Leadership* (Vol. 237). Hoboken, NJ: John Wiley & Sons.

Krigsman, M. (2012, April 10). "Worldwide Cost of IT Failure (Revisited): $3 Trillion." ZDNet.com. Retrieved October 11, 2014, from http://www.zdnet.com/blog/project failures/worldwide-cost-of-it-failure-revisited-3-trillion/15424

Kroeger, O., Thuesen, J., and Rutledge, H. (2002). *Type Talk at Work.* New York, NY: Dell.

Kunas, M. (2013). *Implementing Service Quality Based on ISO/IEC 20000.* 3rd ed. updated. Ashland, OH: ITGP.

Leadership (n.d.). businessdictionary.com. Retrieved December 5, 2014, from http:// www.businessdictionary.com/definition/leadership.html

Levin, G. and Green, A. (2014). *Implementing Program Management.* [Kindle Version]. Retrieved from http://www.amazon.com

Lorange, P. (1980). *Corporate Planning.* Upper Saddle River, NJ: Prentice Hall.

Lounsbury, J., Studham, R., Steel, R., Gibson, L., and Drost, A. (n.d.). "Personality Traits and Career Satisfaction of Information Technology Professionals." eCareerFit .com. Retrieved October 11, 2014, from http://info.ecareerfit.com/eCareerFit/IT%20 Personality%20Traits%20%20Career%20Satisfaction.pdf

Maley, J. and Varner, B. (1994). *Leadership: The Leader and the Group.* Maxwell AFB, AL: Air University Press.

Marter, J. (2013, December 28). "10 Tips for Resolving Conflict." Retrieved June 12, 2015, from http://m.huffpost.com/us/entry/4504510

Maslow, A. (2012a). *A Theory of Human Motivation.* [Kindle Version]. Retrieved from http://www.amazon.com

Maslow, A. (2012b). *Toward a Psychology of Being.* [Kindle Version]. Retrieved from http:// www.amazon.com

Mayer, J. (2014, April 1). "Five Advances in How Psychologists View Personality." Retrieved April 25, 2015, from https://www.psychologytoday.com/blog/the-personality -analyst/201404/five-advances-in-how-psychologists-view-personality

McGregor, D. (1960). *The Human Side of Enterprise.* New York, NY: McGraw Hill.

Merrill, D. and Reid, R. (1981). *Personal Styles & Effective Performance.* Radnor, PA: Chilton Book Company.

Meyers, D. (2007). *Psychology.* New York, NY: Worth Publishers.

Micro Manager. (n.d.). *Investopedia.* Retrieved June 23, 2015, from http://www.investo pedia.com/terms/m/micro-manager.asp#ixzz3dpn2fsZy

Moss, S. (2011, October 2). "Somatic Marker Hypothesis." Psych-it.com. Retrieved May 5, 2015, from http://www.psych-it.com.au/Psychlopedia/article.asp?id=408

Mulqueen, C. (n.d.). "Comparing SOCIAL STYLE® and Myers Briggs." Retrieved July 28, 2015, from http://www.tracomcorp.com/wp-content/uploads/2014/01/SocialStyle -Whitepaper-ComparingSocialStyleandMyersBriggs.pdf

Neile, C. (2015). "Telling Tales at the Office." *Toastmaster Magazine,* (Feb), 26–27.

Newcombe, T. (2014, January 13). "Can Government Avoid Technology Failure?" *Governing the States and Localities.* Retrieved May 17, 2014, from http://www. governing.com/topics/mgmt/gov-can-government-avoid-tech-failure.html

Northouse, P. (2007). *Leadership: Theory and Practice.* London, UK: Sage.

Ogrysko, N. (2015). "OPM IT Infrastructure Plan Still 'High Risk,' IG says." Retrieved September 15, 2015, from http://federalnewsradio.com/opm-cyber-breach/2015/09 /opm-infrastructure-plan-still-high-risk-ig-says/

Olsen, O. (2014, September 14). "Oliver Olsen: Why IT Projects Fail." VTDigger.org. Retrieved September 27, 2014, from http://vtdigger.org/2014/09/23/oliver-olsen -projects-fail/

Paciullo, C. (2015). "Business and Technology: A Love-Hate Relationship." Retrieved September 26, 2015, from http://www.neowin.net/news/business-and-technology-a -love-hate-relationship

Perception. (n.d.) psychologydictionary.org. Retrieved February 7, 2015, from http:// psychologydictionary.org/perception

Porter, L. and Steers, R. (1974). "Role of Task-Goal Attributes in Employee Performance." Retrieved June 16, 2015, from http://files.eric.ed.gov/fulltext/ED094116.pdf

Project Management Institute. (2013a). *A Guide to the Project Management Body of Knowledge (PMBOK® Guide),* 5th ed. Newton Square, PA: Project Management Institute.

Project Management Institute. (2013b). *The Standard for Program Management,* 3rd ed. Newton Square, PA: Project Management Institute.

Project Management Institute. (2000). *Project Management Professional (PMP®) Role Delineation Study.* Newton Square, PA: Project Management Institute.

Rajkumar, S. and KP. (2010). "Art of Communication in Project Management." Project Management Institute. Retrieved from http://www.pmi.org/learning/effective communicationbetter-projectmanagement-6480

"Rational™ Portrait of the Mastermind." (n.d.). Keirsey.com. Retrieved December 13, 2014, from http://www.keirsey.com/4temps/mastermind.asp

Reynolds, M. (2012). "What to Do When Someone Doesn't Like You." *Pschologytoday.com*. Retrieved October 24, 2012, from https://www.psychologytoday.com/blog/wander-woman/201209/what-do-when-someone-doesn-t-you

Riggio, R. E. (2009). "How to Spot a Bad Leader." *Psychologytoday.com*. Retrieved October 24, 2015, from https://www.psychologytoday.com/blog/cutting-edge-leadership/200905/how-spot-bad-leader

Schwalbe, K. (2000). *Information Technology Project Management*. Cambridge, MA: Course Technology.

Self-Image. (n.d.) psychologydictionary.org. Retrieved February 7, 2015, from http://psychologydictionary.org/self-image/

Shriver, M. (2014, May 28). "People Will Never Forget How You Made Them Feel—12 Inspiring Quotes from Maya Angelou." Retrieved February 15, 2015, from http://mariashriver.com/blog/2014/05/maya-angelou-died-people-will-never-forget-how-you-made-them-feel-inspiring-quotes-maria-shriver/

Smith, B. (2014, August 27). "CIOs Share Their Secrets to Project Success." Retrieved from http://www.cio.com/article/2465671/project-management/cios-share-their-secrets-to-project-success.html

Solomon, R. (2006). *Passions: Philosophy and the Intelligence of Emotions*. Chantilly, VA: The Great Courses.

Swenson, R. (2006). "Review of Clinical and Functional Neuroscience." Dartmouth Medical School. Retrieved January 24, 2015, from http://www.dartmouth.edu/~rswenson/NeuroSci/chapter_11.html

"The Big Five Personality Test" (n.d.). Outofservice.com. Retrieved December 4, 2014, from http://www.outofservice.com/bigfive/info/

"The Evolutionary Layers of the Human Brain." (n.d.). McGill University. Retrieved January 24, 2015, from http://thebrain.mcgill.ca/flash/d/d_05/d_05_cr/d_05_cr_her/d_05_cr_her.html

"The Plan, Do, Study, Act (PDSA) Cycle." (2016). The W. Edwards Deming Institute. Retrieved on March 18, 2016, from https://www.deming.org/theman/theories/pdsacycle

The Standish Group International (2013). "The CHAOS Manifesto 2013: Think Big, Act Small." Retrieved December 20, 2014, from http://www.versionone.com/assets/img/files/ChaosManifesto2013.pdf

Thite, M. (1999). "Leadership: A Critical Success Factor in IT Project Management." Retrieved June 22, 2015, from http://www.researchgate.net/profile/Mohan_Thite/publication/3814522_Leadership_a_critical_success_factor_in_IT_project_management/links/0c960532112d65bf3c000000.pdf

Tice, L. (2005). *Smart Talk for Achieving Your Potential: 5 Steps to Get You from Here to There.* [Kindle Version]. Retrieved from http://www.amazon.com

Toastmasters International (2005). *A Practical Guide to Becoming a Better Leader—Competent Leadership Guide.* Mission Viejo, CA: Toastmasters International.

Transformational Leadership (n.d.). Businessdictionary.com. Retrieved December 6, 2014, from http://www.businessdictionary.com/definition/transformational-leadership.html

US Air Force. (2013). "Officer and Enlisted Evaluation Systems." Retrieved September 15, 2015, from http://static.e-publishing.af.mil/production/1/af_a1/publication/afi36-2406/afi36-2406.pdf

Values (n.d.). Psychologyandsociety.com. Retrieved February 7, 2015, from http://www.psychologyandsociety.com/valuesdefinition.html

Vohra, P. and Singh, A. (2013). "A Contrast and Comparison of Modern Software Process Models." Retrieved September 26, 2015, from http://research.ijcaonline.org/icamt/number1/icamt1013.pdf

Walden, D., Roedler, G., Forsberg, K., Hamelin, R., and Shortell, T. (2015). *Systems Engineering Handbook: A Guide for System Life Cycle Processes and Activities.* Hoboken, NJ: John Wiley & Sons.

Walters, S. (2014). *The Biography of Bill Gates: Secrets Behind the Success of the Microsoft Billionaire.* [Kindle Version]. Accessed at http://www.amazon.com/the-biography-bill-gates-billionaire-ebook/dp/B00HTWCFMS

Ward, L. (2014) "What's the Biggest Risk an IT Project Manager Faces?" Projectconnections.com http://blog.projectconnections.com/project_practitioners/2014/10/whats-the-biggest-risk-an-it-project-manager-faces.html

Westcott. R. (2006). *The Certified Manager of Quality/Organizational Excellence Handbook,* 3rd ed. Milwaukee, WI: ASQ Press.

Zimmerer, Th. W. and Yasin, M. M. (1998). "A Leadership Profile of American Project Managers." *Project Management Journal,* 29(1), 31–38.

Further Reading

Andrews, P. and Manes, S. (2013). *Gates: How Microsoft's Mogul Reinvented an Industry and Made Himself the Richest Man in America*, 20th Anniversary ed. Seattle, WA: Cadwallader & Stern.

Barnard, C. I. (1938). *The Functions of the Executive*. Boston, MA: Harvard University Press.

Brady, N. (1990). *Ethical Managing: Rules and Results*. New York, NY: Macmillan.

Burgelman, R. A. and Maidique, M. A. (1988). *Strategic Management of Technology and Innovation*. Homewood, IL: Richard D. Irwin Inc.

Drucker, P. F. (1954). *The Practice of Management*. New York, NY: Harper & Row.

Drucker, P. F. (1986). *Management: Tasks, Responsibilities, Practices*. New York, NY: Truman Talley Books.

Drucker, P. F. (1993). *Post-Capitalist Society*. New York, NY: Harper Business.

Elkington, J. and Hartigan, P. (2008). *The Power of Unreasonable People*. Boston, MA: Harvard Business Press.

Freeman, R. E. (1984/2010). *Strategic Management: A Stakeholder Approach*. Cambridge, UK: HarperCollins/Cambridge University Press.

Freeman, R. E. and Gilbert, D. E., Jr. (1988). *Corporate Strategy and the Search for Ethics*. Englewood Cliffs, NJ: Prentice Hall.

Friedman, M. (1970). The Social Responsibility of Business Is to Increase Its Profits. *The New York Times Sunday Magazine* (September 13), 32–33, 122–124.

Ghemawat, P. (1991). *Commitment: The Dynamic of Strategy*. New York, NY: Free Press.

Green, C. (2000). *Classics in the History of Psychology*. Toronto, ON: York University. Retrieved April 26, 2015, from http://psychclassics.yorku.ca/Maslow/motivation.htm

Grisham, T. (2011). "PMI & IPMA: Differences & Synergies." allpm.com. Retrieved from http://www.allpm.com/index.php/free-resources/94-article/newsletter-article/164-pmiipma

Hamermesh, R. G. (1986). *Making Strategy Work: How Senior Managers Produce Results.* Hoboken, NJ: John Wiley & Sons.

Hillman, A. J. and Keim, G. D. (2001). "Shareholder Value, Stakeholder Management, and Social Issues: What's the Bottom Line?" *Strategic Management Journal,* 22(2), 125–139.

Hosmer, L. T. (1994). "Strategic Planning as if Ethics Mattered." *Strategic Management Journal,* 15(S2), 17–34.

Jackson, I. A. and Nelson, J. (2004). "Values-Driven Performance: Seven Strategies for Delivering Profits with Principles." *Ivey Business Journal,* (Nov/Dec), 1–8.

James, B. (1994). "Narrative and Organizational Control: Corporate Visionaries, Ethics and Power." *The International Journal of Human Resource Management,* 5(4), 927–951.

Jones, T. (1991). "Ethical Decision Making by Individuals in Organizations: An Issue-Contingent Model." *Academy of Management Review,* 16(2), 366–395.

Joyner, B. E. and Payne, D. (2002). "Evolution and Implementation: A Study of Values, Business Ethics and Corporate Social Responsibility." *Journal of Business Ethics,* 41(4), 297–311.

Kelemen, M. and Peltonen, T. (2001). "Ethics, Morality and the Subject: The Contribution of Zygmunt Bauman and Michel Foucault to Postmodern Business Ethics." *Scandinavian Journal of Management,* 17(2), 151–166.

Kennedy, C. (1993). "Changing the Company Culture at Ciba-Geigy." *Long Range Planning,* 26(1), 18–27.

KPMG (2008). *International Survey of Corporate Responsibility Reporting.* Retrieved from http://www.kpmg.com/EU/en/Documents/KPMG_International_survey_Corporate_responsibility_Survey_Reporting_2008.pdf

Kvalnes, Ø. (2014). "Honesty in Projects," *International Journal of Managing Projects in Business,* 7(4), 590–600.

Maddex, R. L. (1995). *Constitutions of the World.* New York, NY: Routledge.

McCafferty, D. (2014, September 18). "Demand Soars for IT Pros with Essential Skills." *Baseline Magazine.* Retrieved February 28, 2014, from http://www.baselinemag.com/careers/slideshows/demand-soars-for-it-pros-with-essential-skills.html#sthash.J6zFc9xz.dpuf

McCoy, C. S. (1985). *Management of Values: The Ethical Difference in Corporate Policy and Performance.* Boston, MA: Ballinger.

Miles, R. E. (1982). *Coffin Nails and Corporate Strategies.* Englewood Cliffs, NJ: Prentice-Hall.

Mintzberg, H. and Quinn, J. B. (1991). *The Strategy Process: Concepts, Contexts, Cases.* Upper Saddle River, NJ: Prentice-Hall.

Ohmae, K. (1982). *The Mind of the Strategist: The Art of Japanese Business.* New York, NY: McGraw-Hill.

Porter, M. E. (1980). *Competitive Strategy: Techniques for Analyzing Industries and Competitors.* New York, NY: Free Press.

Porter, M. E. (1985). *Competitive Advantage: Creating and Sustaining Superior Performance.* New York, NY: Free Press.

Prahalad, C. K. and Doz, Y. L. (1987). *The Multinational Mission: Balancing Local Demands and Global Vision.* New York, NY: Free Press.

Project Management Institute. (n.d.) *PMI® Code of Ethics and Professional Conduct.* PMI.org. Retrieved March 5, 2015, from http://www.pmi.org/codeofethicsPDF

Quinn, J. B. (1980). *Strategies for Change: Logical Incrementalism.* Homewood, IL: Richard D. Irwin Inc.

Robertson, C. J. (2008). "An Analysis of 10 years of Business Ethics Research in *Strategic Management Journal:* 1996–2005." *Journal of Business Ethics,* 80(4), 745–753.

Rumelt, R. P., Schendel, D. E., and Teece, D. J. (1994). *Fundamental Issues in Strategy: A Research Agenda.* Boston, MA: Harvard Business School Press.

Selznick, P. (1957). *Leadership in Administration: A Sociological Interpretation.* Berkeley, CA: University of California Press.

Simon, H. A. (1945). *Administrative Behavior.* New York, NY: Free Press.

Stevens, J. M., Steensma, H. K., Harrison, D. A., and Cochran, P. L. (2005). "Symbolic or Substantive Document? The Influence of Ethics Codes on Financial Executives' Decisions." *Strategic Management Journal,* 26(2), 181–195.

Taylor, H. and Woelfer, J. H. (2011). "Leadership Behaviors in Information Technology Project Management: An Exploratory Study." *Proceedings of the 44th Hawaii International Conference on System Sciences.*

Index

Printed and bound by CPI Group (UK) Ltd, Croydon, CR0 4YY

24/10/2024

01778712-0001